George MacDonald

Divine Carelessness and Fairytale Levity

Daniel Gabelman

BAYLOR UNIVERSITY PRESS

MCI
The Making of the Christian Imagination

Stephen Prickett
general editor

© 2013 by Baylor University Press
Waco, Texas 76798-7363

All Rights Reserved. No part of this publication may be reproduced, stored in a retrieval system, or transmitted, in any form or by any means, electronic, mechanical, photocopying, recording or otherwise, without the prior permission in writing of Baylor University Press.

Jacket Design by theBookDesigners
Jacket images: George MacDonald (1824–1905), Scottish author, poet, and Christian minister, c. 1865, courtesy of Provost Skene's House Museum, Wikimedia; "The Fairy's Tightrope" from "Peter Pan in Kensington Gardens" by J.M. Barrie, 1906, Rackham, Arthur (1867-1939) / Private Collection / The Bridgeman Art Library; "The Fairies have their Tiff with the Birds," 1906 illustration for "Peter Pan in Kensington Gardens" by J.M. Barrie, pub. 1906 (ink and w/c), Rackham, Arthur (1867-1939) / Private Collection / Photo © Chris Beetles Ltd, London / The Bridgeman Art Library

Interior image: The Ecstasy of St. Teresa (marble) (b/w photo). Giovanni Lorenzo Bernini (1598–1680) / Santa Maria della Vittoria, Rome, Italy / Alinari / The Bridgeman Art Library

First issued in paperback in 2023 under ISBN 978-1-60258-783-0

The Library of Congress has cataloged the hardcover as follows:

Gabelman, Daniel, 1979–
  George MacDonald : divine carelessness and fairytale levity / Daniel Gabelman.
  273 pages cm. -- (The making of the Christian imagination)
  Includes bibliographical references and index.
  ISBN 978-1-60258-782-3
 1. MacDonald, George, 1824–1905—Criticism and interpretation. I. Title.
  PR4969.G33 2013
  823'.8--dc23
                                    2012043647

To Josie, Connie, and Beatrice
my divine playfellows

Series Introduction
by Rowan Williams

The current rash of books hostile to religious faith will one day be an interesting subject for some sociological analysis. They consistently suggest a view of religion which, if taken seriously, would also evacuate a number of other human systems of meaning, including quite a lot of what we unreflectively think of as science. That is, they treat religious belief almost as a solitary aberration in a field of human rationality; a set of groundless beliefs about matters of fact, resting on—at best—faulty and weak argumentation. What they normally fail to do is to attend to what it is that religious people actually do and say—and also to attend to the general question of how systems of meaning, or "worldviews," work.

Systems of meaning—philosophies of life, if you must, though the term sounds immediately rather stale—seem to operate by allowing us to see phenomena in connected instead of arbitrary ways. But this means the capacity to see things in terms of other things: it means abandoning the idea that there is one basic and obvious way of seeing the world which any fool can get hold of (and which some people then insist on dressing up with unnecessary complications), and grasping that seeing the world and being able to talk about what it is that we encounter is something we have to learn, a set of skills that allows us to connect and to see one event or phenomenon through the lens of another. At the most severely pragmatic level, this leads to observational generalizations about laws; at a quite different but no less important level, it leads us into the world of metaphor. And in case anyone should think that these are radically separate, consider that "law" itself is a metaphor in the context of natural process....

Metaphor is omnipresent, certainly in scientific discourse (selfish genes, computer modelings of brain processes, not to mention the magnificent extravagances of theoretical physics), and its omnipresence ought to warn us against the fiction that there is a language that is untainted and obvious for any discipline. We are bound to use words that have histories and associations; to see things in terms of more than their immediate appearance means that we are constantly using a language we do not fully control to respond to an environment in which things demand that we see more in them than any one set of perceptions can catch.

All of which is to say that no system of perceiving and receiving the world can fail to depend upon imagination, the capacity to see and speak into and out of a world that defies any final settlement as to how it shall be described. The most would-be reductive account of reality still reaches for metaphor, still depends on words that have been learned and that have been used elsewhere. So it should not be too difficult to see that a map that presents the intellectual world as a struggle between rival pictures, well-founded and ill-founded ways of describing things, literal and fanciful perspectives, or even natural and supernatural vision, is a poor one and one that threatens to devour itself in the long run, if the search is for the unadorned absolute. How shall we move the cultural discussion on from a situation in which religious perspectives are assumed to be bad descriptions of what can be better talked about in simpler terms?

This will involve the discipline of following through exactly what it is that the language of a particular religious tradition allows its believers to see—that is, what its imaginative resources are. When believers are engaged (as they routinely are, despite what may be assumed by the critics of faith) in society and politics and the arts in ways that are recognizable to nonbelievers, how are their perceptions actually and specifically molded by the resources of their tradition? This is not—*pace* any number of journalistic commentators—a matter of the imperatives supposedly derived from their religion. It is about what they see things and persons in terms of, what the metaphors are that propose further dimensions to the world they inhabit in common with nonbelievers.

Characteristically this repertoire of resources—in any religious tradition—is chaotically varied, not just a matter of a few leading ideas or doctrines. It includes the visual and the aural—what is sung and seen as well as said. It includes formative practices, rites, which leave their semantic traces in unexpected settings. And it includes the legacy of others who have engaged the world in the same ways, at various levels of sophistication. The forming of a corporate imagination is something that continues to be the more or less daily business of religious believers, and it needs to be acknowledged that this is a process immeasurably more sophisticated than the repetitive dogmatism so widely assumed to be the sole concern of those who employ religious language.

The way to demonstrate this is to lay out what it means in the practice of specific people; this series is an attempt to exhibit a common imagination at work—and in the process of further refinement and development—in the labors of a variety of creative minds. Because we are in danger of succumbing to a damaging cultural amnesia about what religious commitment looks like in practice, these books seek to show that belief "in practice" is a great deal more than following out abstract imperatives or general commitments. They look at creative minds that have a good claim to represent some of the most decisive and innovative cultural currents of the history of the West (and not only the West), in order to track the ways in which a distinctively Christian imagination makes possible their imaginative achievement. And in doing so, they offer a challenge to what one great thinker called the "cultured despisers" of Christian faith: in dismissing this faith, can an intellectually serious person accept confidently the simultaneous dismissal of the shifts, enlargements, and resources it has afforded the individual and collective imagination? What, finally, would a human world be like if it convinced itself that it had shaken off the legacy of the Christian imagination? The hope of the authors of these volumes is that the answer to that question will be constructively worrying—sufficiently so, perhaps, to make possible a more literate debate about faith and contemporary culture.

CONTENTS

Introduction: The Gravity of a Child at Play   1

Part I: Modalities of Levity

1. The Levity of Saints and Angels   9
2. Ecstasy and Folly   23
   Lightening the Self for Its Journey
3. Vanity and Play   37
   Liberation from Seriousness for Metamorphosis
4. Carnival and Sabbath   51
   A Time for Renewal, Rebellion, and Revelation

Part II: MacDonald's Fairytale Levity

5. "Never so Real as When They Are Solemn"   71
   Victorians and Seriousness
6. Time   107
   Fairyland's Festive Sabbath
7. Space   143
   Fairyland's Ecstatic Cosmology
8. Transformation   173
   "Shall not the Possible Become the Real?"

Conclusion: The Haunting Force of Levity   203

Notes   209
Bibliography   245
Index   257

INTRODUCTION
The Gravity of a Child at Play

Levity is probably not the first word that most readers associate with George MacDonald. On the contrary, unlike his contemporaries Lewis Carroll and Oscar Wilde—fellow writers of fantasy known for their whimsicality—MacDonald tends to be linked with moral and spiritual seriousness rather than lighthearted playfulness. C. S. Lewis, while not the first to emphasize the solemnity of MacDonald, has undoubtedly had the greatest influence in shaping MacDonald's image as a holy, wise, and somewhat dull sage.

In *The Great Divorce*, Lewis' first-person narrator, arriving in heaven with a busload of ghosts, encounters MacDonald in heaven and describes him as follows: "his ageless spirit weighed upon mine like a burden of solid gold: and yet, at the very same moment, here was an old weather-beaten man, one who might have been a shepherd."[1] Lewis confesses that his reading of *Phantastes* was to him "what the first sight of Beatrice had been to Dante."[2] MacDonald thus becomes an odd amalgamation of Virgil and Beatrice, and Lewis thereafter refers to him exclusively as "teacher" or "sir." What one most wants in an otherworldly guide, it appears, is weightiness and solemnity—Dante did not choose Ovid to guide him through the infernal regions. Lewis reinforces this picture of a serious and gentle MacDonald in his introduction to *George MacDonald: An Anthology*. With publishers seeking to harness Lewis' selling power, this short essay now prefaces numerous books of his "teacher," making it even more likely that a reader's first impression of MacDonald is Lewis'. Interestingly, Lewis does in several places speak of MacDonald as "a sunny, playful man" who combined "intellect and imagination and humour and fancy and all the affections," but this vision of MacDonald is almost wholly buried under the avalanche of descriptors of him as wise, weighty, holy, and dull.[3] "Bad pulpit traditions cling" to his style along with "verbosity" and "an over-sweetness."[4] MacDonald hides "his best things [. . .] in his dullest books."[5] Lewis speaks most highly of his "character," "holiness," and "wisdom" and casts over the whole description his own experience of *Phantastes* as having "a certain quality of Death"—a judgment reinforced by J. R. R. Tolkien's brief comment in his seminal essay "On Fairy Stories" that "death was the theme that most inspired George MacDonald."[6] In combination with the brief outline of MacDonald's life—by any account filled with disease, rejection, poverty, and death—MacDonald emerges in the mind of the reader as a pious, ascetic Victorian teacher, donning him in a mantle of hefty seriousness.

Perhaps it should not be surprising, then, to discover that many readers consider MacDonald to be "tall, dark and serious" and think that his greatest works are the ones that dwell on the weighty subject of death, such as *Phantastes*, *Lilith*, and *At the Back of the North Wind*.[7] Readers tend to follow Lewis' lead in finding these darker fantasies to be MacDonald's most significant works of fiction while simultaneously assuming that MacDonald was a solemn preacher at heart.[8] The image of MacDonald that emerges is stereotypically Victorian—straight-laced, humorless, and relentlessly moralistic.

G. K. Chesterton, however, who was both closer to MacDonald chronologically and one of the greatest critics of Victorian literature, depicts MacDonald not as a gloomy sage but as a mystic "half mad with joy."[9] In one of his first essays for *The Daily News*, Chesterton argues that no one has had "so naturally heroic an atmosphere" as MacDonald.[10] MacDonald is like one of his own fairytale characters for whom "the supernatural [is] natural." Unlike other writers of fairytales, "Macdonald enters fairyland like a citizen returning to his home," and this means that his realistic stories are actually hidden fairytales:

> Dr. Macdonald's tales of real life are allegories, or disguised versions, of his fairy tales. It is not that he dresses up men and movements as knights and dragons, but that he thinks that knights and dragons, really existing in the

eternal world, are dressed up here as men and movements. It is not the crown, the helmet, or the aureole that are to him the fancy dress; it is the top hat and the frock coat that are, as it were, the disguise of the terrestrial stage conspirators.

The key to MacDonald, in other words, is not his realistic fiction or his adult fairy romances but his fairytales for the childlike. Unlike writers of moralistic fairytales who put on a façade of play to hide their seriousness, MacDonald puts on a façade of seriousness (in his novels and adult writings) to hide his play. He unveils himself most in his simple and light fairytales. Melancholy did not fascinate MacDonald like it did Yeats and other Celtic mystics of the day because he focused on joy:

> Dr. Macdonald, I fancy, has always known that melancholy is a frivolous thing compared with the seriousness of joy. Melancholy is negative and has to do with trivialities like death: joy is positive and has to answer for the renewal and perpetuation of being. Melancholy is irresponsible; it could watch the universe fall to pieces: joy is responsible and upholds the universe in the void of space. This conception of the vigilance of the universal Power fills all Dr. Macdonald's novels with the unfathomable gravity of complete happiness, the gravity of a child at play.

Here Chesterton inverts the customary polarities of the seriousness of melancholy and the frivolousness of joy and points to a dynamic interplay between gravity and levity in MacDonald's works. You can only play when you take ultimate things seriously; you can only take them fully seriously when you are at play. It is this vital paradox of "the gravity of a child at play" that enlivens MacDonald's fairytales. The heaviness of melancholy is actually ephemeral, whereas the lightness of joy is eternal. Joyous play is not capricious and self-serving, as is ordinarily assumed, rather it responsibly "upholds the universe" while melancholy would frivolously let it all "fall to pieces."

Furthermore, according to Chesterton, MacDonald was profoundly original and yet without followers "in his realisation of the grotesque in the spiritual world." Chesterton characterizes MacDonald's style as "nocturnal anarchy" and "celestial nonsense" before concluding,

> Dr. Macdonald's world of extravagance [. . .] is penetrated through and through with a warmth of world-love, the cosmic camaraderie of the child. Even monsters are pets in that enormous nursery.

Chesterton draws his portrait of MacDonald entirely from the lighter fairytales, yet his argument is that these whimsical and apparently inconsequential works for children are really the most serious things about MacDonald. They suffuse and inform every other aspect of his life and work. Only by understanding MacDonald's levity, it seems, can one truly understand his gravity. In addition, Chesterton here gestures toward a surprising sympathy between light, whimsical things and serious orthodox theology.

The problem then with seeing gravity as the defining characteristic of MacDonald is not just that one might miss out on some exquisite images and humorous passages but that one might misconstrue the nature of MacDonald's gravity itself. Chesterton, interestingly, suffered from the opposite difficulty of people taking levity as his predominant quality and thus discounting his earnest intentions.[11] For Chesterton as for MacDonald, however, there is no insuperable barrier between being serious and being lighthearted, rather the two unite in a higher harmony that is only puzzling to contemporary readers because the modern world has forgotten or abandoned vital theological truths and often prefers quick caricatures to the mysterious nuances of reality.

Therefore, by investigating MacDonald's fairytale levity, this book will not just help to dispel the aura of solemnity surrounding the Victorian writer, bring balance to a reading of MacDonald's works, and open new vistas into his thought and artistic practice; it will also illuminate Christianity's traditional love of lightness and show the dangers of the modern tendency to put playfulness and whimsicality in a ghetto far from the centers of seriousness. In this way, the interpretation of a handful of seemingly inconsequential fairytales connects to larger social and intellectual narratives such as the shift in consciousness from premodern to modern to postmodern and the way in which reason and rationality relate (or do not relate) to faith. In other words, considered broadly, this book seeks to recover the once prevalent premodern understanding that lighthearted modalities are not opposed to serious theological reflection but actually integral to it.

In explaining the plan of *The Everlasting Man*, Chesterton makes the point that after being inside Christianity the next best thing for understanding it is to be really outside of Christianity.[12] Being stuck somewhere between inside and outside is a good way to get thoroughly muddled. Sometimes the quickest way home is to walk around the world. Similarly, to get inside MacDonald's fairyland one must first get lost outside its borders in search of something else.[13] To this end, the story of MacDonald's fairytale levity begins neither with fairies nor with MacDonald but with saints and angels.

PART I

Modalities of Levity

I

THE LEVITY OF SAINTS AND ANGELS

When someone speaks of "levity" today, they are probably referring to something humorous, ridiculous, or frivolous. Used positively, it can mean that which elicits laughter or fleeting joy, or that which calls forth—however briefly—a startling perspective of the world. Used negatively, the word relates to things that are not "serious," not worthy of considering deeply or pursuing whole-heartedly, not pragmatic or useful for the "real" business of life, or not morally trustworthy. Like many words, levity is metaphorical in all of its modern usages, but time and developments in the physical sciences have obscured the original metaphor.

"Levity" comes from the Latin *levitas* meaning "lightness" or "mobility," and is related to words like *levis* ("light in weight") and *levo* ("to lift up, raise" or "to lighten").[1] In English, we can see the word's metaphor more readily in words sharing the same Latin root, such as "elevate" ("to raise up"), "lever" (a tool used to lift up objects), and "leaven" (the process of fermentation which causes bread to rise). Why has "levity" become abstracted and distanced from the core image of "making something light" or "raising up"? Premodern times also used "levity" metaphorically to refer to fickleness, trifling behavior, or moral laxity, as when Shakespeare has Octavius Caesar rebuke Mark Antony and Pompey for wanting to revel in drink and song: "our graver business frowns at this levity" (*Antony and Cleopatra*, II.vii.128).[2] Yet in addition to this usage, there existed a literal, scientific sense to the word:

levity was a positive characteristic opposed to gravity, an abundance of which allowed an object to rise and gave it greater mobility.[3] To the premodern mind, then, what birds, fire, and clouds have in common is levity. With the complete victory of gravity in the physical sciences, however, Western culture abandoned this definition, severing the word "levity" from its primary image. One could thus say that Newton is indirectly responsible for levity's fall into abstraction.[4]

Furthermore, it is interesting to observe the divergence that has occurred in the common usage of "levity" and its closest word-cousin "levitate" since the Enlightenment. According to the *Oxford English Dictionary* (*OED* hereafter), the prevalent sense of levity is now "want of serious thought or reflexion" or "frivolity," while levitate means "to rise by virtue of lightness" but, the *OED* adds, "now only with reference to spiritualism."[5] So while "levity" is for fools, jokesters, and buffoons, "levitate" is the sole (and serious) realm of mystics, saints, and angels. Having in different ways been cut off from the primary meaning and image, both words are now also cut off from each other and hover at opposite ends of the semantic spectrum—one pointing to the silly and superficial, the other to the "seriously" spiritual. G. K. Chesterton wittily plays with this semantic gap in the following passage in order to take the reader by surprise and redirect their thinking:

> Modern investigators of miraculous history have solemnly admitted that a characteristic of the great saints is their power of "levitation." They might go further; a characteristic of the great saints is their power of levity. Angels can fly because they can take themselves lightly.[6]

Following Chesterton, this chapter reexamines the fundamental connection of the commonly opposed connotations of "levity" (humor/play) and "levitate" (spirituality) by looking at saints and angels and focusing on the primary image of "lifting up" and "making light."

Dante the Saintly Pilgrim

A good place to begin an inquiry into the relationship between faith and levity is the *Divine Comedy*. One of the best sources for imaginative depictions of saints and angels, Dante also devotes much of his epic to the imaging of literal levity. Dante's journey continuously enacts vertical motion and physical lightening. Although he initially *descends* into

The Levity of Saints and Angels

hell, this too is a necessary part of levity—he must first understand the weightiness of sin, repent of it, and be purged of its burden before levitation to the heights is possible. In Purgatory, this becomes explicit as an angel inscribes "the scars of seven P's" upon Dante's forehead and tells him, "be sure you cleanse away these wounds" before departing Purgatory (IX, 113–14).⁷ The seven P's stand for the seven deadly sins (*peccatum* is Latin for "sin"), which Dante is about to witness in the circles of Purgatory.⁸ As he leaves each circle, Dante passes by an angel who removes one of the Ps from his brow and lightens both his physical and his spiritual burden. This, for example, is the description of Dante passing the angel of humility at the outskirts to the circle of the proud:

> [The angel] spread his arms out wide, and then his wings.
> > He said: "Come, now, the steps are very close;
> > henceforth, the climbing will be easier."
> To such an invitation few respond:
> > O race of men, born to fly heavenward,
> > how can a breath of wind make you fall back?
> He led us straight to where the rock was cleft.
> > Once there, he brushed his wings against my brow,
> > then assured me of a safe ascent. (XII, 91–99)

With the lightest touch of his wings, the angel removes one of the P's from his forehead, but it is not until Dante begins climbing the stairs that he notices a difference:

> > I seemed to feel myself much lighter now
> > than I had been before on level ground.
> "Master," I said, "tell me, what heavy thing
> > has been removed from me? I feel as if
> > to keep climbing would be effortless."
> He answered: "When the P's that still remain
> > (though they have almost faded) on your brow
> > shall be erased completely like the first,
> then will your feet be light with good desire;
> > they will no longer feel the heavy road
> > but will rejoice as they are urged to climb." (XII, 116–26)

As sin's weight is purged, Dante is enabled to climb, to levitate without hindrance and without becoming weary. Indeed, all of humanity is "born to fly heavenward" (XII, 95). Echoing Aristotle's assertion in his *Physics* that "every perceptible body has either weight or lightness, and tends naturally towards the centre (if it has weight) or upwards (if it has lightness),"[9] Dante says that the natural orientation of all things is to ascend to the "proper distance from their Source" (*Paradise* I, 111).

It is only the burden of sin that keeps us shackled to the ground and subservient to gravity—gravity in this case being the force which pulls us away from the divine and being directly associated with "man's primal drive, / twisted by false desire" that "may bring him down" (I, 134–35). In contrast, levity involves "[seeing] the imprint of Eternal Excellence" and soaring to one's "predestined place" in the cosmic order (I, 107, 124). "This," says Beatrice, "is what carries fire toward the moon, / this is the moving force in mortal hearts" (I, 115–17). Saints free from "every weight" should "be no more amazed / at [their] flight up than at the sight of water / that rushes down a mountain to its base" (I, 136–39). Likewise, in Purgatory Dante exhorts Christians to pray for souls in Purgatory: "[w]e ought, indeed, to help them wash away / the stains they bring from earth, that they may rise, / weightless and pure, into the wheeling stars" (*Purgatory* XI, 34–36). Levity, the ability to rise, is a freedom of movement that comes from having sin eliminated and desire rightly reoriented to God.

While Dante depicts sin in general as a weight, the sin of pride in particular requires purgation through the carrying of heavy stones. Here Dante continues to use the concept of *contrapasso* (opposite suffering), which in Hell meant the slothful were mired in mud and the wrathful tore each other apart. In life, the proud attempted to lift themselves up without God, but since God "looks at every proud man and brings him low" (Job 40:11) in the *lowest* circle of Purgatory, and thus farthest circle from God, these Christians must "bend their bodies toward the ground" (XI, 116).[10] The proud cannot levitate like the saint, purged of her sin, because they have not yet realized that the only motive force for levitation is the power of God himself. The sight of these Christians bowed and hunched by the weight of their own pride causes Dante to comment:

The Levity of Saints and Angels 13

> O haughty Christians, wretched, sluggish souls,
>   All you whose inner vision is diseased,
>   Putting your trust in things that pull you back,
> Do you not understand that we are worms,
>   Each born to form the angelic butterfly,
>   That flies defenseless to the Final Judge?
> Why do your souls' pretensions rise so high,
>   Since you are but defective insects still,
>   Worms as yet imperfectly evolved? (XI, 121–29)

All pretension, all attempts to rise on one's own power result ultimately in crashing back to earth. The lowly worm must recognize itself as a worm before a power beyond itself will give it wings. Yet lightness is what God designed us for—a lightness like the frivolity and insignificance of a "defenseless" butterfly. Spiritual transformation does not make an individual important and self-sufficient; rather it removes defenses and makes people receptive toward and dependent on the Creator.

The ultimate image of the weightiness of sin and pride, however, occurs in the *Inferno*, where there is a unique moment of levity. In the lowest circle of Hell, Satan stands frozen from the chest downward in a lake of ice. After noting the three archtraitors (Judas, Brutus, and Cassius) being gnawed in Satan's mouths, Virgil leads Dante to descend through the ice by clinging to Satan's body:

> He grabbed on to the shaggy sides of Satan;
>   Then downward, tuft by tuft, he made his way
>   Between the tangled hair and frozen crust.
> When we had reached the point exactly where
>   The thigh begins, right at the haunch's curve,
>   My guide, with strain and force of every muscle,
> Turned his head toward the shaggy shanks of Dis
>   And grabbed the hair as if about to climb—
>   I thought that we were heading back to Hell. (XXXIV, 73–81)

A strange inversion has taken place. Upon reaching the center of Satan's body, rather than continuing to descend, the two pilgrims begin ascending. The effect initially confuses Dante as he looks back "expecting I would see / the half of Lucifer I saw before," but instead he sees "his two legs stretching upward" (XXXIV, 88–90). He then naively asks Virgil, "How can he be lodged upside-down?" (103–4). Virgil replies,

> "You think you're still on the center's other side,"
>   he said, "where I first grabbed the hairy worm
>   of rottenness that pierces the earth's core;
> and you *were* there as long as I moved downward
>   but, when I turned myself, you passed the point
>   to which all weight from every part is drawn." (XXXIV, 106–11)

Satan sits at the center of the cosmos, the center of gravity. Like the metaphorical "fall" of Adam and Eve, the Devil has literally *fallen* to the point where he can fall no more in any direction—he has become the embodiment of sin. Interestingly, it is only after Dante and Virgil start to ascend, or levitate—while grappling with sin incarnate—that they must use the "strain and force of every muscle." Gravity is easy to obey and hard to overcome, whereas levity is difficult to obey and easy to overcome. Chesterton articulates this idea and helpfully sums up the spiritual truths embodied in this scene:

> Pride cannot rise to levity or levitation. Pride is the downward drag of all things into an easy solemnity. One "settles down" into a sort of selfish seriousness; but one has to rise to a gay self-forgetfulness. A man "falls" into a brown study; he reaches up at a blue sky. Seriousness is not a virtue. It would be a heresy, but a much more sensible heresy, to say that seriousness is a vice. It is really a natural trend or lapse into taking one's self gravely, because it is the easiest thing to do. It is much easier to write a good *Times* leading article than a good joke in *Punch*. For solemnity flows out of men naturally; but laughter is a leap. It is easy to be heavy: hard to be light. Satan fell by the force of gravity.[11]

Pride and seriousness are closely allied, and neither one is conducive to levity or levitation. Rather, in both spiritual and comic terms, they represent the force of gravity that draw bodies downward and ultimately—if taken to the extreme as with Satan—bring all motion and life to a standstill.[12]

An obvious objection arises at this point—is not the *Divine Comedy* itself "serious"? That is to say, does it not take a sober and earnest attitude toward religion and faith? Here the difficulty centers on the use of the word "serious." Dictionaries are not helpful on this point as they tend to define "serious" as having to do with the "earnest sides of life," but then define "earnest" as relating to "serious consideration."[13] In addition to the circularity, definitions like these only raise more questions such as what are the "earnest sides of life" and how does "serious consideration" differ from normal or trifling thoughts? Oscar Wilde, for one, would be quick to remind us that the vital importance of being earnest does not necessarily include the need to be serious, where "serious" stands for a kind of solemn dignity that despises multiple meanings and hermeneutical complexities. The real problem with "serious" appears to be, as C. S. Lewis suggests, that it "is fatally equivocal" in that it can mean both "solemn" or "grave" and "thoroughgoing, whole-hearted, energetic." For Lewis, discussing different types of reading, this means "the true reader reads every work seriously in the sense that he reads it whole-heartedly, makes himself as receptive as he can," but "for that very reason he cannot possibly read every work solemnly or gravely."[14] The one kind of seriousness precludes the other in cases such as the works of Rabelais, Pope's *The Rape of the Lock*, and Chaucer's *fabliaux*. Moreover, in a culture that highly values both solemnity and wholeheartedness, "serious" becomes essentially a term of approval and success, and as a result loses sight of any clear definition. We might, for example, ask about a popular novel, "is that *serious* literature?" where "serious" does not mean "solemn" or "wholehearted" but is essentially a stand-in for "good." Works might be extremely earnest in their intentions and yet fail miserably in their results. "Camp," for example—which dismantles the distinction between serious and trivial—delights in such pieces.[15] One therefore wonders if levity has been unfairly accused of lacking passion and depth merely because it is the opposite of the "grave" and "solemn" whose "earnestness," at least in lexicons, is unquestioned.

But, to return to the original question, is the *Divine Comedy* "serious" by any or all of these definitions? Obviously, Dante is "serious literature" in the final sense above—his work has lofty goals which he wholeheartedly pursues and successfully achieves. In addition, Dante is also "serious" about religion and faith in the *Comedia* in the sense that he is wholeheartedly in earnest. Yet in other crucial ways, it is emphatically not "grave," "solemn," or "sober." The title *Comedia* itself highlights this. Time and literary fame have obscured the fact that Dante specifically wrote in his vernacular Italian rather than high Latin in order to achieve "an unstudied and low style," and, though not a drama, it follows the genre of comedy in that it proceeds from ignorance to bliss.[16] Moments of laughter might be rare (though as we shall see, they do appear), but moments of levity are not. Indeed, the entire poem is one long ecstatic vision which in the final canto is described as "high fantasy" (*Paradise*, XXXIII, 142). In this final scene, for instance, Dante sounds like Lewis Carroll—that mathematical purveyor of nonsense—as he revels in the paradoxical mysteries of the Trinity:

> Within Its depthless clarity of substance
> > I saw the Great Light shine into three circles
> > in three clear colours bound in one same space;
> the first seemed to reflect the next like rainbow
> > on rainbow, and the third was like a flame
> > equally breathed forth by the other two.
> How my weak words fall short of my conception,
> > which is itself so far from what I saw
> > that "weak" is much too weak a word to use!
> [. . .]
> As the geometer who tries so hard
> > to square the circle, but cannot discover,
> > think as he may, the principle involved,
> So did I strive with this new mystery:
> > I yearned to know how could our image fit
> > into that circle, how could it conform;
> but my own wings could not take me so high. (XXXIII, 115–23, 133–39)

Dante's choice of words and images—rainbows, fire, circles, wings—leaves little doubt about the "light" intent of this passage. There is nothing "grave" or "sober" about this scene. Instead, joy reigns supreme. The power of God's beauty is too strong for mere words and concepts, and rigid rational explanations do not apply in the presence of the Almighty. The ecstasy of levity forces Dante into apophaticism—a stammering and negative gesturing that is the only response to the excesses of divine revelation. Something other than "serious" language appears to be necessary in order to point toward that which transcends the senses. Encountering God in all his majesty and glory is not a crushing, heavy experience but the pinnacle of levity and levitation.

Drunken Angels and Deformed Demons

What about more traditionally recognized forms of levity, like jokes or humor? One instance of humorous levity in Dante's work occurs in canto XXIX of *Paradise* after Dante depicts the angelic hierarchy in the manner described by Pseudo-Dionysius in *The Celestial Hierarchy*:

> The hierarchy of divinities
> > Consists of the Dominions first, and next
> > The Virtues, and the third are called the Powers.
> In the next to last of the last dancing trio
> > Whirl Principalities, and then Archangels;
> > The festive Angels fill the last with play. (XXIX, 121–26)

Angels by their very nature exemplify the connection between levity and levitation. According to Pseudo-Dionysius, one of the most influential theologians of the early church, the lowest circle of celestial beings "are named 'angels' insofar as their hierarchy is more concerned with revelation and is closer to the world"; that is, this lowest rank of beings are the direct intermediaries between God and humanity, and thus are the ones who most immediately reveal God to us.[17] Dionysius' use of words like "hierarchy," "rank," and "order" might suggest to a modern mind that angels are rigid, formal, and ceremonious, but nothing could be further from the truth. For Dante, though all angelic beings dance, it is this lowest circle—the circle most directly in communion with humanity—which is "festive" and filled with "play." Angels delight in the play between earth and heaven; they are intermediary beings whose quickness and lightness make them just as at home on earth as in heaven. This mobility and rapid movement between worlds makes them perfect examples of levity.

Dante goes on to describe the reaction of Pope Gregory I—who had a different view of angelic hierarchy—upon his arrival in heaven: "Gregory, later, disagreed with [Dionysius], / but when he died to waken in this heaven / he saw the truth, and laughed at his mistake" (XXIX, 133–35). The saintly Gregory has no need to be right, but simply finds his earthly blunder comical. His soul—lightened of its desire to be important or correct—is able to see his work for what it is and delight in the joke of his own folly. He is, to use an earlier image, "defenseless" before the truth, a frivolous butterfly content with flitting around his maker.

For Dante, then, Gregory can laugh while Dionysius remains the authority on angels. Along with following Dionysius' angelic hierarchy, Dante also echoes his understanding of the characteristics of angels, one of which, it turns out, is inebriation. When Beatrice raises Dante's senses "beyond their powers" in the final circle of heaven, he witnesses an idyllic scene:

> I saw light that was a flowing stream,
>> Blazing in splendid sparks between two banks
>> Painted by spring in miracles of color.
> Out of this stream the sparks of living light
>> Were shooting up and settling on the flowers:
>> They looked like rubies set in rings of gold;
> Then as if all that fragrance made them drunk,
>> They poured back into that miraculous flood,
>> And as one plunged, another took to flight. (XXX, 61–69)

It takes a second unveiling for Dante to see that these "sparks of living light" are angels who, "like bees," "dip into the flowers" and become "drunk" on the love which ceaselessly flows from God to the saints and back so that "their faces showed the glow of living flame" (XXXI, 7–8, 13). Contrary to popular contemporary images such as Wim Wender's film *Wings of Desire*, angels do not meditatively recline on the tops of buildings, watch humans, and wonder what it would like to be mortal. Instead they participate in drunken, heavenly, sensual play—a divine, neverending carnival.

Static visual depictions have a difficult time conveying the exuberant and frenzied aspect of angels. Typically, they are depicted as soldiers in strict military order, as solemn attendants around the throne of God, as still and meditative melancholics, or as vigilant watchers and guardians. According to Chesterton, however, earlier medieval art was better at capturing the lightness of angels:

> Remember how Fra Angelico represented all his angels, not only as birds, but almost as butterflies. [. . .] It was the one thing that the modern

Pre-raphaelites could not imitate in the real Pre-raphaelites. Burne-Jones could never recover the deep levity of the Middle Ages. In the old Christian pictures the sky over every figure is like a blue or gold parachute. Every figure seems ready to fly up and float about in the heavens. The tattered cloak of the beggar will bear him up like the rayed plumes of the angels. But the kings in their heavy gold and the proud in their robes of purple will all of their nature sink downwards.[18]

Angels have the lightness not just of birds but of butterflies, a fluttering, apparently careless sort of levity. Indeed, according to Dionysius, the closer one gets to divine glory the more seemingly chaotic creatures become. Rather than describing them as disciplined, ordered, melancholic, motionless, meditative, or silent, as many paintings seem to, Dionysius says that angels are characterized by their symbolic association with "fire," "clouds," "winds," and "wings."[19] Like the wind, they have "instant speed with which they operate everywhere" such that they are constantly "coming and going from above to below and again from below to above as they raise their subordinates to the highest peak."[20] Like clouds, angels are "filled in a transcendent way with hidden light," and "they have a generative power, a life-giving power [. . .] for they rain understanding down."[21] Even more striking is their relation to fire:

> [Fire] passes undiluted through everything and yet continues to be completely beyond them. It lights up everything and remains hidden at the same time. [. . .] Yet it is master of everything. It bestows itself upon all who draw near. With kindling warmth it causes renewal. [. . .] It makes distinctions and is nevertheless unchanging. It rises up and penetrates deeply. It is exalted and is never brought low. It is ever on the move, moving itself and others. It extends in all directions and is hemmed in nowhere. [. . .] It is dynamic, powerful, invisibly present in everything. [. . .] It communes joyfully with everything.[22]

From this description, it would seem that angels make perfect witnesses for reexamining the connection between levity and levitation. Like the comic freedom of "levity," they are "ever on the move," "extend in all directions," are "hemmed in nowhere," and "commune joyfully with everything," while like the beneficial religion of "levitation" they "light up everything," "bestow [themselves] upon all who draw near," "kindle warmth," and "cause renewal." By this fiery light, angels look somewhat chaotic. Michel Serres summarizes this resemblance by connecting angels to "volatility," for *volatilis* is Latin for having wings, while volatile also relates to substances "capable of changing very rapidly from one state to another" and to things "which appear and then suddenly disappear."[23] Angels, it would seem, have the attributes of an acrobat, a clown, and a magician rolled into one—they defy gravity, can change forms quickly, and appear and disappear on a whim. This playful frivolity is symbolically linked to their wings, which according to Dionysius represent "their uplifting swiftness, the climb to heaven, the ever-upward journey whose constantly upward thrust rises above all earthly longing." "The lightness of wings," he continues, "symbolizes the freedom from all worldly attraction."[24] The gravity of earthly passions does not restrict creatures that are wholly attuned to God's glory. Rather, a riotous levity empowers them to go where they will and take on whatever shape they please.

Meanwhile, improperly oriented desire, like gravity, binds beings to the earth and limits the power of transformation. Thus in book ten of *Paradise Lost* when Satan returns triumphantly to Hell and tells the other fallen angels of his victory, something unexpected occurs:

> All yet left of that revolted rout
> Heav'n-fall'n, in station stood or just array,
> Sublime with expectation when to see
> In triumph issuing forth their glorious chief;
> They saw, but other sight instead, a crowd
> Of ugly serpents; horror on them fell
> And horrid sympathy; for what they saw,
> They felt themselves now changing; down their arms,
> Down fell both spear and shield, down they as fast,
> And the dire hiss renew'd, and the dire form
> Catch'd by contagion, like in punishment,
> As in their crime. (X, 534–45)

In a kind of *contrapasso*, the forsaking of God and his weighty glory (Hebrew *kabod* translates literally as "heaviness") leads to abject subservience to earthly gravity. The repetition of words like "fall" and "down" drives home the realization that these once brilliant and godlike beings have become like Dante's "defective insects" rather than "angelic butterflies." Their rebellion, according to Milton's contemporary Henry More, "changed their pure Ethereal Bodies into more Feculent and Terrestrial."[25] A transformation has occurred, but not a glorious one. Instead they metamorphose into slow, dirt-crawling snakes without even the liberty of arms and legs, let alone wings.

Falling and crashing into the depths is the fate of all creatures who aspire to rise by their own power rather than trusting in God's. In this way, stories like those told of Icarus and Babel—which depict the desire to ascend to the heavens by human effort—are not contradictory but complimentary to the claim that levity's metaphor is related to a kind of carelessness toward the self, because just like Milton's devils, Icarus and Babel end with the utter downfall of pride. To find a lasting levity, it would appear that one must abandon the seriousness of the self and allow God to do the lifting, as Jesus in his anger against the proud of his day makes clear: "whoever exalts himself will be humbled, and whoever humbles himself will be exalted" (Matt 23:12).

Hell therefore might imaginatively seem filled with a vibrant and creative anarchy to people like William Blake, but, according to Milton's more orthodox view, it is populated with the bland and banal, with worms trying to work out a petty pecking order. A perfect liberty meanwhile permeates heaven, a liberty that comes from focusing wholly on the divine, with the result that angels have eerie similarities with fairy tricksters.

It would seem, then, that levity and levitation are not quite as disparate as their current usage might suggest. Angels sometimes behave like drunken revellers, while saints end up stammering giddily and flying like "defenseless butterflies" to their heavenly Father. Indeed they both come off rather foolishly by the world's standards.

The Ecstasy of St. Teresa (marble) (b/w photo). Giovanni Lorenzo Bernini (1598–1680)
Santa Maria della Vittoria, Rome, Italy / Alinari
The Bridgeman Art Library

2

ECSTASY AND FOLLY
Lightening the Self for Its Journey

One of the most famous visual representations of a saint and an angel levitating is Bernini's sculpture *The Ecstasy of St. Teresa* (see facing page). Despite its massive heft of white marble and gilded metal, this is probably one of the lightest works of art ever created. The two central actors in Bernini's sculpted drama float between the grounded level of the viewer and the heavenly dome above where angels sport and play. Effortlessly using just thumbs and forefingers, the angel lightly lifts and holds Teresa with one hand and with the other delicately pinches a golden arrow. Teresa's form is a contrast between the flowing, wavy folds of her garment—which melds into the flame-like apparel of the angel—and the three realistically presented anatomical parts that emerge from the frenzied folds (foot, hand, and face). The limp hand and extended foot reach down below the cloud as if to show the still-present connection to the lower earthly realm, while the face points fully toward the heavenly sphere. Her slightly parted lips and half-open eyes convey the ambiguity of a pain that is also the sweetest of pleasures. The sumptuous Cornaro chapel that holds this sculpture at its heart participates in the drama, making the whole feel like a lunatic's fanciful dream. The walls and pillars evoke a sensation of erratic motion and chaotic upheaval with their motley colors and lawless shapes. Even the skeletons depicted in the marble floor have awoken and are moved to exuberant gestures in response to the scene above them. The sculpted drama lifts all things upward including the viewer by initiating a kind of liturgical lightness: it reformulates the liturgy's command to "lift up your hearts" and the psalmic enjoinder to "lift up your eyes" (Ps 121).

The spiritual experience depicted, however, seems oddly similar to madness or insanity by normal standards. Here is Teresa of Avila's description of the event:

> It pleased the Lord that I should see this angel in the following way. He was not tall, but short, and very beautiful, his face so aflame that he appeared to be one of the highest types of angel who seem to be all afire [. . .] In his hands I saw a long golden spear and at the end of the iron tip I seemed to see a point of fire. With this he seemed to pierce my heart several times so that it penetrated to my entrails. When he drew it out, I thought he was drawing them out with it and he left me completely afire with a great love for God. The pain was so sharp that it made me utter several moans; and so excessive was the sweetness caused me by this intense pain that one can never wish to lose it, nor will one's soul be content with anything less than God. It is not bodily pain, but spiritual, though the body has a share in it—indeed, a great share.[1]

This passage is easily susceptible to psychoanalysis and other forms of criticism, and it might be tempting for Christianity to distance itself from such experiences because ecstasy seems foolish from a secular point of view. Yet as Hans Urs von Balthasar argues, "to be transported belongs to the very origin of Christianity," and, speaking of humanity's transformation by God, David Bentley Hart adds, "becoming is an ecstasy, and nothing besides."[2] There is thus something about this experience of being "caught up" or lifted out of oneself and ascending toward the divine that is both original to Christianity and central to its being. What is it about ecstasy that is so significant, and why is it so foolish?

A Strange Witness
Folly Praising Ecstasy

Holy fools have a strange predilection for ecstasy and levitation. For example, St. Andrew the Fool—one of the first holy fools in the Eastern Orthodox tradition—embraced folly as his life calling after an ecstatic vision of Christ in which Jesus told him to "run the good race naked" and "become a fool for my sake."[3] Andrew complied and became an object of ridicule in Constantinople during the reign of Leo I (457–474), but in his private devotions he was seen "suspended in the air while he prayed."[4] Meanwhile, Joseph of Cupertino (1603–1663) was a less intentional fool than Andrew, being naturally clumsy, inept, and unintelligent, but people mocked him and treated him the same way. Yet, according to *Butler's Lives of the Saints*, his "life was one long succession of ecstasies, miracles of healing and supernatural happenings on a scale not paralleled in the reasonably authenticated life of any other saint."[5] He apparently levitated on over seventy occasions, often in the presence of notable and reliable authorities (including Pope Urban VII and a Spanish ambassador). Commenting on the spiritual significance of levitation, Butler says it is "a special mark of God's favour whereby it is made evident even to the physical senses that prayer is a raising of the heart and mind to God."[6] It would seem that God gives a special lightening grace to fools who disregard the weightiness of this world. Those who truly "lift up their hearts" out of the burdens of earthly existence find their bodies echoing the upward inclination. Are these stories anomalous within Christianity or do they point to something more essential?

Speaking through a mask of folly, Erasmus claims that "the entire Christian religion seems to bear a certain natural affinity to folly" precisely because of its ecstatic impulses.[7] He culminates *In Praise of Folly* with a discussion of ecstasy, observing how "the ultimate reward for which [Christians] strive is nothing but a kind of madness" in that they long for the time when "the whole man will be outside himself, will be utterly happy at being outside himself."[8] Here Erasmus articulates a Christian version of an idea that originated in ancient Greece and particularly with Plato.[9]

For Plato, ecstasy occurs when a soul catches sight of the beautiful and then experiences an intense longing (*eros*) for it. Like a lover who ignores all concerns and distractions except the beloved, the person in a state of ecstasy does not live in themselves but in the beloved, and it is for this reason that they are said to be "outside themselves."[10] Plato speaks of ecstatic contemplation of the beautiful and the good as the soul's means of "recovering its plumage"; it is the motive force that allows a soul to "soar aloft" into the higher regions of being.[11] The emphasis on wings, feathers, and flying draws attention to the lightening effects of ecstasy.[12]

Christian thinkers such as Augustine and Pseudo-Dionysius modified Plato's description of ecstasy somewhat in order to avoid a gnostic view of the body as intrinsically evil, but they kept the same language of levity to describe its goals and effects.[13] Speaking of the vision that he had with his mother at Ostia, Augustine says that they "lifted themselves" beyond even heaven itself and "soared higher yet by inward musing" on God's works.[14] Christian theologians further reinforced the lightening effects of ecstasy by connecting it with rapture, which comes (via Latin *rapere*, "to seize") from the Greek *arpazein* meaning "to catch up." St. François de Sales expresses this clearly when he says, "Ecstasy is called rapture because through it God draws us and raises us up to him; and rapture is called ecstasy in that, by it, we come out of ourselves, remain out of ourselves and above ourselves, in order to unite ourselves to God."[15] By this description, ecstasy is not just for mystics and saints. All Christians must experience its levity. Unlike with Plato, however, the goal in Christian ecstasy is not to escape the body, but to "come out of ourselves" and lightly remain "above ourselves."[16] How does this aid one along the spiritual journey?

Closely connected with the ecstatic concept of living "outside ourselves" (Latin, *extra se*) seems to be Augustine's image of human sinfulness as an inward bent within the self (*homo incurvatas in se*). The fall of Adam, says Augustine, happened not when he ate the forbidden fruit but when he "turned towards himself."[17] By turning away from God and bending inward upon himself, Adam also become "less real" because he was no longer adhering "to him who exists in a supreme degree."[18] Augustine then comments on how "it certainly appears somewhat paradoxical that exaltation abases and humility exalts." The reason for this is that humility makes a person subject to God; it turns the mind back toward the source of all existence, whereas pride bends a person further inward upon themselves, a condition that one scholar describes as "the gravity of sin."[19] This orientation is for Augustine the defining characteristic of the city of God: "in one city love of God has been given first place, in the other, love of self."[20] Ecstasy, then, when it lifts individuals outside themselves, helps them overcome the inward bend of humanity and reorient them to "him who exists in a supreme degree." Ecstasy provides the velocity to escape the crushing gravity of the self and ascend to the divine. Yet as Augustine points out, there is a kind of paradoxical logic by which the only path up is down. The only way to levitate to the heights is to abase oneself—in other words, to become a fool.

Christ Jesus
The Floating Fool

As opposed to ecstasy's general affiliation with ascent, folly relates to descent. John Chrysostom calls the fool "the one who is slapped at public expense."[21] Theatrical fools debase themselves for the entertainment of others, frequently through bodily abuse or physical falls. Folly as a concept only exists within a clear hierarchy—it is the lower partner of wisdom. To enter into folly, therefore, is a clear descent either from normalcy or wisdom. Nonetheless, prophets and wise men often utilize folly as a means of shocking or startling people into an awareness of the truth. Hosea, for example, after God commands him to marry a whore and love her in the midst of her sin, comments, "The prophet is a fool; the man of the spirit is mad, because of your great iniquity and great hatred" (Hos 9:7). In this ambiguous instance, the prophet is a fool either as a means of forcing people to see undesirable truths or because his righteousness stands out so starkly from the standard of iniquity. In both cases, though, folly inverts expectations and reveals itself to be a higher form of wisdom. Similarly, medieval court fools—depicted so memorably by Shakespeare in characters like Touchstone and Feste—enjoyed, on account of their debased position, a sort of prophetic freedom to speak unpleasant truths.[22] Folly thus functions as a subversive method of getting at a higher truth; it descends in order that it might truly ascend and help others to do so as well.

With Christ, however, this heuristic trick becomes not just a method but a model, a paradigm of ultimate reality. In other words, Jesus was the universe's most foolish fool. From a purely Platonic perspective, God, as the highest and only self-sufficient being, is indifferent to everything below him.[23] Therefore, for God to go outside of himself, even toward the beings closest to him, is foolishness. It lessens his perfect goodness and beauty. This is why the message of Christ crucified is "folly to the Gentiles" (1 Cor 1:23), for in Christianity, as

Pseudo-Dionysius makes clear, ecstasy begins with the self-emptying of God, who incarnates himself in the historical person of Jesus the Messiah: "the transcendent has put aside its own hiddenness and has revealed itself to us by becoming a human being."²⁴ God becomes the greatest fool when he leaves the highest heights of beauty, goodness, and infinity for the lowest low of a human baby born to peasants in a backwater province within an otherwise unimportant moment in history for the purpose of raising humans up to the Father. The Supreme Being makes himself a lowly servant, as St. Paul recounts in Philippians:

> Though he was in the form of God, Christ did not count equality with God a thing to be grasped, but made himself nothing, taking the form of a servant, being born in the likeness of men. And being found in human form, he humbled himself by becoming obedient to the point of death, even death on a cross. Therefore God has highly exalted him and bestowed on him the name that is above every name. (2:6-9)

This establishes the proper pattern of ascent revealing how the downward movement of folly is at the heart of cosmic levitation. The phrase "made himself nothing" translates the Greek *kenosis* ("self-emptying"). God's love for the world elicits his ecstasy—he foolishly, like a mad lover, empties himself of his weighty glory and enters into finitude. And according to David Bentley Hart, "Christ's *kenosis* is not diremption but expression, the very shape of God's eternal life."²⁵ The incarnation, in other words, is not anomalous but constitutive of God's essence; it reveals that the interior life of the trinity is also one of ecstatic love.

Jesus' life, then, is simultaneously the greatest ecstasy and the greatest folly. Moreover, this overarching description is true of Jesus' specific mode of engaging with the world as well. Thus in Mark 3 as Jesus is beginning his ministry, his family arrives to take him home saying, "he is out of his mind," and in the next verse the wise from Jerusalem add, "he is possessed by Beelzebub" (Mark 3:21-22).²⁶ Almost as if prompted by these assertions, Jesus immediately begins teaching in parables (Mark 3:23-4:9), much in the same way that a medieval fool might have spoken in riddles. Fools prefer forms like riddles and parables because they are "polyvalent," "playful," and indirect; they force people either to attend carefully or to receive nothing.²⁷ Unlike expositional teaching, parables demand an imaginative act on the part of the audience. When asked why he teaches in parables, Jesus replies, "to those on the outside everything is said in parables so that 'they may be ever seeing but never perceiving, and ever hearing but never understanding; otherwise they might turn and be forgiven'" (Mark 4:11-12). Given the context, "those on the outside" likely refers to the scribes and Pharisees—the wise and powerful of the day. The foolishness of parables subverts earthly wisdom and power thereby excluding the worldly wise, but it also invites the response of humility. If an individual Pharisee were to empty himself of his comfortable wisdom and enter into the unsettling world of the parable, then Jesus would forgive him, and he would no longer be outside the kingdom (cf. Nicodemus in John 3). In this way, parables "shatter the structural security of the hearer's world and therein and thereby render possible the kingdom of God."[28]

An instructive example of how parables function is Jesus' interaction with a Gentile woman who begs him to heal her possessed daughter. Jesus responds in the manner of a fool by debasing her:

> "First let the children eat all they want," he told her, "for it is not right to take the children's bread and toss it to their dogs."
>
> "Yes, Lord," she replied, "but even the dogs under the table eat the children's crumbs."
>
> Then he told her, "For such a reply, you may go; the demon has left your daughter." (Mark 7:27-29)

It is hard to imagine a character more foolish by Jewish standards of wisdom—a Gentile, a woman, and a mother whose daughter is possessed by an "unclean spirit."[29] Reflecting these social attitudes, Jesus' initial ironic reply uses parabolic imagery to hide from her request and seemingly establish her as one of "those outside" (but also to rebuke indirectly the Jewish attitude toward outsiders). This is a fool's tactic—responding to a demand with a ridiculous polyvalent metaphor. Instead of taking offense, however, the woman accepts her ignoble designation and enters into Jesus' game of folly, trusting not in her own dignity but in Jesus' graciousness—that is, she makes herself "defenseless," opens herself to Jesus, and joins his frivolity. Indeed, she is the only person in the gospels to respond to one of Jesus' parables with a parable of her own, and Jesus loves her for it (cf. Matt 15:28: "Woman, you have great faith!") and grants her request. Jesus' ready love for the woman's witty playfulness is also a sort of proof of his humor, for it is only those with a sense of humor who can recognize and applaud it in others.[30] The foolishness of Jesus reveals those who are willing to lower their defenses, humbly accept their creaturely designation as "worms" or "dogs," and receive the transformative power of levity to raise them to "butterflies" or "children." In this way, Jesus is the paradigmatic "holy fool" who calls others to be fools for his sake—a calling which as we have seen became a sacred tradition especially in eastern Christianity.[31] Folly also characterizes many other aspects of Jesus' life. Peter Berger, for instance, notes the foolish overtones of Jesus' passion in how he entered Jerusalem riding on a donkey, and how "the Roman soldiers took him and subjected him to a mock coronation" such that just before his crucifixion, "Jesus was crowned as a king of folly."[32] Certainly death on a cross—the punishment reserved for slaves and criminals— was the lowest possible debasement for the king of infinite glory, and thus the greatest possible "folly to Gentiles" (1 Cor 1:23). As the perfect act of self-emptying and loving movement toward the world, this folly was simultaneously an ecstasy, yet Jesus also had at least one experience that we would more readily identify with ecstasy—the transfiguration. Whereas most of Jesus' recorded life seems characterized by struggle and earnestness, the transfiguration was a moment of divine bliss on the eve of his passion. The event has all the trappings of theophanic ecstasies: ascending to the top of a mountain, brilliant light emanating from his clothes and body, a voice from the bright overshadowing cloud, and angelic visitors. In comparison to more standard Platonic ecstasies, however, there are several key distinctions. First, there is the ambiguity of Jesus both experiencing ecstasy himself and eliciting it in others. He is simultaneously the participant in a theophany, as his ecstatic love for the Father overflows in physical manifestations of glory, and himself the theophany, as the disciples encounter his divinity revealed. In this way, Jesus' ecstasy is both private and corporate. His personal bliss does not make him indifferent to others, rather in the midst of his own uplifting he still condescends to lift the disciples up as well. Thus, when they "fell on their faces and were terrified, Jesus came and touched them, saying, 'Rise, and have no fear'" (Matt 17:7). There is a strange irony in that Jesus' metamorphosis into the form of God actually makes his lowly form clearer. Hans Urs von Balthasar observes that this transformation of "the divine form into the form of a servant" will actually "teach the disciples to read and understand the servant-form as the very form of God."[33] Not only is ecstasy folly, it also reveals folly to be the form of the divine, specifically the folly of ignoring the interests of the self (even and especially in its ecstasy) and attending to the needs of others.

The other key distinction from Platonic ecstasy is the bodily element. Instead of escaping the body, Jesus unveils the glory and lightness of bodily existence. Hence our existential experience of heaviness and limitation is not to be attributed to the mere fact that we have bodies, but to a disharmony between body and spirit. The impulse of Plato toward levity and "pluming the soul" would therefore seem to be correct, but the problem is not the body per se. Though it is not recorded in the gospels, tradition frequently depicts the transfigured Jesus floating, as for example in Raphael's *Transfiguration*. This is not just artistic license; rather it intuits the workings of a body and spirit fully in harmony with each other and the world. Thomas Aquinas suggests this interpretation when, in explaining the miraculous clarity of the transfiguration, he connects it to Jesus' walking on water: "the refulgence, which appeared in Christ's body then, was miraculous: just as was the fact of His walking on the waves of the sea." Aquinas goes on to quote Pseudo-Dionysius who says that "Christ excelled man in doing that which is proper to man: [. . .] in the unstable waters bearing the weight of material and earthly feet."[34] Humans as God intended them to be could levitate on water, and Jesus in his transfiguration merely manifests the lightness of this original and eschatological relationship between body and soul. Even Peter experiences this bodily levity briefly when in a fit of divine carelessness he foolishly and ecstatically leaps out of the safety of a boat in order to draw near to Jesus on the tumultuous sea (Matt 14:28-33).[35] His childlike trust in Jesus miraculously harmonizes his body and spirit allowing him to float on the waves, but when prudent concern for safety returns him to himself he once again feels the inexorable pull of gravity.

In some ways, then, Jesus' transfiguration is a foretaste in the midst of his earthly life of the ultimate triumph of levity over gravity in the resurrection and ascension. Like the Neoplatonic journey of ascent,

Jesus' final resting place is lifted up on high at the right hand of the Father (Acts 2:33), but Jesus' journey of ascent includes as a necessary element a willing descent into folly. Thus, as Mark McIntosh describes it, "Christ embodies both God's ('descending') love in pursuit of the other who turns away, and also God's ('ascending') love within the other, uplifting and drawing her or him into the embrace of peace."[36] In both cases, however, love shows itself to be a lightening force, emptying the self of its weightiness and lifting the lowly up to the divine.

Active Knowing and Loving
St. Paul's Foolish Ecstasy

In the midst of his "fool's speech"—beginning in 2 Corinthians 11 with "I wish you would bear with me in a little foolishness" and ending almost two chapters later with "I have been a fool!" (12:11)—Paul inserts the following description of an ecstatic experience:

> I will go on to visions and revelations of the Lord. I know a man in Christ who fourteen years ago was caught up to the third heaven—whether in the body or out of the body I do not know, God knows. And I know that this man was caught up into paradise—whether in the body or out of the body I do not know, God knows—and he heard things that cannot be told, which man may not utter. (12:1-4)

An intriguing interplay of knowledge and ignorance animates this passage. Paul knows "a man in Christ" (unanimously interpreted to be Paul himself) who was "caught up" to both the third heaven and paradise, yet in both instances he does not know "whether in the body or out of the body." This is interesting because "the third heaven" connects more readily with the spiritual realm whereas "paradise" has resonances with the bodily realm,[37] but in both cases Paul refuses to give the knowledge that his audience might most want to know, given that the Greek mystical tradition was so interested in the soul leaving the body.[38] Like the fool he is playing, Paul claims ignorance. This rhetorical strategy has the effect of subverting controversy before it begins and refocusing his audience's attention on what actually matters. The fool's folly thus serves the community by making irrelevant the endless arguments of the wise—including the wise of the future. Hence after long and careful discussions of "whether in the body or out of the body," Augustine is forced to say, "if the Apostle doubted the matter, who of us will dare to be certain?" and Aquinas acknowledges, "we must assert that both before and after he ignored whether his soul were separated from his body."[39] Paul's apparently foolish carelessness leaves open the possibility that God could use any type of ecstasy (in body, out of body, waking, dreaming) and subtly reorients the audience from philosophical debate to direct encounter with God.

Paul does definitely "know," however, that he was "caught up" to the "third heaven" and "paradise." According to Aquinas, the third heaven "pertains to the contemplation of the intellect" whereas paradise "pertains to the appetite," such that Aquinas is able to speak of rapture as both "cognitive" and "appetitive," that is, as including both knowing and loving. In this way, Aquinas also avoids the accusation that being "caught up" or "raptured" is an entirely passive annihilation of the self. Much like the Neoplatonic goal of annihilation of the self through union with the "One," certain forms of Christian mysticism divorce knowledge from love and relinquish responsibility to the world for an increasingly interior experience of the divine.[40] Rowan Williams argues that this was at least partially the fault of the church for not supplying a proper theological vocabulary for expressing "the basic principle of its life, the *ekstasis*, emptying, displacement of self in response to the self-emptying love of God, the communion of God and humanity by the presence of each in the other." Though they sometimes go too far, mystics try to remind the church that "Christian speculation is properly inseparable from engagement of a personal and demanding kind with the paradoxes of cross and resurrection."[41] As Paul would say, understanding all mysteries and knowledge without love is worth nothing (1 Cor 13:2).

What Aquinas' interpretation of Paul's rapture as including both the "appetitive" and "cognitive" powers suggests, meanwhile, is that true ecstasy unites love and knowledge as well as activity and passivity. Much like an erotic touch, there is a heightened sense of engagement that goes hand in hand with a defenseless vulnerability. *Kenosis*, then, is a sort of letting go of the self, in the same way that one lets a caged bird go free. The paradox, though, is that the self is both the caged bird and the one letting it go free. As Jesus indicates, letting go of the self is the only way for the self to become a true self: "unless a kernel of wheat falls into the earth and dies, it remains alone; but if it dies, it bears much fruit" (John 12:24).

This might help explain why Paul seems to hold his ecstasies so lightly and only discuss them when playing the fool. To do otherwise might arouse rivalry or jealousy and would overly focus attention on himself.[42] From ascending to the heights of heaven in the third person ("a man in Christ"), Paul instantly descends to the first-person foolish depths of "weaknesses, insults, hardships, persecutions, and calamities," for in weakness "the power of Christ may rest upon me" (12:9-10). Perhaps in donning the fool's mask, Paul realized the truth articulated by Dostoevsky's fool, Myshkin: "it's sometimes quite a good thing to be absurd. Indeed, it's much better, it makes it so much easier to forgive each other and to humble ourselves."[43] By creating ironic distance from himself and subverting the importance of visions, Paul avoids the pitfalls on either side of ecstatic experience. He neither clings to them tightly as his private possessions nor aggrandizes himself through boasting in their greatness. In love and out of a desire to correct the knowledge and behavior of the Corinthians, Paul offers his most intimate secrets as a public and embarrassing spectacle. "We have become a spectacle to the world, to angels and to men," says Paul in his first letter to the Corinthians, "we are fools for Christ's sake" (4:9-10). Thus his ecstasy becomes his folly and his folly his ecstasy, but in such a light and mobile way that he takes neither with ultimate seriousness. The mask of folly means that Paul, in the words of Balthasar on fools, "is never quite 'in his right mind,' never quite 'all there,' [so that] he lacks the ponderousness that would tie him down to earth."[44] Both his ecstasy and his folly lighten his self so that he is lifted up—whether in the body or out of the body—to heaven, yet his foolish performance of love also lifts others up, drawing them out of their selfish concerns and into community with God and each other.

Paradoxically, then, it is precisely the descending motion of public Christlike folly that enables the ascending movement of private ecstasy. Following Paul's lead, St. John of the Cross says, "all visions, revelations, heavenly feelings, and whatever is greater than these, are not worth the least act of humility, being the fruits of that charity which neither values nor seeks itself, which thinketh well, not of self, but of others."[45] The reverse, however, is also true. The knowledge of God received in private ecstasy and the love that sets the heart "aflame" transforms the mystic into a public fool that helps to lift others out of a domesticated relationship to God and their neighbors. Thus, to return to *The Ecstasy of St. Teresa*, the saint's intimate encounters with God become a foolish spectacle for the world. Her face forever displays her orgasmic joy, and everyone has permission to stare. Like the parables of Jesus demanding an individual response, this folly forces a viewer either to accept the cynical wisdom of the crowd or to enter personally into the divine drama of foolishly letting go of the self and lightly ascending to God.

3

VANITY AND PLAY
Liberation from Seriousness for Metamorphosis

Commenting on one of the effects of ecstatic experience, Augustine and his mother describe how their attitude toward the things of this world changed during their rapture at Ostia:

> In that day when we were speaking of these things, this world with all its delights became, as we spake, contemptible to us, and my mother said, "Son, for mine own part I have no further delight in any thing in this life."[1]

After a vision of God's glory, immutability, and eternity, the mystics see the world clearly for what it is—fleeting, transient, perishable, fallen. This gaze of contempt reduces what it looks at to vanity, and, for Augustine, vanity affects "whatsoever exists in transition," that is, the entire created order and all of existence.[2] On first consideration, it might seem that a gaze that reduces everything to vanity would be antagonistic to levity—that which sees emptiness and decay everywhere could have nothing to do with the lighthearted, playful, or humorous. Here certainly, we might say, gravity and solemnity are in full force, for contempt is the opposite of joy and humor. Something similar, however, also seems to happen when one plays, as Friedrich Schiller indicates in *On the Aesthetic Education of Man*:

> [Play denotes] everything that is neither subjectively nor objectively contingent, and yet imposes neither outward nor inward necessity. As our nature finds itself, in the contemplation of the Beautiful, in a happy midway point between law and exigency, so, just because it is divided between the two, it

is withdrawn from the constraint of both alike. [. . .] In a word, as it comes into association with ideas, everything actual loses its seriousness, because it grows *small*; and as it meets with perception, necessity puts aside its seriousness, because it grows *light*.[3]

Like a mystic in ecstasy, a player is "withdrawn" from common constraints, laws, and exigencies such that everything becomes "small" and "light" and seriousness is undermined. Play induces a vision of vanity, which in return makes play possible. It would seem, then, that in strange ways vanity and play are interrelated. To explore this connection, let us begin by looking at the most famous preacher of vanity, the Qoheleth of Ecclesiastes.

The Lightness of Being

"Vanity of vanities, says the Preacher, all is vanity" (Eccl 1:2; 12:8). Thus begins and ends Qoheleth's rambling, exhaustive examination of the world and human life. Qoheleth's gaze pierces everyone, everything, everywhere, and every time and declares it all to be vanity. Wise men along with fools, young and old, man and beast, past and future, dreams and words, wealth and poverty, righteousness and wickedness, novelty and tradition, pleasure and pain, weather and nature, Qoheleth's roving eye strikes them all.[4] Moreover, unlike Job, whose lament is for the loss of goods, people, health, and position; or the psalmist, whose cry "how long O Lord?" (Ps 13:1) looks for the fulfilment of a promise, Qoheleth in his role as Solomon, Israel's most prosperous king, lacks nothing and is if anything sated, bored. Vanity is not a longing for what is absent but a way of seeing the hollowness of what is present.[5] Is Qoheleth simply bored with existence?

A clue that might help to provide an answer is the strong connection between Ecclesiastes and the first four chapters of Genesis.[6] In addition to the thematic parallels between the two texts,[7] there are striking verbal similarities, most notably between Genesis 2:7, "the Lord God formed the man from the dust of the ground and breathed into his nostrils the breath of life," and Ecclesiastes 12:7, "the dust returns to the earth as it was, and the breath returns to God who gave it." This quotation, Qoheleth's last statement before the concluding "vanity of vanities" (12:8), suggests that in interesting ways Ecclesiastes dwells upon the interplay between those two substances so radically different from each other and yet each so vital for creation, "dust" and "breath." Hence even though it includes the effects of the fall, the gaze of vanity is a creational gaze. Like God in the first few chapters of Genesis, vanity takes a global perspective that can simultaneously hold in view the entirety of nature and human existence.

This vantage point on the world can seem fatally pessimistic. In various ways, Qoheleth constantly reminds his readers, in an echo of Genesis 3, "all are from the dust, and to dust all return" (Eccl 3:20). As Macbeth's line from his famous monologue indicates, "all our yesterdays have lighted fools the way to dusty death" (V.v.22), inert dust often prompts meditation on mortality. Divorced from breath, the perspective of dust is death. According to one scholar, "death is the dominant motif in Ecclesiastes" in that "it is human mortality that most commonly occasions [Qoheleth's] conclusion that all is vanity."[8] Death pervades Qoheleth's thinking not only in the obvious sense of being the end of physical life, but also in the way it makes everything appear futile. Why work or be wise or be righteous when ultimately all things come to the same end? Not even fame endures, for, as Milan Kundera, in a quote that echoes Qoheleth, observes, "history is as light as individual human life, unbearably light, light as a feather, as dust swirling into the air, as whatever will no longer exist tomorrow."[9] The dustiness of death discloses the lightness of being, but it is an "unbearable" lightness. While it reveals all things to be light as dust, death, as the most "serious" and weighty of subjects, also burdens Qoheleth's discourse with an inescapable gravity.

It is, then, somewhat surprising to discover that Ecclesiastes is one of the most artful and literarily playful books in the Bible. Scholars call Ecclesiastes "the sphinx of Hebrew literature."[10] Grammatical riddles and linguistic oddities abound—more so proportionally than in any other book in the Hebrew canon.[11] As we have already seen with "dust," "breath," and "vanity" but including words like "toil," "wind," "gift," and "lot" as well, the play of language—with all its ambiguous sensuousness—animates the text in a way that resonates with Jacques Derrida's concept of "free play," prohibiting the finalizing of interpretation.[12]

In addition to this structural and verbal play, the author of Ecclesiastes also uses fictional masks to play various roles. This masking is signaled in 1:12 when the speaker names himself ("I the Preacher

[Qoheleth]") and takes on a kingly persona ("have been king over Israel"). The initial act of role-playing then leads on to more and more costume changes as Qoheleth attempts the ludicrous task of "seeing everything" (1:14). This ceaseless striving to see everything is either an attempt to imitate the omniscience of God (Qoheleth sees "all the living who move about under the sun" [4:15] and "all the work of God" [8:17]) or is a way of taking on as many human perspectives as possible (he sees wise and foolish, righteous and wicked, rich and poor, old and young).[13] In either case, Qoheleth appears to parody more traditional and straightforward genres such as wisdom literature through this taking on of different guises (cf. 7:15-17). Mikhail Bakhtin, who has written perceptively on the use of masks, reminds us that "the mask is connected with the joy of change and reincarnation, with gay relativity and with the merry negation of uniformity and similarity" because "it contains the playful element of life."[14] In other words, Qoheleth's play with masks reveals that he is more than just a morbid cynic. While on the one hand the creational gaze of Qoheleth prompts his ruminations on dust, death, and the ephemerality of life on earth, on the other it evokes the ludic perspective of "breath."

Indeed, like wisdom, who in the creation account of Proverbs 8 was "ever at play in [God's] presence, at play everywhere on his earth, delighting to be with the children of men" (8:31-32 New Jerusalem Bible), Qoheleth's creational understanding of frolicsome "breath" informs the other dominant theme of Ecclesiastes—delight. The concluding frame narrator, for example, summarizes Qoheleth's work by saying, "The Preacher sought to find words of delight" (12:10). If Qoheleth were merely "a confused, sceptical wise man," as some critics argue, this would be a strange synopsis, but in addition to his playful literary mode Qoheleth endorses a life of simple enjoyment as well.[15] "There is nothing better for a person," says Qoheleth in 2:24, "than that he should eat and drink and find enjoyment in his toil" for "this is from the hand of God, for apart from him who can eat or who can have enjoyment?" In the final of seven such "joy passages,"[16] there is a complex dance of solemnity and play:

> Light is sweet, and it is pleasant for the eyes to see the sun. So if a person lives many years, let him rejoice in them all; but let him remember that the days of darkness will be many. All that comes is vanity. Rejoice, O young man,

Vanity and Play

in your youth, and let your heart cheer you in the days of your youth. Walk in the ways of your heart and the sight of your eyes. But know that for all these things God will bring you into judgment. (Eccl 11:7-9)

Here Qoheleth appears to play provocatively with a verse from the Torah: "Remember all the commandments of the LORD, to do them, not to follow after your own heart and your own eyes, which you are inclined to whore after" (Num 15:39). In fact, Qoheleth's play with this verse almost kept Ecclesiastes out of the Hebrew canon since the rabbis feared the direct contradiction of the Torah.[17] Qoheleth exhorts joy and freedom of action, even dangerously playing with key passages of the Law to do so, but immediately juxtaposes this with a harsh (and orthodox) affirmation of God's judgment. Joy and playfulness, then, mix gamesomely with death and judgment, much in the same way that "breath" comes together for a brief span with "dust" to form *Homo Ludens*, man the player. Like dust, breath unveils the lightness of being, but unlike dust, breath does not find this lightness "unbearable" but joyful and liberating. How exactly does vanity create this effect?

Suspending Seriousness
The "As if" and "As not" of Vanity

The English word "vanity" translates the Hebrew *hebhel*, which outside of Ecclesiastes is usually "breath" or "vapor," as in Psalm 39:6: "Surely, all mankind stands as a mere breath."[18] Jean-Luc Marion argues that this word "cannot be translated by 'nothingness' but suggests the image of steam, a condensation, a breath of air."[19] Hence when Qoheleth's gaze strikes something with vanity, "no reality disappears, but only a certain aspect of the reality."[20] In particular, what disappears is the appearance of seriousness, the pretence of all things to be self-sufficient and enduringly significant. Contrary to his assumptions, "man does not weigh a lot: under the breath of the spirit, he flies to pieces, dissipates, is undone."[21] In comparison with God, all things are light and airy, and man's "presence floats, in suspension, in the flux that comes to him from elsewhere."[22] Seeing with the eyes of vanity is a way to remember that we "are a mist that appears for a little time and then vanishes" (James 4:14). For Marion, vanity places all things in suspension, and "suspension itself marks everything with the indication of caducity," which means that "all *can* fall and disappear," that is, "the possibility of falling" saturates every instant.²³ Vanity marks all creation with "the very possibility of disappearing."²⁴ To put this another way, vanity is a mode of seeing what is *as if* it were not.²⁵ The vision of vanity sees all that pretends to seriousness—the real, the important, and the weighty—as if it were artful, frivolous, and light. Interestingly, St. Paul says something very similar to the Corinthians:

> The appointed time has grown very short. From now on, let those who have wives live as if they had none, and those who mourn as if they were not mourning, and those who rejoice as if they were not rejoicing, and those who buy as if they had no goods, and those who deal with the world as if they had no dealings with it. For the present form of this world is passing away. I want you to be free from anxieties. (1 Cor 7:29-32)

The recognition of vanity that "the present form of this world is passing away" leads Paul to exhort not only a mode of seeing *as if* but also a mode of living *as if*. This way of living and seeing "renders the world strange, deranged, a stranger to itself."²⁶ Or perhaps, as Giorgio Agamben suggests, it is better to translate ως μη as "as not," for "the messianic vocation is the revocation of every vocation."²⁷ Jesus' messianic call strikes all things with vanity and reveals the false gravity of other claims so that a believer can be liberated from worldly seriousness.

Thus Paul clearly states the purpose of this imaginative mode: "I want you to be free from anxieties." Anxiety makes gravity more difficult to overcome and binds people within themselves. The German theologian Jürgen Moltmann observes how "the mechanism of fear and worry always keeps men down on the ground," whereas "freedom begins when men suddenly find themselves to be without fear." For Moltmann, therefore, "the game of theology [is] the liberating game of faith with God against the evil bonds of fear and the grey pressures of care which death has laid upon us."²⁸ Fear and worry immobilize, bind, and burden mankind. But the "game of faith" liberates; it frees us from the fear of death and allows us to overcome the "grey pressures of care." Thus Christ says that he comes to bring freedom and levity: "come to me all who labour and are heavy laden and I will give you rest [. . .] for my burden is light" (Matt 11:28-30). The "as not" of vanity loosens and lightens so that human existence becomes a kind of game, as Moltmann argues:

> Because the world does not provide firm ground under our feet, it does—and for that very reason—give us the playground for freedom. Because equilibrium seems to be so uncertain, the figures of the game are moveable and the players must be lighthanded and limber. When the heavy burdens of earth pull the players down, they lose their place in the game. We are playing in the world and with the world, and we are trying through free play to make ourselves fit for the totally-other.[29]

Vanity, then, helps overcome the crushing gravity of seriousness. It does this not by dissolving the material world like a gnostic mystic but by removing a certain manner of its appearing—the manner by which it claims permanence. Swiss theologian Karl Barth thus says, "as God's children we are in fact released from the seriousness of life and can and should simply play before God."[30] Both Moltmann and Barth suggest that vanity is primarily a force of liberation *from* seriousness, but they also hint that this liberation is not arbitrary freedom for its own sake but liberation *for* something else. For Moltmann, it is "to make ourselves fit for the totally-other" while for Barth it is "growing up to be the child of God that I am," but both agree it is liberation for metamorphosis.[31]

Ludic Transformations

Scholars frequently interpret Qoheleth's experience of vanity as cynicism or boredom, but as we have seen it is also an incitement to play. In modern times, few writers have understood this dual aspect of vanity better than Lord Byron, who even justifies his mischievous epic *Don Juan* by the canonical authority of Qoheleth:

> Ecclesiastes said, that all is vanity—
> Most modern preachers say the same, or show it
> By their examples of true Christianity;
> In short, all know, or very soon may know it;
> And in this scene of all-confessed inanity,
> By saint, by sage, by preacher, and by poet,
> Must I restrain me, through the fear of strife,
> From holding up the Nothingness of life? (*Don Juan*, VII, 6)[32]

While many declare the "nothingness of life," few partake in the joyous freedom that this revelation provides, but for Byron it legitimates his poetic play. Vanity clears the ground of false pretension and opens an empty space, a formless void in which new creations can take shape. For Byron, this means the formation of a particularly playful muse:

> Good company's a chess-board—there are kings,
> Queens, bishops, knights, rooks, pawns; the world's a game;
> Save that the puppets pull at their own strings;
> Methinks gay Punch hath something of the same.
> My muse, the butterfly, hath but her wings,
> Not stings, and flits through ether without aim,
> Alighting rarely:—were she but a hornet,
> Perhaps there might be vices which would mourn it. (XIII, 89)

The revelation of vanity that "the world's a game" licenses the gamesome butterfly muse whose movement is light and ethereal. After exhorting his muse, "if you cannot fly yet flutter," Byron adds, "and when you may not be sublime, be arch" (XV, 27). Unlike the belligerent hornet or the task-oriented bee, butterflies seem sublimely careless, but Byron's play can take more roguish forms of frolicking as well ("be arch") when other modes falter. The important thing for play is to perpetuate its own motion.

Thus Plato speculated that play originated because "the young of all creatures cannot be quiet in their bodies" and "are always wanting to move and cry out [. . .] some leaping and skipping, and overflowing with sportiveness and delight."[33] The semantic starting point of most words for play in every language is the concept of swift movement.[34] Hans-George Gadamer observes that "what [play intends] is to-and-fro movement that is not tied to any goal that would bring it to an end."[35] This explains why insentient things such as light and water are frequently described as playing, as for example in W. H. Auden's poem "Streams":

> Dear water, clear water, playful in all your streams,
> As you dash or loiter through life who does not love
> To sit beside you, to hear you and see you,
> Pure being, perfect in music and movement?[36]

Auden goes on to say that "*Homo Ludens*, surely is [water's] child." The anthropomorphism evident in this analogy is revelatory. Humans feel a playful kinship with water because of its agility, litheness, and ability to take on various aspects and forms. Water can cascade down mountain falls, glisten peacefully in still lakes, crystallize into drifting snowflakes, or vaporize and ascend into the sky. More than any other earthly element, it is constantly in motion, ever perpetuating its play between earth, sea, and sky through many ludic transformations.

One such transformation that Byron draws attention to in *Don Juan* because of its similarity to human life is the mixing of water and air to form bubbles:

> Amidst the court a Gothic fountain play'd,
> Symmetrical, but deck'd with carvings quaint—
> Strange faces, like to men in masquerade,
> And here perhaps a monster, there a Saint:
> The spring gush'd through grim mouths, of granite made,
> And sparkled into basins, where it spent
> Its little torrent in a thousand bubbles,
> Like man's vain glory, and his vainer troubles. (XIII, 65)

The image of bubbles encourages the reader to hold both glory and troubles lightly. Vanity, symbolized perhaps by the emptiness at the heart of bubbles, highlights the brevity and fragility of human existence, but it is also what makes bubbles light, mobile, and free. Like humans formed of "dust" and "breath," bubbles combine two light substances with the result that they are lively creatures of two worlds, air and water, but are not wholly at home in either. Humans, says Byron, share a similar fate:

> Between two worlds life hovers like a star,
> 'Twixt night and morn, upon the horizon's verge:
> How little do we know that which we are!
> How less what we may be! The eternal surge
> Of time and tide rolls on, and bears afar
> Our bubbles; as the old burst, new emerge (XV, 99)

Like bubbles upon the waves, humans are caught between two worlds, knowing neither what "we are" nor "what we may be." It is this space of uncertainty between worlds that gives birth to play.

Indeed, as Friedrich Schiller argues, play is the force that mediates between the two dominant impulses of humanity, the "sensuous" and the "formal," that is, between body and spirit.[37] These two impulses seemingly "exhaust the conception of humanity" and both claim a sort of ruling seriousness.[38] The sensuous impulse, concerned as it is with finitude, time, and materiality, is interested in the practicality of things, whereas the formal impulse, concerned as it is with the infinite and the absolut,e is interested in the purpose of things. Play, meanwhile, aims at "the reconciliation of becoming with absolute being, of variation with identity."[39] By its quick and ceaseless movement between the two impulses, play remains simultaneously outside of and inside of both. Play herein holds the "twofold nature" of humanity in tension, keeping the two poles distinct yet unified. Hence Schiller boldly concludes, "Man plays only when he is in the full sense of the word a man, and *he is only wholly Man when he is playing.*"[40] What Schiller's argument suggests is that play is liberation *for* humanity's actual transformation into its ideal. Play somehow bridges the gap between "what we are" and "what we might be"; it helps bring infinity into finitude. How does it accomplish this feat? Perhaps a fairytale—that playful form that delights in transformation—might provide some clues.

In "The Happy Hypocrite," Max Beerbohm tells the story of the dissolute and debauched Lord George Hell, a man entrenched in his sinful ways. While attending a performance, Cupid shoots Lord George, and he falls in love with the childlike Jenny Mere. The result is a mixture of ecstasy, folly, and vanity: "of his comrades, his synicism [*sic*], his reckless scorn—of all the material of his existence—he was oblivious now."[41] Despite his earnest request for her hand in marriage, however, Jenny rebuffs him because his face is "as a mirror long tarnished by the reflection of this world's vanity" and she can only marry a man "whose face is wonderful as the faces of the saints."[42] Downcast, Lord George asks a mask-maker to affix the mask of a saint to his face so that he might play the part of a saint and thereby convince Jenny to marry him. The result is a complete transformation:

> When Lord George looked through the eyelets of his mask into the mirror that was placed in his hand, he saw a face that was saintly, itself a mirror of true love. How wonderful it was! He felt his past was a dream. He felt he was a new man indeed.[43]

By putting on the mask—like the original hypocrites in Greek drama—and entering into a world of play, Lord George finds himself liberated from his past patterns of behavior and liberated for a new mode of engaging with the world. Gadamer explains, "play draws [a player] into its dominion and fills him with its spirit. The player experiences the game as a reality that surpasses him."[44] Play is thus not a mere disguise, "rather, play itself is a transformation of such a kind that the identity of the player does not continue to exist for anybody."[45] Lord George, for example, finds that none of his former friends or acquaintances recognize him (except his former lover La Gambogi). In other words, as a condition of entry into the realm of play, a player must let go of self and embrace the rules and attitude of the play sphere. This explains the characteristic feeling of lightness that accompanies play. "The ease of play," says Gadamer, "is experienced subjectively as relaxation [because] the structure of play absorbs the player into itself, and thus frees him from the burden of taking the initiative, which constitutes the actual strain of existence."[46] The structure of play lifts and bears the weight of decision making. Play liberates us from the existential heaviness of liberty and provides a satisfying pattern in which we can move with ease. In other words, play induces a sort of beneficent carelessness of the self and the "seriousness" of the world.

After Lord George successfully woos Jenny Mere and in marriage changes his name to George Heaven, he plays the part of a saint and gives up his former mansion and wealth for a simple cottage in the forest where he and Jenny live in happy simplicity. As time goes by, George grows "reconciled to his mask" so that "it seemed to become an integral part of him, and, for all its rigid material, it did forsooth express the one emotion that filled him, true love."[47] Inevitably, though, George's former lover La Gambogi finds the couple and after a fierce struggle unmasks George: "but, lo! His face was even as his mask had been. Line for line, feature for feature, it was the same. 'Twas a saint's face."[48] As a pattern or structure for movement and development, play actually transforms individuals into its likeness. Far from being deceptive, therefore, play is instead intimately related to truth. According to Gadamer, play "is not enchantment in the sense of bewitchment that waits for the redeeming word that will transform things back to what they were; rather, it is itself redemption and transformation into true being." Play, he continues, "produces and brings to light what is otherwise constantly hidden and withdrawn."⁴⁹ Something ontological happens when people play. As an individual conforms in beneficent self-carelessness to the structure of play, real and true transformation is effected.

This is not just good fantasy but good developmental psychology, too. Psychologists have long recognized how play in children stimulates and develops the brain while a lack of play stunts their physical, emotional, and intellectual growth.⁵⁰ It is also good theology.

Playing before God

After alluding to "The Happy Hypocrite" in a chapter entitled "Let's Pretend," C. S. Lewis goes on to describe how the Christian life is similar to a kind of game. He observes how the very first words of the Lord's Prayer are "Our Father" before continuing:

> Do you now see what those words mean? They mean quite frankly, that you are putting yourself in the place of a son of God. To put it bluntly, you are *dressing up as Christ*. If you like, you are pretending.⁵¹

Christians as "little Christs" are happy hypocrites playing at something they are not. Yet as Lewis points out, both Jesus and St. Paul command this mode of play. Paul even turns Jesus into a kind of costume when he tells believers in Romans to "clothe yourselves with the Lord Jesus Christ" (13:14). Even more important, however, God calls believers to be born again as his children. For Barth, this means that the believer is "in process of change" for "there is an obedience that consists in letting go here and now in time, in growing up to be the child of God that I am."⁵² There is, therefore, an eschatological tension between what we presently are and what we one day will be, and the only way to bridge this gap between *is* and *ought* is to let go of the seriousness of ourselves and play at being God's children. As Moltmann describes it, "we are then no longer playing merely with the past in order to escape it for a while, but we are increasingly playing with the future in order to get to know it."⁵³ Christian play is not a nostalgic longing for a lost Eden; it is the bringing into being of the hoped-for future.

Despite the intensity and all-inclusive nature of his call, Jesus can truthfully say that his yoke is easy and his burden is light because

God ultimately bears the existential weight of existence. In playing before God as his children, we learn in Barth's words that "one can walk before God in full seriousness only when one realizes that God alone is fully serious."[54] The "as not" game of vanity frees us from the appearance of seriousness that all things naturally put forward, but play also frees us for transformation into the eschatological reality of the kingdom of God. Hence, to quote Barth once more, "play is not the opposite of serious decision," but "it is decision taken gladly, willingly, and cheerfully along the lines of the command and in opposition to the present reality in which we stand."[55] What disappears through vanity and play, in other words, is not seriousness as such but a certain deceptive mode in which things in our present world tend to appear. The best way, simultaneously, to dispel this illusion and to participate in the seriousness of God's kingdom—joy, transformation, love—might, therefore, be with a bit of child's play.

4

CARNIVAL AND SABBATH
A Time for Renewal, Rebellion, and Revelation

Hidden in the midst of Qoheleth's discussions of the vanity of being is one of his most famous reflections:

> For everything there is a season, and a time for every matter under heaven:
> A time to be born, and a time to die; [...]
> A time to break down, and a time to build up;
> A time to weep, and a time to laugh;
> A time to mourn and a time to dance; [...]
> He has made everything beautiful in its time. (Eccl 3:1-4, 11)

By drawing attention to the evanescence of existence, vanity not only liberates an individual for present playfulness but also discloses the importance of different times and seasons. Weeping cannot take precedence over laughter nor death over life, for God has "made everything beautiful in its time." Time is not one undifferentiated whole but is made up of rhythms and undulations.

Christianity accentuates this rhythm in various ways but perhaps most notably in the concept and observance of the Sabbath and in the liturgical calendar of feasts and fasts. As Charles Neaves—a nineteenth-century Scottish theologian—remarks in his poem "Let Us All Be Unhappy on Sunday," though, Christianity's special times are often staunchly solemn:

> We zealots, made up of stiff clay,
> The sour-looking children of sorrow,
> While not over-jolly to-day,
> Resolve to be wretched to-morrow.
> We can't for a certainty tell
> What mirth may molest us on Monday;
> But, at least, to begin the week well,
> Let us all be unhappy on Sunday.[1]

Worshipping God, it would seem, is a serious affair that requires a long and grave face. Perhaps this is why unofficial times of frivolity are necessary, to offset the gravity of official religious rituals. Byron, for example, at the beginning of *Beppo* describes a particular season of revelry in which play predominates:

> 'Tis known, at least it should be, that throughout
> All countries of the Catholic persuasion,
> Some weeks before Shrove Tuesday comes about,
> The people take their fill of recreation,
> And buy repentance, ere they grow devout,
> However high their rank, or low their station,
> With fiddling, feasting, dancing, drinking, masquing,
> And other things which may be had for asking.
> [. . .]
> This feast is named the Carnival, which being
> Interpreted, implies "farewell to flesh":
> So call'd, because the name and thing agreeing,
> Through Lent they live on fish both salt and fresh
> But why they usher Lent with so much glee in
> Is more than I can tell. (*Beppo* 1, 6)

For a brief period, an alternative sphere of play appears in which high and low mix and delighting oneself and others is the goal. Byron observes that this world of carnival connects in some way with the Catholic faith but appears somewhat baffled by the practice of wild revelry immediately preceding the ascetic season of Lent, offering as his only explanation "'tis as we take a glass with friends at parting" (6). The extreme contrasts are difficult to reconcile, and it seems, as Byron suggests, that carnival is a mere release, a last hurrah, a short rebellion against the harsh commandments of faith. Is it possible, however, that the revels of carnival are more than merely anarchic, that they are actually an important aspect of faith? And conversely, could it be that instead of constricting festivity the Sabbath somehow enables a more joyful mode of living?

Beguiling Lazy Time

In the fifth act of *A Midsummer Night's Dream*, as the three couples await the coming of night and their joyous nuptial unions, Theseus asks Philostrate, his master of revels: "what abridgement have you for this evening? What masque, what music? How shall we beguile the lazy time, if not with some delight?" (V.i.45–48). Time has the uncanny ability to appear to us in different modes—it can "fly," "crawl," or "stand still," just to name a few of the most obvious. Perhaps the most normal mode of time that humans experience, however, is what Theseus calls "lazy time," the span between significant moments, time stretched out in what appears to be uniform monotony. It is this mask of time that needs to be beguiled—tricked into revealing one of its more congenial faces.

Feasting is a particularly good way of enchanting time. Feasts, according to the Russian literary theorist Mikhail Bakhtin, are "always essentially related to time" in that they are "breaking points in the cycle of nature or in the life of society and man" that elicit "a festive perception of the world."[2] Unfortunately, says Bakhtin, official feasts often fail to create this effect because they "sanction the existing pattern of things" rather than leading people into a second world where different rules apply. The tone of the official feast is thus "monolithically serious" for it uses the past in order to consecrate the present.[3] Instead of beguiling lazy time, these official feasts reinforce lazy time as a means of placating people and securing the authority of those in power. Carnival, then, as the unofficial feast of the people is "the true feast of time, the feast of becoming, change, and renewal."[4] In this way, carnival arose in the Middle Ages as a kind of parodic mirror of the official serious world. It created what Bakhtin calls a "two-world condition"—though we might also call it a "two-time condition"—for it drew people into a separate sphere of reality where the rules of the "serious" world were inverted.

A clear literary example of this carnivalesque "two-time condition" appears in *A Midsummer Night's Dream*. Each word of the title signals the play's concern with times, seasons, and different modes of chronological experience. In the opening lines Theseus declares,

> Now, fair Hippolyta, our nuptial hour
> Draws on apace: four happy days bring in
> Another moon; but, O! methinks, how slow
> This old moon wanes; she lingers my desires. (I.i.1–4)

Shakespeare establishes Theseus as the emblem of the official, rational, daytime world who is highly conscious of the laziness of time. Hippolyta then responds:

> Four days will quickly steep themselves in night;
> Four nights will quickly dream away the time
> And then the moon, like to a silver bow
> New-bent in heaven, shall behold the night
> Of our solemnities. (I.i.7–11)

Whereas the experience of time in the day can be tedious and exacting, at night time is swift, agile, and light. The desert father Evagrius observes how "the noonday demon" makes it appear that "the sun moves slowly or not at all, and that the day seems to be fifty hours long."[5] The feminine world of night, on the other hand, "quickly dreams away the time." Hippolyta here foreshadows the nighttime realm of the fairy forest, which is the sphere of dreams, play, and freedom. In contrast to Theseus' sphere of rigid hierarchical laws, which orders everything and stifles love in favor of patriarchal rights, the fairy forest turns everything on its head and engenders freedom. Hermia and Lysander enter the forest to be free from "the sharp Athenian law" (I.i.162), while the tradesmen actors go to the forest so they will not "be dogged with company" (I.ii.82). The magic wood looses and reorients the fixed vows of romantic love, resulting in a frustration that causes the lovers to abandon their polite formality for insults. This carnivalesque world displays a freedom in relation to the ordered daytime world that is at once liberating and chaotic.

In this chaotic play, the nighttime realm of the fairies hearkens back to something akin to creational time, an elemental moment filled with infinite hopes and limitless possibilities. Writing on festivals, Roger Caillois aptly summarizes the forest's atmosphere when he describes "primordial" or "mythical" time as "the ideal place for metamorphoses and miracles as nothing has yet been stabilized, no rule pronounced, and no form fixed."[6] Rather than merely appealing to the past to solidify the present rule of "lazy time," true festivals such as carnival usher participants into mythical time thereby lightening the existential burden of conventional chronology. For Bakhtin, the function of the "carnival-grotesque" is "to consecrate inventive freedom, to permit the combination of a variety of different elements and their rapprochement, to liberate from the prevailing point of view of the world, from conventions and established truths, from clichés, from all that is humdrum and universally accepted."[7] A clear element of deconstruction imbues the carnival spirit. A desire for freedom drives the participants to break down walls and to shed the normal restraints of society in an act of joyous rebellion. This rebellion, however, is not blind, random, or vindictive, rather it targets all that is "immortalized and completed," that is, "the old authority and truth [which] pretend to be absolute, to have an extratemporal importance."[8] At first glance, then, carnival appears to be opposed to faith and the church, for the church claims to be authoritative and the guardian of truth.[9] Is carnival a rebellion against faith?

Here we must be careful to distinguish between what Bakhtin calls "religiosity" and true faith, for Christianity itself levels its harshest criticisms against the hypocrisies of religious authority. Indeed, Christ's proclamation of the kingdom of God has striking resemblances to the carnival "two-time condition" and its rebellion against traditional authority. Shortly after beginning his ministry, Jesus enters the synagogue in his hometown of Nazareth on the Sabbath and reads from Isaiah:

> The Spirit of the Lord is upon me, because he has anointed me to proclaim good news to the poor. He has sent me to proclaim liberty to the captives and recovery of sight to the blind, to set at liberty those who are oppressed, to proclaim the year of the Lord's favour. (Luke 4:18-19)

Jesus then audaciously claims that he has fulfilled this Old Testament promise in their midst. While the text that he reads is Isaiah 61, what

Jesus is proclaiming is the "year of Jubilee" outlined in Leviticus 25, the Sabbath of Sabbaths, the ultimate time of liberty, rest, and renewal. Like the topsy-turvydom of carnival, in the year of Jubilee creditors forgive debts, masters free slaves, the rich return land to the poor, and farmers let the fields rest. It is a year of joyous liberty that returns people to the creational moment of limitless potentiality when God declared everything to be "very good" and rested to complete his creation. Karl Barth argues that in the Sabbath God shows that he "was not content merely to create the world but that when he had created it He associated Himself with it once for all and always as the Lord of glory that He is."[10] By announcing the year of Jubilee, therefore, Jesus recalls the era when creation was in harmony with itself and God and reminds of God's ever-present nearness to his creation (cf. "the kingdom of God is at hand," Mark 1:15).

Jesus also, however, inaugurates a new sort of time; he does not announce *a* Jubilee but *the* Jubilee. In the words of Jürgen Moltmann, "the messianic year of liberty is the beginning of messianic time; and the messianic time is time without end."[11] The futural aspects of messianic time will be discussed in a later section, but here we should observe how, like carnival, Jesus establishes a different mode of time within time; he creates a "two-time condition" where the new experience of time is in direct contrast to conventional chronology. As the herald and emissary of this oppositional kingdom, Jesus finds himself in conflict with the traditional power structures—the Jewish religious authorities, the Roman government, and the social, ethnic, and economic boundaries of his age. He does this not for his own aggrandizement but for the freedom of others. Summarizing a theological understanding of this kingdom, Moltmann says that "the Trinitarian doctrine of the kingdom is the theological doctrine of freedom," for "God is the inexhaustible freedom of those he has created."[12] It would seem that Jesus' inauguration of the kingdom of God's Jubilee has quite a few affinities with carnival, including their initiating of an alternate time within time and their emphasis on freedom. Both "beguile lazy time" and free participants for a wilder chronological modality.

Transgression and the Preposterous

How does carnival bring about freedom? Commenting on games and the carnival spirit, Bakhtin says, "games drew the players out of the bounds of everyday life, liberated them from usual laws and regulations, and replaced established conventions by other lighter conventionalities."[13] Participants cross the boundaries of "normal life" and enter into a second sphere where "lighter conventionalities" apply. Elsewhere, Bakhtin discusses the carnival principle of "degradation, that is, the lowering of all that is high, spiritual, ideal, abstract."[14] Again, the idea of boundary crossing is crucial as carnival seeks to transgress social, economic, political, and religious boundaries in order to level all things. Transgression and freedom, by this account, go hand in hand. Carnival can even seem synonymous with destruction.[15] As we will see, it is unfair to reduce the carnivalesque to transgression; nevertheless its love of boundary crossing cannot be denied.

In *A Midsummer Night's Dream*, Puck, the fairy trickster, is the clearest exemplar of transgression. Puck is the "merry wanderer of the night" who plays tricks on the likes of "the wisest aunt, telling the saddest tale" in order to make others laugh (II.i.43, 51). Puck is literally a free spirit who delights solely in play and finds the human pretension to seriousness to be one of his greatest sports, saying to Oberon about the lovers, "Shall we their fond pageant see? / Lord, what fools these mortals be!" (III.ii.114–15). Combining the roles of Cupid and Mercury, Puck puts "a girdle round about the earth in forty minutes" to find the magic flower of love that causes so much mischief (II.i.175–76). He moves between the world of the lovers, the tradesmen actors, and the fairy monarchs with the greatest of ease, playing his merry tricks at every opportunity. "The trickster," according to Jan Kott, "is the personification of mobility and changeability and transcends all boundaries, overthrowing all hierarchies. He turns everything upside-down."[16] A favorite game of Puck's is chasing and leading the mortals astray by transforming himself. Disrupting the "hempen homespun" actors, he declares,

> I'll follow you: I'll lead you about a round,
> Through bog, through bush, through brake, through briar;
> Sometime a horse I'll be, sometime a hound
> A hog, a headless bear, sometime a fire,

> And neigh, and bark, and grunt, and roar, and burn,
> Like horse, hound, hog, bear, fire at every turn. (III.i.88–93)

Both form and locality are lightly transgressed, much to the bewilderment of the actors. He boasts that he is "feared in field and town" (III.ii.398). Puck enjoys the sport, but mortals often do not. Transgression can have a disturbing, unsettling, and terrifying side to it. Bakhtin calls Puck's type of character the "rogue" and claims it has a vital function in carnivalesque literature: "They grant the right *not* to understand, the right to confuse, to tease, to hyperbolize life; the right to parody others while talking, the right to not be taken literally, not 'to be oneself'; [. . .] the right to act life as a comedy and to treat others as actors."[17] Frequently utilizing an agent of transgression, the carnivalesque destabilizes monolithic norms and disorients traditional modes of being.

This disorientation often occurs through an inversion of order or a reversal of expectations. Puck claims that "those things do best please me / that befall prepost'rously" (III.ii.120–21). Typically thought to mean simply "absurd," "preposterous" literally relates to "placing last what should be first" or vice versa.[18] Whereas the mechanicals *begin* their play within a play with "if we offend, it is with our good will" (V.i.115), Puck *ends* with an oddly inverted sentiment:

> If we shadows have offended
> Think but this, and all is mended,
> That you have but slumber'd here
> While these visions did appear. (V.i.417–20)

Unlike the plea for preemptive absolution on the basis of good intent, Puck, having already offended, offers no apologies but a final trick. An inversion of perspective from reality to dream will "restore amends" (V.i.432). It is, however, this final trick couched in terms of friendship that is the most disconcerting. Chesterton observes how, after dispelling the dreams of the forest in the "happy and generous rationalism" of Theseus' house:

> The play seems naturally ended. It began on the earth and it ends on the earth. [. . . But] then there comes a faint sound of little feet, and for a moment, as it were, the elves look into the house, asking which is the reality. "Suppose we are the realities and they the shadows." If that ending were

acted properly any modern man would feel shaken to his marrow if he had to walk home from the theatre through a country lane.[19]

It is this final preposterous inversion which, according to Chesterton, "makes the play colossal" and potentially "the greatest of [Shakespeare's] plays."[20]

Connections here between carnivalesque transgression, preposterous inversions, and a theological understanding of the kingdom of God are not hard to find. Harvey Cox, for instance, has written of how Christ is "like the jester" in how he "defies custom and scorns crowned heads," "like a wandering troubadour" in that "he has no place to lay his head," and "like a minstrel" in the way that "he frequents dinners and parties."[21] Jesus was an inveterate boundary crosser. He scorned ethnic, religious, and gender boundaries when he spoke with the Samaritan woman at the well (John 4). He crossed social barriers by eating with tax collectors and allowing prostitutes to wash his feet. He delighted in little children and mocked the powerful religious authorities. He destabilized rigid conventions, such as Sabbath and ritual purity laws (Mark 2 and 7). When in Luke 4 Jesus declares the time of Jubilee, he disorients and angers the crowd by claiming that God's love transgresses ethnic and religious barriers, and then, after they "brought him to the brow of the hill" so that they could "throw him down the cliff," Jesus mysteriously and nonchalantly escapes ("but passing through their midst, he went away," 4:30). Subsequent to his resurrection—the ultimate act of transgression, crossing the boundary of death—he behaves rather like Puck at times, passing through walls (John 20:19, 26), appearing disguised (Luke 24:16; John 21:4), disappearing at will (Luke 24:31), and finally ascending into the clouds (Acts 1:9). The picture of Jesus as the transgressive "rogue" or "trickster" is surprisingly easy to paint.

Jesus also seems best pleased by those things "that befall prepost'rously." He declares that "the last will be first and the first last" (Matt 20:16) and that "unless you change and become like little children, you will never enter the kingdom of heaven" (Matt 18:3). Jesus' most preposterous trick, however, is his final inversion of the human story. Ending with his tragic and innocent death, Jesus could have been like Socrates, a noble teacher, a vibrant example of how to defy corruption and live virtuously. Instead, like the fairies returning to the stage when "the graves, all gaping wide, / Every one lets forth his sprite" (V.i.371–72), Jesus rises from the grave, preposterously placing death not at the end of all things but at the beginning of new life. This single assertion has haunted and beguiled the world for almost two thousand years.

Moreover, according to Karl Barth, Jesus' resurrection had an additional preposterous effect. In accordance with the Genesis creation account, the Jewish week ends with the Sabbath. Since Jesus rose again on the day after the Jewish Sabbath, however, Christians now celebrate Sabbath on the first day of the week rather than the last. Barth explains:

> This first day of this new time had to become literally as well as materially the day of rest which dominates life in this new time. [. . .] Man after this day was not set on the way to a Sabbath still to be sanctified, but on the way from a Sabbath already sanctified; from rest to work; from freedom to service; from joy to 'seriousness' of life. Rest, freedom and joy were not just before him. [. . .] He had already sat at the divine wedding-feast, and having eaten and drunk could now proceed to his daily work. The "Lord's Day" was really his first day.²²

By preposterously placing Sabbath at the beginning of the week rather than the end, Jesus turns time on its head and shows that joy and rest are not the rewards of work but the festive place of its commencement. Seriousness thus becomes the secondary and derivative experience rather than primary. "Each week," says Barth, "instead of being a trying ascent, ought to have been a glad descent from the high-point of the Sabbath."²³ While it is still in some sense an interruption into normal "lazy time," Sabbath reveals itself as being (and always having been) "the true time from which alone [man] can have other time."²⁴ The preposterous herein unmasks itself as the true order. Given the fallen or inverted nature of humanity, carnivalesque and Sabbath inversions are not only liberating and beguiling but also apocalyptic, unveiling true reality.

Apocalyptic Lightness

The revelations of carnival are not received through reason and seriousness but through laughter and enjoyment. Bakhtin comments that "laughter is essentially not an external but an interior form of truth; [. . .] laughter liberates not only from external censorship but first of all from the great interior censor; [...] laughter [opens] men's eyes on that which is new, on the future."²⁵ Carnivalesque laughter not only releases, it also reveals, and, as Bakhtin points out, it does so primarily from within the individual. It is a change of perspective, a new and different way of seeing reality, one which is oriented toward the future.

In *A Midsummer Night's Dream*, Puck through the magic flower forces a similar change of perspective upon the lovers. They find themselves donning and stripping various romantic masks, trying on foreign attitudes and seeing with different eyes. Demetrius sees the cruelty of his former behavior toward Helena and repents of it; Lysander learns how frustrating it is to pursue someone who does not return his love; Hermia and Helena exchange positions—the former to see how miserable it is to be rejected by her lover and the latter to learn how undesirable it is to have two men fighting over her. These scenes are laughable primarily because the mask of romantic love, which claims to be eternal and wholly authentic, turns out to be ephemeral and mutable. In being laughed at, however, romantic love is not ultimately scorned, for as Bakhtin says, "True ambivalent and universal laughter does not deny seriousness but purifies and completes it; [...] it liberates from fanaticism and pedantry, from fear and intimidation, from didacticism, naiveté and illusion, from the single meaning, the single level, from sentimentality."²⁶ Though not shown laughing, the lovers by the light of day see the ridiculousness of their nighttime behavior. In impersonating each other, they have learned something about themselves and are better prepared for their future marriages. In the words of one critic, it is as if "no one has ever known his or her face until seeing it in caricature."²⁷ They have become conscious of a dialogic vision:

> Demetrius: These things seem small and undistinguishable,
> Like far-off mountains turned into clouds.
> Hermia: Methinks I see these things with parted eye
> When everything seems double.
> Helena: So methinks;
> And I have found Demetrius, like a jewel,
> Mine own, and not mine own.
> Demetrius: Are you sure
> That we are awake? It seems to me
> That yet we sleep, we dream. (IV.i.184–91)

Their masks are not forgotten; they can still see "with parted eye" and remember what it was like to have had their love altered or thwarted. They are therefore more aware that love is a gift that always remains a gift—"mine own, and not mine own." The carnivalesque exchange of masks and perspectives, in Bakhtin's words, "restores this ambivalent wholeness" allowing the characters to be transformed and reintegrated into the joyful community.[28]

Laughter could thus in some sense be said to bring one to a place of confession, for "the ability to laugh at oneself," as Reinhold Niebuhr observes, "is the prelude to the sense of contrition" and "a vestibule to the temple of confession."[29] Laughter teaches individuals to let go of their seriousness and therein prepares them for acknowledging and repenting personal failings. John Donne in his Easter Day sermon from 1622 rhapsodizes:

> Man is but a vapour; but a glorious, and a blessed vapour, when he is attracted, and caught up by this Sun, the Son of Man, the Son of God. O what a blessed alleviation possesses that man! and to what a blessed levity [. . .] to what a cheerefull lightnesse of spirit is he come that comes newly from Confession, and with the seale of Absolution upon him![30]

As the Sabbath of Sabbaths, Easter discloses the lightness of being, a lightness that causes "a holy cheerefulnesse of spirit" in one who has unburdened heavy sins through confession. In this way, what Barth calls the "renouncing faith" of Sabbath shows itself not as strenuous asceticism but as "blessed alleviation" and "cheerefull lightnesse." Like carnivalesque laughter, Sabbath forces an individual to change his perspective, to put on certain masks, but only in order to reveal his true nature and bring about a metamorphosis of levity:

> It demands that he know himself only in his faith in God, that he will and work and express himself only in this imposed and not selected renunciation, and that on the basis of this renunciation he actually dare in it all to be a new creature, a new man.[31]

Sabbath so lightens a self of its seriousness—all that binds the self to itself—that it can "actually dare" that most audacious of things, to transform into a new, more liberated creature.

Messianic Time and the Grotesque

There is, of course, an actual metamorphosis in *A Midsummer Night's Dream* involving Bottom and an ass' head, which brings out a further aspect of carnival—its love of the grotesque and the body. The already-mentioned carnival principle of degradation, "the lowering of all that is high, spiritual, ideal, abstract," is "the essential principle of grotesque realism" in that it transfers ideals and abstractions "to the material level, to the sphere of earth and body."[32] W. H. Auden describes this phenomenon in terms of the relationship between body and spirit:

> Carnival celebrates the unity of our human race as mortal creatures, who come into this world and depart from it without our consent, who must eat, drink, defecate, belch, and break wind in order to live, and procreate if our species is to survive. Our feelings about this are ambiguous. [. . .] We oscillate between wishing we were unreflective animals and wishing we were disembodied spirits, for in either case we should not be problematic to ourselves.[33]

We are beings laden with both spiritual aspirations and physical urges. It is this contradiction which the grotesque plays upon. In addition, there is a recognition that revelation only comes through the body. The spirit—much to its chagrin—is dependent upon the body for the knowledge that it craves and cannot in its search after truth, goodness, and beauty escape the grossness of bodily needs and functions.

Looking again at Shakespeare's play, we find that Bottom is a perfect example of a character caught between body and spirit. Chesterton says that he "has a huge and unfathomable weakness, his silliness is on a great scale, and when he blows his own trumpet it is like the trumpet of the Resurrection."[34] Having been "translated" into the spiritual realm of Titania and crowned with an ass' head, Bottom's concern is not love for the beautiful fairy queen but rather more basic bodily things like having his head scratched and procuring honey-bags, "a peck of provender," or "good dry oats" (IV.i). He thus frustrates Titania's attempt to "purge thy mortal grossness so / that thou shalt like an airy spirit go" and remains a stubborn ass stuck somewhere between body and spirit (III.i.166–67). The ass mask is, according to Bakhtin, "one of the most ancient and lasting symbols of the material bodily lower stratum, which at the same time degrades and regenerates," and

Jan Kott adds that "the bodily meets with the spiritual in the *figura* and the masque of the ass."³⁵ The comedy of this scene consists in the coincidence of these opposites—high and low, spirit and body—and the tensions that exist within Bottom as he struggles to reconcile these impulses:

> I have had a most rare vision. I have had a dream, past the wit of man to say what dream it was. Man is but an ass if he go about to expound this dream. Methought I was—there is no man can tell what. Methought I was—and methought I had—but man is but a patched fool if he will offer to say what methought I had. The eye of man hath not heard, the ear of man hath not seen, man's hand is not able to taste, his tongue to conceive, nor his heart to report what my dream was! I will get Peter Quince to write a ballad of this dream; it shall be called 'Bottom's Dream', because it hath no bottom. (IV.i.200–209)

Bottom here misquotes 1 Corinthians 2:9-10: "Eye hath not seen, nor ear heard, neither have entered into the heart of man, the things which God hath prepared for them that love him. But God hath revealed them unto us by his Spirit: for the Spirit searcheth all things, yea, the deep things of God" (KJV). The mystery both in Bottom's speech and in Corinthians is how revelation occurs. Spiritual revelation conveys knowledge that the bodily senses alone could never discover, and yet revelation in both cases seeks form and enters into the sensible realm. Interestingly, as Jan Kott has pointed out, both the Tyndale (1534) and Geneva (1557) translations of 1 Corinthians 2:10 read, "the Spirite searcheth all things, ye the botome of Goddes secretes."³⁶ Bottom potentially acquired his ambiguous name from this verse—he is a low, bodily person caught up in the difficulties of interpreting high spiritual revelation. Humanity is in the position of Bottom ever striving to unify these distant poles but only succeeding in comic ways. With its intermingling of opposites, these scenes with Bottom and Titania depict the grotesque principle of degradation, yet Christianity offers an even more extreme example—the incarnation.

Though it is frequently overlooked or forgotten, the Christian faith has the grotesque at its heart, what Slavoj Žižek calls "the perverse core of Christianity."³⁷ The belief that the creator of the universe lowered himself, became human, died upon a cross, and then was resurrected resonates perfectly with the grotesque principle of degradation. In the incarnation, the perfection of spiritual revelation takes bodily form and becomes subject to all the inconveniences and embarrassments of flesh and blood. God urinated, defecated, belched, was sick, broke wind, masticated food, bled, cried, and died. Paul mentions only the last of these when he acknowledges that the grotesque idea of God being subject to death is scandalous to non-Christians: "we preach Christ crucified, a stumbling block [*skandalon*] to Jews and folly to Gentiles" (1 Cor 1:23). By taking on flesh, God affirms the goodness of physical existence and shows that it is the right means for receiving revelation. Not only did God lower himself to become human, but as noted in our discussion of folly he also became the lowest of humans, taking on the role (mask) of a servant. The result of his *kenosis*, his self-emptying, is to make a lowly servant the king of creation: "Therefore God has highly exalted him and bestowed on him the name that is above every name" (Phil 2:9). By this logic, the idea behind the feast of fools—that the lowliest fool should be king for a day—will eventually be the governing principle of reality. The future Sabbath will fulfill carnival expectations.

Such eschatological hope is essential to Sabbath and to carnival. Festive laughter, says Bakhtin, "expresses the people's hopes of a happier future, of a more just social and economic order, of a new truth."[38] Likewise, in the words of Barth, the "meaning and basis of the holy day" is "eschatological," in that it is a "reminder of the special history of the covenant and salvation [and] undoubtedly points us to the ultimate consummation of this history."[39] Both look to the future not with intangible abstraction, but in a way that begins to actualize it in the present. Messianic time as seen in the Sabbath, according to Giorgio Agamben, "implies an actual transformation of the experience of time that may even interrupt secular time here and now," for "it is that innermost disjointedness within time through which one may— by a hairsbreadth—grasp time and accomplish it."[40] In preposterously overcoming death in the resurrection, Jesus creates the real possibility of playing with the future. As Moltmann argues, "Easter opens up the boundary-crossing freedom to play the game of the new creation" meaning that "faith is a new spontaneity and a light heart."[41] With humanity liberated from its past sins and the future freed from the determinism of death, "lazy time" is thoroughly beguiled, and humanity can participate in the inexhaustible delight of being lighthearted children of God.

Concluding Interlude
MacDonald on Merriment

As our discussion shifts from general modes of levity to George MacDonald's specific fairytale levity, it might perhaps be helpful to be preposterous and give a glimpse of the end at the beginning. The reader might be convinced that levity is a significant and polyvalent theological and literary concept and yet still see the transition from lightness to the "tall, dark and serious" George MacDonald as something of a hermeneutical chasm.[42] Many people view MacDonald more as Charles Neaves' "zealot of stiff-clay" and "sour-looking child of sorrow" than one frequently "molested by mirth." Like Neaves, however, MacDonald was critical of the Scotch Sabbath and its tendency to make Sundays dull and lifeless. He writes, "One grand aim of the reformers of the Scottish ecclesiastical modes appears to have been to keep the worship pure and the worshippers sincere by embodying the whole in the ugliest forms that could be associated with the name of Christianity."[43] For MacDonald, this attitude toward the Sabbath misses the essential truth that the Lord does not give "bare existence" but "is ever working, even by suffering, to render life more rich and plentiful" and to "be lavish to his brethren."[44] Writing about Jesus' turning of water into wine, MacDonald says:

> There is a glad significance in the fact that our Lord's first miracle was this turning of water into wine. It is a true symbol of what he has done for the world in glorifying all things. With his divine alchemy he turns not only water into wine, but common things into radiant mysteries, yea, every meal into a eucharist, and the jaws of the sepulchre into an outgoing gate. [. . .] From all that is thus low and wretched, incapable and fearful, he who made the water into wine delivers men, revealing heaven around them, God in all things, truth in every instinct, evil withering and hope springing even in the path of the destroyer.[45]

Jesus did not come to limit celebration but to increase it by liberating humanity of its sins and false gods. The carnivalesque atmosphere of the wedding does not elicit Jesus' righteous anger but his extravagant generosity. Reflecting further on this miracle, MacDonald speculates:

> I wonder how many Christians there are who so thoroughly believe God made them that they can laugh in God's name; who understand that God invented laughter and gave it to his children. Such belief would add a keenness to the zest in their enjoyment, and slay that sneering laughter of which a man grimaces to the fiends, as well as that feeble laughter in which neither heart nor intellect has a share. It would help them also to understand the depth of this miracle. The Lord of gladness delights in the laughter of a merry heart.[46]

In the light of these statements about Jesus' love of laughter and festivity, maybe we can begin to see why Chesterton attributed a range of carnivalesque attributes to MacDonald, calling him "a nocturnal anarchist" who is "half-mad with joy" and whose style could be characterized as "celestial nonsense."[47] Perhaps in a preposterous reversal, seriousness and solemnity are the secondary, derivative things for MacDonald, while festive joy and laughter are the true realities.

PART II

MacDonald's Fairytale Levity

5

"Never so Real as When They Are Solemn"
Victorians and Seriousness

While most modern cultures set up levity and seriousness as diametrical opponents, this has not always been the view of every society. Medieval Catholic Europe, for instance, though girded round with strict laws and hierarchical structures, gave laughter and play a prime position within its cultural life both in institutional ceremonies such as the Feast of the Ass and in the everyday life of the people.[1] Of the forces that brought about the breakdown of medieval Catholic Europe and its attitude toward levity, two in particular are paramount to the discussion of Victorian seriousness—the Reformation and the Enlightenment.

The historical irony of the Reformation is that its attempt to liberate humanity from the works-righteousness of the most excessive elements of the Catholic Church ended in a new form of legalism. Jürgen Moltmann notes how after fighting against the "system of penances, indulgences and almsgiving on the ground of a new faith which justified without the works of the law," the Reformation went on to "abolish the holidays, games and safety valves of that society. This led to the establishment of the Puritan society of penny pinchers and to the industrial workaday world among the very people who had at first insisted on believing that men are justified by faith alone."[2] It is as though humanity has an incredible difficulty bearing the lightness of grace, and finds it easier to assert the primacy of seriousness in various forms and guises. The anonymous 1693 book *A Call to Seriousness in*

Religion exhorts its readers, "Thou hast a God to mind, a Soul to save, and Heaven to seek, and Hell to flee from; Warnings to take notice of; and all the solemnities and results of an Awful Day of Judgment to prepare for and expect."[3] It would appear that some Protestants, in the words of Charles Neaves, "with sermons from morning till night / strive to be decent and dreary."[4]

The Enlightenment emphasis on reason and rationality led to a different sort of solemnity, but one which was similarly destructive to a spirit of levity. According to Friedrich Engels, in the age of Enlightenment "cogitative reason became the yardstick of all that existed."[5] Philosophers set reason on a lonely monolithic throne, denigrating tradition and religion as superstition and eschewing laughter and merriment as manifestations of humanity's "self-incurred immaturity."[6] From her lofty position, reason then identified categorical imperatives and mandated solemn duties which everyone had to perform without the help of humor or enjoyment.[7] "Laziness and cowardice" were the only possible reasons for people not engaging in the serious and solemn business of becoming autonomous individuals.[8] Thus, as with Protestantism, followers of the Enlightenment often ridiculed light or grotesque forms and espoused a negative attitude toward levity.

Such quick summaries of two complex ages like the Reformation and the Enlightenment can be little more than evocative caricatures, yet Victorians were still wrestling with the legacies left by these movements. Consider, for instance, the following excerpt from John Henry Newman, writing in 1850 five years after his conversion from Anglicanism to Catholicism about the religious attitude of Victorian Britain:

> They keep the exhibition of their faith for high days and great occasions, when it comes forth with sufficient pomp and gravity of language, and ceremonial of manner. Truths slowly totter out with Scripture texts as their elbow, as unable to walk alone. Moreover they know, if such and such things *be* true, what *ought* to be the voice, the tone, the gesture, and the carriage attendant upon them; thus reason, which is the substance of their faith, supplies the rubrics, as I may call them, of their behaviour. This, some of you, my brethren call reverence; though I am obliged to say, it is as much a mannerism, and an unpleasant mannerism, as that of the Evangelical party, which they have hitherto condemned. They condemn Catholics, because, however religious, they are natural, unaffected, easy and cheerful, in their

mention of sacred things; and they think themselves never so real as when they are solemn.[9]

Gravity and solemnity, according to Newman, connect with the "real" in the minds of Victorians. Assaulted on the one side by the earnest moral and spiritual tradition of the Reformation and on the other by the grave rationalistic mindset of the Enlightenment, the Victorians were constantly tempted to associate "seriousness" with the only reality and to see an "easy and cheerful" attitude toward "sacred things" as somehow inauthentic. As much as any age before or since, Victorians were haunted by "seriousness." They argued about it, extolled its virtues, rebelled against it, tried to escape it, and worshipped at its temple. Such a conclusion about the Victorians, however, might at this point seem too general, so let us take a few moments to explore more thoroughly some contours of the Victorian intellectual landscape. Doing so will help to place MacDonald within his context and illustrate how remarkable his fairytale levity was in contrast to the heavy earnestness of his contemporaries.

A Humorous Age?

One objection to the suggestion that the Victorians were obsessed with seriousness is the prominence of popular comic literature in the period. As Donald Gray observes, "the first point to be made about Victorian laughter is simply that there was so much of it."[10] Chesterton, likewise, claims that one of the primary characteristics of the period was "the deep Victorian sense of humour" and that the "[Victorian] was really a humourist."[11] In addition to the more famous periodicals like *Punch* and its main rival *Fun*, there were more than 300 comic periodicals published in Great Britain between 1832 and 1900.[12] Many famous writers began on or edited one of these comic journals, including William Thackeray (who wrote for both *Fraser's Magazine* and *Punch*) and Thomas Hood, the humorist poet who edited the *Comic Annual* (1830–1842). In addition to large numbers of writers, these journals also required a small army of comic illustrators such as George Cruikshank—more famous for his illustrations of *Grimms' Fairy Tales* (1823) and several Dickens novels (e.g., *Sketches of Boz*, 1836; and *Oliver Twist*, 1838)—and John Leech, *Punch*'s most renowned Victorian artist.

And yet, perhaps the most interesting aspect of this massive comic output was its relationship to the "serious" issues and questions of the time. Donald Gray points out that "the political and social opinions championed in comic journals tended to be huddled discreetly near the middle of the road" and that "comic journalists were most often content to exploit rather than to try to change or enlarge the opinions of their readers."[13] Jokes and laughter were seen as pardonable and innocuous as long as they did not touch upon questions of politics, morality, or religion. Unlike the medieval topsy-turvy, which was not only unafraid to laugh at the king and pope but delighted in doing so, most Victorian humor was tame and fearfully kept to its place. Even so, more-respectable Victorians often had harsh words to say about the genre of "light literature" and its lack of seriousness, as did, for instance, the Christian Socialist and poet Gerald Massey in discussing the lamentable imitators of Thomas Hood:

> This ambition to say smart things, and be thought funny, is working fatally in the literature of the day, and is sapping the very root of all earnestness. A man will soon have to be ashamed of all serious earnestness in the presence of these modern Samsons, who wear such long hair, and slay with the jawbone of an ass. Nor can we tolerate all the senseless levity that in certain quarters is fast eating out the sturdy spirit of our glorious Saxon language, or, without protest, permit these eunuchs of thought to replace the lofty English of Shakspeare, and Milton, and the great divines, with the slang of the cider-cellars, and the cantology of puppydom. We have had all too much of this irreverence and losel levity. Life is too real, too earnest, too solemn a thing, to be spent in producing or in reading such *light* literature. We want something more of the Ironside earnestness in individual character, in our books, and in the national life. Earnestness is the root of greatness and heroism. "They were in earnest," and not "They were only joking," is the epitaph which history has inscribed in letters of light, or of blood, on the tombs of her illustrious—the heroes, martyrs, and teachers.[14]

Earnestness and levity cannot mix, according to Massey, without earnestness losing its power and vitality. Here again we find the association of life and the "real" with an earnest solemnity. Gravity is true and substantial; levity is false and ephemeral, and those models that one should look to—heroes, martyrs, and teachers—were all in deadly earnest.

This attitude toward humor existed not just within a small group of social and moral elitists—the humorists themselves shared it. While defending Thomas Hood as a "serious" poet, Gerald Massey perceptively observes Hood's own relationship with his humor: "Hood always appears to me to have so deep a sense, such a painful sense of the terrible earnestness of existence, that it would be unbearable if he could not get some humour out of it, and *phantasie* some light and merry moods of mind."[15] Humor, in other words, is an escape, a momentary forgetting of the heavy seriousness of existence. Similarly, Chesterton says of Hood that "poverty and illness forced him to the toils of an incessant jester"—humor was not a joy but a job.[16] Hood himself confirms these opinions when he writes in the preface to a work that he wanted to be taken "seriously": "because I have jested elsewhere, it does not follow that I am incompetent for gravity."[17] Here Hood implies that he does not consider his light and comic works to have any "serious" import—they are mere distractions and entertainments. No doubt Hood undersells himself and does not fully value the serious significance of his light modes, but the attitude is intriguing. And, according to Gray, this was the common belief of humorists: "professional humourists similarly manifested their mistrust of the seriousness of laughter when they chose unequivocally grave forms in which to speak their earnest selves."[18] Even humorists took it for granted that "seriousness" was the real business of life. While they might toil for their daily bread by making light of things, comic writers too felt "never so real as when they were solemn."

But what was it precisely that the Victorians were so solemn about? One Victorian humorist who did mix seriousness and levity—and recognized the value of both—presciently identified and laughed at some of the more tyrannical forms of seriousness, and his characters serve as useful illustrations of these Victorian attitudes.

Gradgrind and Bounderby
Utilitarian Apostles

Dickens' *Hard Times* begins with the following monologue by Thomas Gradgrind: "Now, what I want is, Facts. Teach these boys and girls nothing but Facts. Facts alone are wanted in life. Plant nothing else, and root out everything else. You can only form the minds of reasoning animals upon Facts: nothing else will ever be of any service to them."[19] In Britain, the Enlightenment exaltation of reason led to the Utilitarianism of Jeremy Bentham and his followers—notably James Mill, and his son John Stuart Mill. Gradgrind was actually a thinly veiled caricature of James Mill, who famously took Bentham's Utilitarian principles and attempted to raise his children solely by reason. Speaking of his upbringing, John Stuart Mill wrote in his *Autobiography*, "I do not believe that any scientific teaching ever was more thorough, or better fitted for training the faculties, than the mode in which logic and political economy were taught to me by my father."[20] James Mill intended this education to turn his son into a model for a new sort of humanity—one based on Gradgrind's facts and which sought to perfect society and its structures without personal prejudice. Bentham posited the quantitative principle of utility—the greatest happiness to the greatest number—as the only fully rational means of resolving the economic, political, and moral issues of society.[21] Whereas subjective self-interest motivated most people, Utilitarians saw themselves as objective, not swayed by the vagaries of emotion or desire.

These beliefs manifestly equate reality with solemnity and illusion with any form of levity. In *Hard Times* when Sissy Jupe uses the common phrase "I fancy," Gradgrind flies into a fury: "You are to be in all things regulated and governed by fact. [. . .] You must discard the word Fancy altogether. You have nothing to do with it. You are not to have, in any object of use or ornament, what would be a contradiction of fact."[22] In a similar incident, his daughter Louisa says to her brother, "Tom, I wonder," at which Gradgrind cries, "Louisa, never wonder!" and the narrator comments, "herein lay the spring of the mechanical art and mystery of educating the reason without stooping to the cultivation of the sentiments and affections. Never wonder."[23] This is why Gradgrind is so upset when he finds his children peeping under the tent of the circus. Fancy and wonder—those two vital elements of the imagination—have no role in a serious, fact-based reality.

Thomas Gradgrind's closest "friend" in *Hard Times* is the large "bully of humility" Josiah Bounderby, who takes Gradgrind's Utilitarian principles beyond education and into the economic and social spheres. Bounderby, who owns the bank and the manufacturing plant, essentially controls Coketown. Roughly based on a mid-nineteenth-century

Lancashire town, Coketown is "a triumph of fact," and Bounderby is the chief cause of this triumph. Dickens here shows capitalism arm in arm with the scientific materialism of Utilitarianism. While Gradgrind often displays tenderness toward the poor and oppressed (taking in the abandoned Sissy), Bounderby is entirely self-interested and behaves heartlessly toward the lower classes, believing that their misfortune is due to an inadequate work ethic. In the Utilitarian gospel—as for Victorians more generally—work was the grace given everyone.[24] If someone is struggling to survive, many Victorians thought, it must be because they are not working hard enough. "Know thy work and do it," says Thomas Carlyle in *Past and Present* (1843), "is the latest Gospel in this world."[25] Bounderby feels no sympathy for the troubles of the poor because they seem to him to have neglected work as their means to salvation. Though obviously a caricature, Dickens portrays in Bounderby and Coketown the harsh economic and social realities that dominated much of the Victorian experience.

The Industrial Revolution left Britain with many Coketowns that were "triumphs of fact." These towns and cities served as the basis for the new wealth and power of the British Empire, but as Philip Davis comments, "this man-made world seemed to be gaining power over the men and women within it, like a machine that had developed beyond the control of its own inventors."[26] The move from the rural community life to urban individual existence was a key factor in the development of the Victorian consciousness and also one that led to the creation of new problems and the exacerbation of old ones. Overcrowded cities put strains on water and food sources. Existing sanitation could not handle the increased waste. The coal-burning plants that created jobs and opportunity also spewed out clouds of black soot. Such was the strain put on cities that "in 1851, a child born in inner Liverpool could expect to survive to the age of only 26, whereas a child born in the small market town of Okehampton could hope to live more than twice as long, to the age of 57."[27] Facts were facts, and the facts of urban life were often painful and always serious. "The time for levity, insincerity, and idle babble and play-acting, in all kinds, is gone by," says Thomas Carlyle in *Past and Present*, for "it is a serious, grave time."[28] How could anything be more real than the poverty, sickness, and death that were ever present in these toxic environments? Levity in the midst of such suffering, thought the Victorians, was surely worse than frivolous, it was inhuman and heartless. For Carlyle, the seriousness of the times proved that life was "not a May-game [. . .] but a battle and a march, a warfare with principalities and powers. [. . .] It is a stern pilgrimage through burning sandy solitudes, through regions of thick-ribbed ice."[29] Victorian life was far more akin to Dante's purgatory or hell than it was to his paradise. Surely, however, the religious attitudes of the time must have promoted a more joyful mode of being? Unfortunately for the Victorians, this was rarely the case.

A Grave God
Evangelicals and Matthew Arnold

After observing that everything in Coketown is "severely workful," Dickens turns to "eighteen religious persuasions" who each built "a pious warehouse of red brick, with sometimes (but this is only in highly ornamental examples) a bell in a birdcage on the top of it."[30] There is, however, a "perplexing mystery" about these religious groups: "Who belonged to the eighteen denominations? Because, whoever did, the labouring people did not." This upsets the religious people to such an extent that they send representatives to the House of Commons "indignantly petitioning for acts of parliament that should make these people religious by main force."[31] Dickens is hardly exaggerating here about the diversity and enthusiasm of these religious groups. By 1882 the city of London had 1,251 churches associated with 30 denominations while nationwide there were over 180 different brands of Christianity.[32] Despite an 1851 census that showed less than half of the population attending church (and to the chagrin of Anglicans more than half of those were nonconformist), church building continued at a frenetic pace in the second half of the century. Anglicans, for example, spent over £80.5 million on building projects from 1860 to 1885—with the result that "where in 1851 there was seating for 85% of the population, by 1881 the population had doubled, yet church and chapel seating was said to have exceeded it, and churches were less full in 1881 than in 1851."[33] In response to this social decline of religion, Christians, especially evangelicals, seemed to become increasingly grave.

Evangelicals, of course, did not need additional encouragement to be solemn—it came naturally. Half a century before the Victorian era,

William Cowper articulated the evangelical admiration of seriousness in describing the ideal preacher:

> I would express him simple, grave, sincere;
> In doctrine uncorrupt; in language plain,
> And plain in manner; decent, solemn, chaste,
> And natural in gesture; much impress'd
> Himself, as conscious of his awful charge,
> And anxious mainly that the flock he feeds
> May feel it too. (*The Task*, Book II, 399–405)

Right moral behavior was the duty of all earnest Christians, and evangelicals thought that any deviation from solemnity in these matters was an attack on goodness and God himself. Parodying the Clapham Society, a prominent evangelical sect, William Thackeray in *The Newcomes* describes their compound:

> It was a serious paradise. As you enter the gate, gravity fell on you; and decorum wrapped you in a garment of starch. [. . .] The rooks in the elms cawed sermons at morning and evening; the peacocks walked demurely on the terraces; the guinea-fowls looked more quaker-like than those savoury-birds usually do. The lodge-keeper was serious, and a clerk at a neighbouring chapel.[34]

Furthermore, a heavy emphasis on judgment and predestination, especially in the Calvinism of Scotland, gave people the impression that God himself was stern, earnest, and rigid, like the black-clad prophets in the pulpit. Revivalist preacher Rowland Hill complained that "because I am in earnest, men call me an enthusiast. [. . .] When I see eternal destruction ready to fall upon poor sinners, and about to entomb them irrevocably in an eternal mass of woe, and call aloud on them to escape, shall I be called an enthusiast now?"[35] In the face of humanity's awful destiny, unbelievers were to tremble and believers were to remain ever sombre and vigilant, searching their souls for traces of sin and boldly pointing out the sins of their neighbors. "Labouring under an intense sense of mission," says Ian Bradley, "[evangelicals] believed that their task was to call their fellow men to seriousness."[36]

As the nineteenth century moved on, however, traditional Christian faith became difficult to affirm. The ability of scientific inquiry to explain in purely naturalistic terms the geological history of the earth or the origins of life shook the foundations of religious belief. Tennyson's *In Memoriam*—described by George MacDonald as "*the* poem of the hoping doubters, *the* poem of our age"[37]—captured the conflicted mood of the period:

> [Man] trusted God was love indeed
> And love Creation's final law—
> Tho' Nature, red in tooth and claw
> With ravine, shriek'd against his creed. (55)

Increasingly, the arguments of evangelicals like Anthony Nesbit (E. Nesbit's grandfather)—who in *Essay on Education* (1841) said the dinosaurs were the animals left out of Noah's ark—and Philip Gosse—who in *Omphalos* (1847) argued that God created the world six thousand years ago but with a ready-made geological past—seemed untenable to thoughtful individuals.[38] To a person like Matthew Arnold, this trend to abandon traditional religious belief was both positive and worrying.

In his 1873 work *Literature and Dogma*, Arnold described the growing disbelief of "the masses" in the Bible:

> Is what this story asserts *true*, they are beginning to ask; can it be verified?—since experience proves, they add, that whatever for man is true, man can verify. And certainly the fairy-tale of the three Lord Shaftesburys no man can verify. They find this to be so, and then they say: The Bible takes for granted this story and depends on the truth of it; what, then can rational people have to do with the Bible? So they get rid, to be sure, of a false ground for using the Bible, but they at the same time lose the Bible itself, and the true religion of the Bible: righteousness, and the method and secret of Jesus.[39]

Forget about a historically revealed God and the mythology of the Bible, says Arnold, but do not forget its moral and ethical teachings.[40] The Bible, in other words, behind the fairytales is solemnly serious. Earlier in the same work, Arnold makes similar condescending remarks about fairytales and faith:

> That men should, by help of their imagination, take short cuts to what they ardently desire, whether the triumph of Israel or the triumph of Christianity, should tell themselves fairy-tales about it, should make these fairy-tales

> the basis for what is far more sure and solid than the fairy-tales, the desire itself,—all this has in it, we repeat, nothing which is not natural, nothing blameable. [. . .] In religion, above all, *extra-belief* is in itself no matter, assuredly, for blame. The object of religion is conduct.[41]

Not only are form and content separable for Arnold, but it is the duty of enlightened humanity to distill the essence from the Bible.[42] The fairytales of faith were fine when humanity was still in its infancy and adolescence, but now that humanity has come of age it is time to be reasonable: discard the fancy and hold ever more firmly to the truth therein embodied. In Arnold's mind, this abstract truth was the morality of "high seriousness."

Arnold believed that he was defending the importance of religion in the modern age against the more extreme elements of naturalism and positivism, but as Chesterton quips, "[he] may have thought that he was building an altar to the Unknown God; but he was really building it to Divus Caesar."[43] Religion, for Arnold, is "the greatest and most important of the efforts by which the human race has manifested its impulse to perfect itself."[44] When this impulse succeeds, its result is "high seriousness," although for Arnold such an achievement is extremely rare in the history of culture and literature—not even Chaucer rises high enough:

> The substance of Chaucer's poetry, his view of things and his criticism of life, has largeness, freedom, shrewdness, benignity; but it has not this high seriousness. Homer's criticism of life has it, Dante's has it, Shakespeare's has it. It is this chiefly which gives our spirits what they can rest upon; and with the increasing demands of our modern ages upon poetry, this virtue of giving us what we can rest upon will be more and more highly esteemed.[45]

Arnold restates this phrase "what we can rest upon" several times in his comparison of the relative virtue of Byron and Wordsworth: "[Wordsworth's] poetry gives us more which we may rest upon than Byron's,—more which we can rest upon now, and which men may rest upon always."[46] A generation earlier, Thomas Carlyle said something similar in *Sartor Resartus* when he commanded the reader, "close thy Byron; open thy Goethe."[47] In the exclusion of Byron and Chaucer from the pantheon of "high seriousness," it is difficult not to think that Arnold is denigrating laughter and levity as things which cannot "be rested upon"—that is, as less "real" than seriousness. Indeed in "My Countrymen" (1866), Arnold says that "with frivolity you can do nothing; but with seriousness there is always hope."[48] Like most Victorians, Arnold too seems to find himself and his culture "never so real as when they are solemn." Though Arnold shucks the mythological husk of the traditional Christian God, his kernel God ends up being just as solemn and grave as the evangelicals who prefer eating the seed whole.

On Griffins
Eliot vs. Ruskin

In literature, one consequence of the dominance of seriousness was the rise of realistic fiction. Evangelical earnestness caused writers like George Eliot and John Ruskin—both of whom were evangelical by upbringing but later rejected it—to have an "extra-literary anxiety and concern which gave their works their tense realist seriousness."[49] It is slightly ironic that evangelical earnestness and solemnity by promoting "tense realist seriousness" might have contributed to the rising difficulty that Victorians had in believing in the supernatural. Interestingly though, it is George Eliot, the writer of creative fiction, who sometimes looked down upon the supernatural and fanciful imaginative modes and John Ruskin, the writer of nonfiction criticism, who often found himself defending the grotesque and the fanciful.

After her childhood evangelicalism, George Eliot embraced many principles of Utilitarianism and positivism. Though she never accepted in their entirety the teachings of Auguste Comte—the founder of positivism, who taught that knowledge was only accessible through sensory experience and hence scientific investigation—she knew his work well and was constantly in contact with more avid disciples—notably George Lewes, her long-time lover, and her neighbor Richard Congreve, the founder and first priest of the "Church of Humanity," which was an outgrowth from positivism.[50] This association comes out clearly in Eliot's attitude toward the supernatural and the grotesque, which she reveals in *Adam Bede* (1859):

> I am content to tell my simple story, without trying to make things seem better than they were; dreading nothing, indeed, but falsity, which, in spite of one's best efforts, there is reason to dread. Falsehood is so easy, truth so difficult. The pencil is conscious of a delightful facility in drawing a griffin—the

"Never so Real as When They Are Solemn"

longer the claws, and the larger the wings, the better; but that marvellous facility which we mistook for genius, is apt to forsake us when we want to draw a real unexaggerated lion.[51]

It may be pleasant, fun, and easy to draw an imaginary creature, but it is hardly truthful. Truth, for Eliot, as for the Positivists, comes through the mediation of direct sensory experience, and since no one has ever seen a griffin, there is little if any truth in a picture of one. Indeed, Eliot's main criticism of Dickens rests on this distinction between the truthfulness of material reality and the falsity of imaginative constructs: "he scarcely ever passes from the humorous and external to the emotional and tragic, without becoming as transcendent in his unreality as he was a moment before in his artistic truthfulness."[52] Dickens' sentimental characters are little more than deceitful, and dangerously so, to Eliot's way of thinking.[53] Like griffins, characters that are not true to reality are not truthful.

In 1856, three years before Eliot published *Adam Bede*, John Ruskin came out with the third volume of his well-received *Modern Painters*, in which he too discusses griffins in art. Providing two depictions of griffins, Ruskin calls one a piece of "true grotesque" and the other "false grotesque":

> "Well, but," the reader says, "what do you mean by calling *either* of them true? There never were such beasts in the world as either of these?" No, never: but the difference is, that the Lombard workman did really see a griffin in his imagination, and carved it from the life, meaning to declare to all ages that he had verily seen with his immortal eyes such a griffin as that; but the classical workman never saw a griffin at all, nor anything else; but put the whole thing together by line and rule.[54]

Ruskin then defines why the Lombard griffin is "true" and "real" in some sense beyond the merely physical. The classical workman followed formal rules to combine the two forms of the eagle and the lion and created a lifeless image, but the Lombard workman "simply saw the beast" and joined the two animals in such a way that it "has the united *power of both*." Moreover, this imaginative seeing is a seeing of truth: "taking the truth first, the honest imagination gains everything; it has griffinism, and grace, and usefulness, all at once: but the false composer, caring for nothing but himself and his rules, loses everything,—griffinism and grace and all."⁵⁵ Ruskin, in other words, would tell Eliot that if she thinks long claws and large wings make a good griffin, then *she* has not seen the truth of griffins—positivism or naturalism or some other rationalistic principle was keeping her from a whole other dimension of truth. Far from being a less real mode, then, the grotesque is for Ruskin, in the words of Alison Milbank, "the realist mode par excellence because it witnesses to the fallen and divided nature of humanity as half beast and half angel by representing hybrid forms."⁵⁶

Moreover, in her offhand allusion, Eliot seems to be oblivious to the most famous griffin in Western literature—that of Dante in the climactic scene of the Purgatorio. Standing before the griffin that bore Beatrice's chariot from heaven, Dante looks in Beatrice's eyes and beholds something strange:

> Like sunlight in a mirror, shining back,
>   I saw the twofold creature in her eyes,
>   Reflecting its two natures, separately.
> Imagine, reader, how amazed I was
>   To see the creature standing there unchanged,
>   Yet, in its image, changing constantly,
> My soul, delighted and amazed,
>   Was tasting of that food which satisfies
>   And, at the same time, makes one hungrier. (XXXI, 115–29)

Viewed directly, the griffin remains one creature, but reflected in Beatrice's eyes Dante can see that the griffin is not half eagle and half lion but both creatures simultaneously and fully—it is "unchanged" yet "changing constantly." Stephen Prickett comments that whatever the precise allegorical meaning, "Dante seems to be trying to describe a paradox at the centre of a great deal of 'religious' experience—and of the language of that experience."⁵⁷ The paradox is the playful movement from "unchanged" to "changing constantly" that results from the limitation of human perception and expression. Divine reality is so layered and fecund that it requires the viewer to maintain apparently contradictory perceptions simultaneously. This paradoxical vision "satisfies" one intellectually and spiritually, but it also "makes one hungrier," thereby provoking an individual to seek further experiences of the transcendent. At the same time, the truth expressed

"*Never so Real as When They Are Solemn*" 85

in this double vision continually nourishes because it can never be exhausted.

Unlike Eliot, Ruskin is very aware of Dante when he discusses griffins, saying, "in its unity of lion and eagle, the workman of the middle ages always meant to set forth the unity of the human and divine natures."[58] Such a paradoxical conception of truth is foreign to George Eliot. Though she unquestionably saw and depicted realistic settings and psychologies as well as anyone in her age or any other, she, like so many of her contemporaries, sadly did not allow herself the truthful levity of looking at griffins.

Ruskin, on the other hand, is emblematic of another type of Victorian, a much rarer breed who was more skeptical of the connection between solemnity and reality. The greatest among them were Lewis Carroll, Oscar Wilde, and George MacDonald. These men were much more conscious of the possibility and importance of what Newman calls "that mixture of seriousness and levity."[59] In an age utterly convinced that gravity was the only "real" force in the universe, the works of these men are all the more remarkable in their insistence that play, fairytales, and nonsense can be just as "real" as straightforward solemnity.

A Lack of Morals?

At the beginning of the nineteenth century, Maria Edgeworth remarked happily in *Practical Education* that fairytales "are not now much read," and yet she still insisted on emphasizing the superiority of "real" stories:

> The history of realities, written in an entertaining manner, appears not only better suited to the purposes of education, but also more agreeable to young people, than improbable fictions. We have seen the reasons why it is dangerous to pamper the taste early with mere books of entertainment; [. . .] Natural history is a study particularly suited to children: it cultivates their talents for observation, applies to objects within their reach, and to objects which are every day interesting to them. The histories of the bee, the ant, the caterpillar, the butterfly, the silkworm, are the first things that please the taste of children, and these are the histories of realities.[60]

History and reality are best for children, not imaginative places or grand adventures, for these create unrealistic expectations and desires that hinder a child's future ability to be satisfied with commonplace occupations and lives. Edgeworth herself produced examples of these types of stories in her *Moral Tales*, intended for adolescents, in which she provided clear summarizing morals such as "it is possible for a lady of sixteen to cure herself of the affectation of sensibility, and the folly of romance."[61] Numerous other writers such as Sarah Trimmer and Anna Barbauld similarly wrote stories for children that were explicitly intended to teach moral lessons that grounded children in reality. Trimmer, for example, though she wrote of talking birds in her *Fabulous Histories*, very anxiously asserted that birds do not actually talk and that the only purpose of using such a technique is "to convey moral instruction."[62] This desire to make morality unambiguously clear to young readers and to connect stories directly with reality led to the assumption that any story whose contents were unabashedly fantastic or whose message was ambiguous was itself immoral, or, at best, a trivial distraction. Easily identifiable "morals" were the mark of a moral story.

Drawing on both the utilitarian focus on practical education and the evangelical moral emphasis, this idea of the function of stories for children persisted into the Victorian period. The famous illustrator of *Grimm's Fairyt Tales*, George Cruikshank, rewrote fairytales like "Jack and the Beanstalk" and "Tom Thumb" in order to promote a specific social agenda. The giant was really a drunkard, and Tom greatly benefited from a thorough education. In his essay "Frauds on the Fairies" (1853), Dickens chides "our dear moralist" for using fairytales in order to propagate "the doctrines of Total Abstinence, Prohibition of the sale of spirituous liquors, Free Trade, and Popular Education." Dickens calls these crudely inserted moral messages "weeds" in the fairytale garden, for they are "a thing growing up in the wrong place."[63] Yet this was a difficult idea for the serious-minded Victorians to accept, and so both morals and morality—or rather morals as morality—remained dominant in the literature intended for children.

In *Alice's Adventures in Wonderland* (1865)—first read in manuscript form to George MacDonald's children—Lewis Carroll parodies this belief during an episode in which Alice converses with the Duchess in the midst of the Queen's croquet match (and, incidentally, moments before she meets a griffin):

"Never so Real as When They Are Solemn" 87

> "You're thinking about something, my dear, and that makes you forget to talk. I can't tell you just now what the moral of that is, but I shall remember it in a bit."
>
> "Perhaps it hasn't one," Alice ventured to remark
>
> "Tut, tut, child!" said the Duchess. "Everything's got a moral, if only you can find it."[64]

Even though she can't remember the moral, the Duchess is certain there must be one, and in their further conversation she reveals her facility in finding out the morals in everything:

> "The game's going on rather better now," [Alice] said, by way of keeping up the conversation a little.
>
> "'Tis so," said the Duchess: "and the moral of that is—'Oh 'tis love, 'tis love, that makes the world go round'!"
>
> "Somebody said," Alice whispered, "that it's done by everybody minding their own business!"[65]

In their first meeting, the Duchess had rebuked Alice after Alice had criticized the Duchess' handling of her baby ("If everybody minded their own business the world would go round a deal faster than it does"[66]), but the Duchess is oblivious to this allusion and merely agrees:

> "Ah well! It means much the same thing," said the Duchess, digging her sharp little chin into Alice's shoulder as she added "and the moral of *that* is—'Take care of the sense and the sounds will take care of themselves.'"
>
> "How fond she is of finding morals in things!" Alice thought to herself.[67]

The Duchess is, interestingly, the only child-rearing figure in the book—and not a very good one. As observed, her uninterested and harsh treatment of her baby caused Alice some concern in their first encounter, and the song she sings to her child as she tosses it "violently up and down" is not exactly tender: "I speak severely to my boy, / I beat him when he sneezes / For he can thoroughly enjoy / The pepper when he pleases!" Indeed, it is hard to think of a character that Carroll displays less sympathetically than the Duchess. Not surprisingly, this severe parent, like many Victorian parents, is obsessed with finding the "moral" in everything—an attitude which Carroll clearly finds absurd. Carroll echoes this criticism of his contemporaries in an 1867 letter to Lily MacDonald (George's eldest daughter) when he says of a book he gave her, "the book is intended for you to look at the outside, and then put it away in the bookcase: the *inside* is not meant to be read. The book has got a moral—so I need hardly say it is *not* by Lewis Carroll."[68] Taking a view opposite to his culture, Carroll finds that clear "morals" do not make for good stories. Instead, Carroll seems to suggest that nonsense literature possesses a vitality and dynamism that might just be closer to "real" life than moralizing realism.

This is not to say, however, that these moralless stories lacked morality. Oscar Wilde's works were often accused of being "immoral," partially on account of their playful ambiguity, to which he replied in his preface to *The Picture of Dorian Gray*, "there is no such thing as a moral or an immoral book. Books are well written, or badly written. That is all."[69] This might seem to imply that Wilde was simply amoral, but if Wilde was anything, he was not simple. This complex relationship between morals and morality appears in his fairytale "The Devoted Friend," in which a Linnet tells a story with a moral to a Water-rat—much to the Water-rat's consternation:

> "I am afraid you don't quite see the moral of the story," remarked the Linnet.
>
> "The what?" screamed the Water-rat.
>
> "The moral."
>
> "Do you mean to say that the story has a moral?"
>
> "Certainly," said the Linnet.
>
> "Well, really," said the Water-rat, in a very angry manner, "I think you should have told me that before you began. If you had done so, I certainly would not have listened to you; in fact, I should have said 'Pooh,' like the critic. However, I can say it now"; so he shouted "Pooh" at the top of his voice, gave a whisk with his tail, and went back into his hole.[70]

The story referred to does indeed have a clear moral message—a rich and selfish Miller prides himself on his grand ideas of friendship but treats his best friend Hans, a poor and selfless gardener, horribly, and ultimately Hans dies as a result of the Miller's treatment. The Water-rat has obvious affinities with other Wildean characters (such as Lord Henry Wotton) and with Wilde's own public persona (the Water-rat is only interested in witty statements and pleasing ideas). The above passage, therefore, would seem to be a clear repudiation of both morals

"Never so Real as When They Are Solemn"

and morality; however, the final lines of the story, in which the Linnet speaks with a mother Duck, unsettle this interpretation:

> "I am rather afraid that I have annoyed him," answered the Linnet. "The fact is, that I told him a story with a moral."
> "Ah! that is always a very dangerous thing to do," said the Duck.
> And I quite agree with her.[71]

The heretofore unheard-from narrator intrudes in the story's last line and declares his sympathy with the Duck rather than the Linnet *or* the Water-rat. After teasing the reader with the interpretation of a character readily identified with himself, Wilde intentionally distances himself from any of the positions advocated in the story, except that of the motherly Duck, whose opinion is decidedly ambiguous toward morals but whose morality is not in question (in contrast to the Duchess, her view of child-rearing is that "parents cannot be too patient").[72] What Wilde resists, then, is not morality as such, but the overpowering influence of a constricting didacticism upon stories, a didacticism that might itself be more "dangerous" than any lack of clear morals.[73] Therefore, by liberating his stories from the narrowness of straightforward morals, Wilde in some sense also allows for a more subtle moral functioning of the story in that readers must exercise their individual consciences to identify the tale's meaning. The light indeterminacy gives readers room to play and to discover for themselves the nature of right and wrong.

While most Victorians were solemnly going about trying to teach people morals and how to live in this grave "reality," people like Carroll and Wilde playfully rose above this solemnity, and, in so doing, often sparked imaginations and inspired more joyful modes of being in the world. This same project was also at the core of George MacDonald's life and work.

Defying the Plumb Line of Gravity

Earlier in the chapter in which he discusses the true and false griffins, Ruskin outlines three different kinds of grotesque art: the noble grotesque, which arises "from the confusion of the imagination by the presence of truths which it cannot grasp"; the evil-enjoying grotesque, which arises "from irregular and accidental contemplation of terrible things or evil in general"; and the playful grotesque, which arises "from healthful but irrational play of the imagination in times of rest."⁷⁴ Though he speaks at greater length about both the evil-enjoying grotesque and the noble grotesque (the one he prefers and advocates), Ruskin has only the following to say of the playful grotesque:

> The form arising from an entirely healthful and open play of the imagination as in Shakspere's [*sic*] Ariel and Titania, and in Scott's White Lady, is comparatively rare. It hardly ever is free from some slight taint of the inclination to evil; still more rarely is it, when so free, natural to the mind; for the moment we begin to contemplate sinless beauty we are apt to get serious; and moral fairy tales, and such other innocent work, are hardly ever truly, that is to say, naturally imaginative; but for the most part laborious inductions and compositions. The moment any real vitality enters them, they are nearly sure to become satirical, or slightly gloomy.⁷⁵

Ruskin writes so little about this type of grotesque because he believes it is the most difficult to achieve and maintain. Artists who begin in this form have a hard time keeping it up, for the "real vitality" of seriousness makes it difficult to uphold the light and playful atmosphere, forcing the artist—except in the most exceptional of occasions—to become either "satirical" or "gloomy." Truly light and playful fairytales, therefore, are rare and highly skillful literary creations.

In an afterword to a 1966 edition of "The Golden Key," W. H. Auden points out MacDonald's unique place within this body of imaginative literature:

> George MacDonald's most extraordinary, and precious, gift is his ability, in all his stories, to create an atmosphere of goodness about which there is nothing phony or moralistic. Nothing is rarer in literature. As Simone Weil observed:
>
>> "Imaginary evil is romantic and varied; real evil is gloomy, monotonous, barren, boring. Imaginary good is boring; real good is always new, marvelous, intoxicating. 'Imaginative literature,' therefore, is either boring or immoral or a mixture of both."
>
> George MacDonald's tales are a proof that this is not necessarily the case. That is why, though there are many writers far greater than he, his permanent importance in literature is assured.⁷⁶

"Never so Real as When They Are Solemn" 91

Weil says explicitly what was implicit in Ruskin's comments—the problem with imaginative literature is that either it indulges in the pleasures of imaginary evil and thus becomes immoral or it leans so heavily on the side of morality that it becomes boring. But MacDonald, according to Auden, is a rare and delightful exception. His fairytales are both good and playful, full of truth and "seriousness" but not thereby weighed down and immobilized from being quick, lively, and inspirational. This is what is so rare. They display true levity, in that they retain contour and heft even as they fly with seeming ease. In Chesterton's words, MacDonald's fairytale writings evince a profound "realization of the grotesque in the spiritual world."[77]

Yet even though MacDonald is a well-known fantasist, who along with William Morris helped found and shape the modern fantasy genre, people still do not often think of him as "light." Unlike Lewis Carroll, readers associate MacDonald more closely with his strong religious outlook than with free-spirited writing for children. Scholars in the past century have routinely recognized MacDonald's peculiar gift for the "mythopoeic," but they have tended to focus on the heavier and more openly "adult" (and thus "serious") works of *Phantastes* and *Lilith*, or when they have investigated the shorter fairytales have often only looked for the "serious" content—what they say about death, child rearing, class structure, psychoanalysis, or other themes.[78]

To a certain extent, this approach is valid, for MacDonald was undoubtedly a product of his Victorian culture and its interest in seriousness. Born in 1824 into a strict Calvinist family in the far north of Scotland, MacDonald's childhood was far from easy. His experience of death began early as his mother died of tuberculosis when he was eight.[79] Never very healthy, MacDonald was the weakest of the four boys who survived childhood (though he lived the longest—until 1905), and in letters from his early childhood he often referred to physical illness and weakness. In a letter written in 1834 when he was nine (also referring to his ill health), MacDonald proudly tells his father how he refused to drink gin and thus "did not break any of the Rules of the Temperance Society."[80] At the age of thirteen, he founded and became president of the Huntley Juvenile Temperance Society, whose declaration was "to abstain from distilled spirits except for medicinal purposes."[81] Greville MacDonald, George's eldest son and first biographer, comments on his father's young enthusiasm for temperance that "spirit drinking was then as now the curse of Scotland."[82] Whatever the reasons, there can be no doubt that young George was extremely earnest and concerned about the "serious" issues of his day. Of his early religious feelings, MacDonald was later to write: "I have been familiar with the doctrines of the gospel from childhood. I always knew and felt that I ought to be a Christian, and repeatedly began to pray, but as often grew weary and gave it up. The truths of Christianity had no *life* in my soul."[83] Duty and morality weighed very heavily upon the young MacDonald—a burden that was not in any way lightened by the consolations of faith.

This is not to say that MacDonald's was an unhappy childhood. Greville takes great pains to point out how MacDonald's "keener vision everywhere disclosed fairyland and bewitchment, chivalry and devotion."[84] While this might extend beyond the evidence, there seem to have been enough trips to the beach, kite flying, game playing, horse riding, hill climbing, pantomimes, and mock battles to make the memory of childhood especially dear to MacDonald in later life.[85] And yet the cares of everyday life were always pressing. At thirteen, MacDonald was already "thinking of what I should betake myself to," and after briefly considering becoming a sailor due to his love for the ocean, it was decided that he should go to university.

At the University of Aberdeen, MacDonald studied chemistry and natural philosophy and became well versed in the science of the day. Inwardly, MacDonald experienced great turmoil during this period as he wrestled with the apparently competing claims of science, art, religion, and society. Thus, like his contemporaries George Eliot and John Ruskin, MacDonald too struggled to reconcile the two dominant forces of the time—Enlightenment naturalism and reformation religion. In a letter to his father in 1847, MacDonald wrote how it was "a mercy I was not allowed to follow out Chemistry" because it allowed him finally to come to true religion: "What should I be now without religion? With nothing here to make me happy besides, with health bad enough to make me generally feel miserable, though nothing is seriously the matter with me. Yet I am able to trust and thank God for all these, for thus I hope he has led me to find joy of being—the *real existence*."[86] MacDonald goes on to explain how he was finally able to reconcile his romantic love of nature and religion:

> One of my greatest difficulties in consenting to think of religion was that I thought I should have to give up my beautiful thoughts & my love for the things God has made. But I find that the happiness springing from all things not in themselves sinful is much increased by religion. God is the God of the Beautiful, Religion the Love of the Beautiful, & Heaven the House of the Beautiful—nature is tenfold brighter in the sun of righteousness, and my love of nature is more intense since I became a Christian, if indeed I am one.[87]

Uniting nature, art, and God, MacDonald finds that they are mutually enriching, and that faith, rather than dampening his enthusiasm for beauty, rather increases it. Joy is at the heart of MacDonald's faith, which leads him to rejoice in all things "not in themselves sinful." This emphasis on the "joy of being" as "the real existence" contrasts very strongly with Newman's comment about Victorians who were "never so real as when they are solemn," and, I think, is the key to MacDonald's fairytale levity.

Rejoicing in all things allows MacDonald to find meaning and worth in works and modes that others commonly ignored or considered low. In his first published essay (1853), MacDonald praises Robert Browning's nonconventional and playful poem "Christmas Eve" and simultaneously lays out several principles that were to inform his own artistic practice. Browning himself anticipated the critical objection to his poem in its penultimate lines:

> if any blames me,
> Thinking that merely to touch in brevity
> The topics I dwell on, were unlawful,—
> Or worse, that I trench, with undue levity,
> On the bounds of the holy and the awful,—
> I praise the heart, and pity the head of him,
> And refer myself to THEE, instead of him,
> Who head and heart alike discernest
> Looking below light speech we utter,
> When frothy spume and frequent sputter
> Prove that the soul's depths boil in earnest! (XXII, 106-16)

Though the intention of guarding the holy from low things is noble, it springs from a confused mind. The levity of "frothy spume" and "sputter" can be the result of a soul boiling in the most profound earnest. MacDonald opens his defence of Browning's poem with one of his own translations of a Goethe poem:

> Poems are painted window panes.
> If one looks from the square into the church,
> Dusk and dimness are his gains—
> Sir Philistine is left in the lurch!
> The sight, so seen, may well enrage him,
> Nor anything henceforth assuage him.
>
> But come just inside what conceals;
> Cross the holy threshold quite—
> All at once 'tis rainbow-bright,
> Device and story flash to light,
> A gracious splendour truth reveals.
> This to God's children is full measure,
> It edifies and gives you pleasure![88]

From the outside, many things appear dim or even ugly. "Such," says MacDonald, "is the world itself, as beheld by the speculative eye; a thing of disorder, obscurity, and sadness: only the child-like heart, to which the door into the divine idea is thrown open, can understand somewhat the secret of the Almighty."[89] Revelation occurs only by entering in, with the twofold result of pleasure and edification—and MacDonald, unlike many of his contemporaries, is never willing to sacrifice pleasure on the altar of moral teaching. Browning's poem may initially seem obscure, difficult, and unconventional, but, MacDonald argues, "that form of expression, which is most easily understood at first sight [is not] necessarily the best" because "it will not, therefore, continue to move; nor will it gather force and influence with more intimate acquaintance."[90]

MacDonald thus defends Browning's use of humor and other forms of levity in a work focused on spiritual reflection:

> Objection may, probably, be made to the mingling of the humorous, even the ridiculous, with the serious; at least, in a work of art like this, where they must be brought into such close proximity. But are not these things as closely connected in the world as they can be in any representation of

it? Surely there are few who have never had occasion to attempt to reconcile the thought of the two in their own minds. Nor can there be anything human that is not, in some connexion or other, admissible into art. The widest idea of art must comprehend all things. A work of this kind must, like God's world, in which he sends rain on the just and on the unjust, be taken as a whole and in regard to its design. [. . .] Here the thing is real, is true, is human; a thing to be thought about.[91]

Wholeness gives vitality and power to a work and justifies the "mingling of the humorous, even the ridiculous, with the serious." Like Ruskin, MacDonald believes that rather than being escapist or deceptive, the grotesque in art is a means of exploring universal reality. If God joins these apparently incongruous things in humanity and the world, thinks MacDonald, why should not art do the same? MacDonald goes further, however, when he says that the light form chosen by Browning is the best one possible for his subject:

> One of the most wonderful things in the poem is, that so much of argument is expressed in a species of verse, which one might be inclined, at first sight, to think the least fitted for embodying it. But, in fact, the same amount of argument in any other kind of verse would, in all likelihood, have been intolerably dull as a work of art. Here the verse is full of life and vigour, flagging never. [. . .] The poem is full of pathos and humour; full of beauty and grandeur, earnestness and truth.[92]

Lightness is not just artistically acceptable; sometimes it is the best way of addressing certain questions and presenting certain subjects. In *The Gay Science*, Friedrich Nietzsche wonders, "is it a fact that a thing has been misunderstood and unrecognized when it has only been touched upon in passing, glanced at, flashed at?" To which he answers, "there are truths of a peculiar shyness and ticklishness which one can only get hold of suddenly, and in no other way."[93] MacDonald seems to be saying something similar about Browning. The levity of Browning's verse is not incidental nor does it bespeak a deficiency of thought or craft, rather there are things of a "peculiar shyness and ticklishness"—which are nevertheless still "real"—that can only be approached lightly. In MacDonald's creative work, the form that best embodies a comparable light mode is the fairytale.

As the Wind Assails an Aeolian Harp
The Lightness of Fairytales

Whereas "Browning's 'Christmas Eve'" (1853) was MacDonald's first published essay, "The Fantastic Imagination" (1893) was his last. It might seem odd putting these two essays together, but in interesting ways "The Fantastic Imagination" picks up on some of the same questions about the nature of artistic lightness first raised in the earlier essay. Instead of approaching the issue as a reader of someone else's work, however, MacDonald addresses the question from the perspective of an author advising prospective readers about the "peculiar shyness and ticklishness" of his favorite light form, the fairytale.

Critics sometimes use "The Fantastic Imagination" to illustrate MacDonald's ideas about the Christian imagination or fantasy generally, but, strictly speaking, it is an essay that attempts to get at the form of the fairytale. This is significant because although MacDonald wrote around thirty full-length novels, he never once commented on the form of the novel or his mode of writing them. His body of fairytales may be dwarfed by his novelistic output, but they held a unique place in his imagination. As William Raeper, a recent MacDonald biographer, says, "the fairytale was a special kind of construct which enabled him to express his particular view of life."[94] This is undoubtedly true, but not enough has been done to show why this particular form was so significant to him.

One of the most vital characteristics of a fairytale according to MacDonald is its ability to generate meaning lightly. "A fairytale," he says, "like a butterfly or a bee, helps itself on all sides, sips at every wholesome flower, and spoils not one."[95] Fairytales do not convey a definite, limited amount of information or ideas; rather their playful form lightly fertilizes the mind of a reader and initiates a dynamic imaginative exchange that proliferates signification. Everywhere in the essay MacDonald is concerned with how fairytales "suggest," "wake," and "arouse" meaning rather than with directly convincing through logic or unambiguous content, as in the following key passage:

> Where [a writer's] object is to move by suggestion, to cause to imagine, then let him assail the soul of his reader as the wind assails an aeolian harp. If there is music in my reader, I would gladly wake it. Let fairytale of mine go for a

firefly that now flashes, now is dark, but may flash again. Caught in a hand which does not love its kind, it will turn to an insignificant, ugly thing, that can neither flash nor fly. The best way with music, I imagine, is not to bring the forces of our intellect to bear upon it, but to be still and let it work on that part of us for whose sake it exists. We spoil countless precious things by intellectual greed.[96]

The fairytale reverses the subject/object relationship such that instead of a reader attempting to grasp intellectually the interpretation of a text as intended by the author, a reader must be open and willing to receive the light touch of the fairytale which assails the soul "as the wind assails an aeolian harp." Without the playful cooperation of the reader, fairytales will "neither flash nor fly" because unlike heaviness, which forces its singular meaning upon its audience, lightness involves a kind of elected vulnerability that moves by invitation and suggestion. It evokes the desires, images, and experiences of each individual in order to make them consorts in the imaginative encounter.

This necessarily means that authorial intention is cast down from its hermeneutical throne and signification is allowed to flourish. In this sense, MacDonald sounds like a Derridean poststructuralist in the way that he talks about the author's inability to control meanings because "there is layer upon layer of ascending significance" and one "cannot help his words and figures falling into such combinations in the mind of another as he had himself not foreseen, so many are the thoughts allied to every other thought, so many are the relations involved in every figure, so many the facts hinted in every symbol."[97] Instead of being concerned by this, however, MacDonald seems to revel in the indeterminacy, for it is precisely the mobility and multiplicity of meaning that makes the fairytale so potent. "The greatest forces," he says, "lie in the region of the uncomprehended," and it is only lightness that can tickle these things out of people.[98] Like the parables of Jesus—which the wisdom of the world labels as "foolishness"—fairytales avoid a finalizing discourse and attempt to keep things open so that there is always room for readers to play within their worlds and in their playing to tap into "the region of the uncomprehended." By signaling the inadequacy of their own representations, therefore, fairytales simultaneously point toward and attempt to keep open their connection to vital energies beyond themselves.

The seeming weakness of fairytale levity—that it chooses the vulnerability of indeterminacy and needs the assistance and good will of others—thus reveals itself as superior strength (much as holy folly turns out to be true wisdom). As Chesterton observes, "the promptest and boldest agencies are also the most fragile or full of sensibility" for "in perfect force there is a kind of frivolity, an airiness that can maintain itself in the air."[99] The apparent carelessness of fairytales does not reflect a weak and reckless irresponsibility; it is instead a "divine carelessness" that lets go of the constricting insecurities of solemnity in order to preserve an adequately capacious place for large things like joy, truth, and beauty.

If MacDonald is right about the light, semiotic playfulness of fairytales, it would explain one of the underlying problems with many approaches to the genre. Any method that reduces the fairytale to its sociological, psychological, or ideological content—what the story is "about" or what it "means"—is in a crucial sense missing the point, or rather is unwittingly falling into the trap laid by the fairytale. All of the five major schools of fairytale scholarship—philological, functional, psychological, structuralist, and poststructuralist—have a tendency to constrict and limit the meaning of a story to a narrow interpretation that aligns with their hermeneutical agendas.[100] Critics often see what they set out to find, for the frolicsome fairytale invites them into a semiotic dance and lets them lead it wherever they want to go. But the fairytale focuses ultimately on the dance (and helping its readers to dance), rather than the destination (at least not in the same way as the critics). The fact that it can convincingly accommodate whole schools of criticism suggests that in interesting ways the fairytale is larger than all of them.

Indeed, MacDonald's elusive refusal to define discursively the fairytale generally or his own fairytales specifically gestures toward his belief that the fairytale is a form that helps envisage the grand and majestic sweep of reality. Thus he begins "The Fantastic Imagination" by talking about metaphysical concepts like "law," "truth," "creation," "harmony," "beauty," and "morality," prompting his imagined interlocutor to comment, "you write as if a fairytale were a thing of importance."[101] This fictional speaker seems to represent the typical Victorian attitude toward seriousness that we have been tracing throughout this chapter. The questions he poses are earnest attempts to control meaning and limit the power and significance of the seemingly foolish fairytale. Like a solemn Evangelical, he worries that "a man may then imagine in your work what he pleases," disclosing his fear that without careful oversight, morality might degenerate. And like a good descendant of Enlightenment rationality, he desires hermeneutical certainty: "how am I to assure myself that I am not reading my own meaning into it, but yours out of it?" But perhaps most importantly, he does not want to look foolish in front of his children: "suppose my child ask [sic] me what the fairytale means, what am I to say?" Despite these entreaties, however, MacDonald continues to frustrate his interlocutor, for in MacDonald's mind not only are these the wrong questions, but to answer them would do harm to the person's experience of fairytales. At one point, MacDonald admits that he does not write for earnest adults (those who, in Newman's phrase, "think themselves never so real as when they are solemn") any more than he writes for children, "but for the childlike, whether of five, or fifty, or seventy-five."[102] In this, MacDonald eschews the traditional categories of child and adult and insists upon a third thing—the childlike.

Expanding the Playground
The Childlike

MacDonald's concept of the "childlike" reverberates throughout every work of his poetry, fiction, and nonfiction. It is the structure that holds up every idea and image in his vast *oeuvre*.[103] And yet it is of even more importance to his fairytales, for in them MacDonald consciously writes for and thereby tries to construct a "childlike" audience.

Much of MacDonald's idea of the "child" is borrowed from the Romantics, particularly Wordsworth. MacDonald was fond of quoting Wordsworth's line "The Child is father of the Man," even making it the motto for the journal he edited for three years (1870–1873), *Good Things for the Young of all Ages*, the same journal in which he first published many of his works for children, including *The Princess and the Goblin* and *At the Back of the North Wind*.[104] In his initial editorial statement of intent, MacDonald tells of how he wishes to speak to both child and man: "We wish to do something towards the culture of that natural piety which should bind our days together. The Child is father of the Man; the Man himself is to be a Child again."[105] MacDonald here begins with Wordsworth but immediately goes beyond him. Rather than stopping at nostalgic longing for a lost past, he looks forward in hope to a promised future. The final note of melancholy in Wordsworth's poem "Intimations of Immortality"[106] is theologically unacceptable for MacDonald, and so he turns to Henry Vaughan to complete his vision of childhood:

> What we feel is wanting in Wordsworth's [poem is] the hope of return to the bliss of childhood. We may be comforted for what we lose by what we gain; but that is not a recompense large enough to be divine: we want both. Vaughan will be a child again. For the movements of man's life are in spirals: we go back whence we came, ever returning on our former traces, only upon a higher level, on the next upward coil of the spiral, so that is it a going back and a going forward ever and both at once. Life is as it were, a constant repentance, or thinking of it again: the childhood of the kingdom takes the place of the childhood of the brain, but comprises all that was lovely in the former delight. The heavenly children will subdue kingdoms, work righteousness, wax valiant in fight, rout the armies of the aliens, merry of heart as when in the nursery of this world they fought their fancied frigates, and defended their toy-battlements.[107]

Though he uses Vaughan's poem "The Retreat" as a justification for this reflection, MacDonald actually goes beyond Vaughan as well. Whereas Vaughan desires merely "by backward steps to move" and thereby return to childhood, MacDonald's spiral is not a two-dimensional, linear reverting but a liberated three-dimensional ascension as he extends the spatial metaphor and thus preemptively disarms the psychoanalytic criticism of "regression." Childhood for MacDonald is, as John Pridmore puts it, "a continuing moral and spiritual goal."[108] In journeying to this goal, a person expands the playground of reality and thereby overcomes false oppositions and binaries such as innocence/experience and serious/playful. The childlike, for MacDonald, transcends these categories not by repudiating them but by incorporating them into itself with room still left to play. Thus "heavenly children" are grown-ups who do the "serious" work of "subduing kingdoms" and "working righteousness," but they do it "merry of heart" as when they played in the nursery. Within the spacious world of the childlike, moral earnestness and lighthearted play are united.

"Never so Real as When They Are Solemn"

This expansive inclusion of apparent opposites represents an important distinction between MacDonald and other Victorians fantasists. U. C. Knoepflmacher argues that "the self-divided Victorians found themselves 'wandering between two worlds' in their Janus-like split between progress and nostalgia" and that they attempted to "balance" or "see-saw" between the two realms of innocence and experience.[109] Charles Dodgson's double life as Lewis Carroll provides a ready example of this approach—one name and style for those things pertaining to the world of grown-ups and one for those pertaining to children. From Dodgson delivering hour-long sermons with "intense solemnity and earnestness" on "the duty of reverence and the sin of talking carelessly of holy things" to Carroll writing the playful nonsense of Alice, the two realms could not be more separate and distinct.[110]

Carroll's view of childhood is closer to that of Wordsworth than MacDonald though, as can be seen in his dedicatory poem in *Through the Looking Glass*:

> Child of the pure unclouded brow
> And dreaming eyes of wonder!
> Though time be fleet, and I and thou
> Are half a life asunder,
> Thy loving smile will surely hail
> The love-gift of a fairytale.

The poem works both as an address to Alice Liddell—from whom Carroll had been estranged—and to his general child audience. Children and grown-ups are "half a life asunder" and yet can meet in the edenic form of the fairytale. Carroll goes on to talk about summer days "whose echoes live in memory yet, / Though envious years would say 'forget'" before the poem takes a slightly darker turn:

> Come, hearken then, ere voice of dread,
> With bitter tidings laden,
> Shall summon to unwelcome bed
> A melancholy maiden!
> We are but older children, dear,
> Who fret to find our bedtime near.

> Without, the frost, the blinding snow,
> The storm-wind's moody madness—
> Within, the firelight's ruddy glow,
> And childhood's nest of gladness.
> The magic words shall hold thee fast:
> Thou shalt not heed the raving blast.

Carroll depicts childhood as a "nest of gladness" which is somehow distant from the "voice of dread" and the "moody madness" of the world. The echoes of Eden still resound in the blithe and protected sphere of childhood. Grown-ups, "older children," can also return to this "nest of gladness" through the vehicle of the fairytale. As with Wordsworth, it is the faculty of memory that allows this communion between the adult and childhood. And yet it is clearly a retreat, not a MacDonald-like progression. While Carroll promises in the final stanza that the outside storms and "the shadow of a sigh" "shall not touch with breath of bale, / the pleasance of our fairy-tale," the reader has been made aware that this "fairy-tale" is a sort of holiday or hovering, in which one can only remain so long, either because the adult must eventually return to his world or because the child must eventually grow up.

No doubt MacDonald's levity might also seem at first glance to be indistinguishable from a motionless "floating between" two worlds—a snapshot of a hovering bird might look identical to a bird ascending toward the clouds—but this optical illusion vanishes once the overall trajectory is perceived.[111] MacDonald, in any case, did not articulate the "childlike" in terms of fine balance:

> There is a childhood into which we have to grow, just as there is a childhood we must leave behind; a childlikeness which is the highest aim of humanity, and a childishness from which but few of those who are counted the wisest among men, have freed themselves in their imagined progress toward the reality of things.[112]

Here is no static hovering but an adventurous journey to a desired destination. Growth—the enlargement of one's reality—and hope are always operative in MacDonald, and if one is not progressing toward the divine childlikeness, then one is regressing toward the childish and inhuman.[113] Belief in the goodness of the Creator and the hope of our ultimate restoration to a divine childhood is so essential to

MacDonald that "if there be no such live Ideal, then a falsehood can do more for the race than the facts of its being; then an unreality is needful for the development of the man in all that is real, in all that is in the highest sense true."[114] Development needs hope, even if it is imaginary. "Those that hope little," he says, "cannot grow much."[115] If progress is impossible, MacDonald would prefer believing an illusion.

What characteristics, then, does MacDonald ascribe to childlikeness? Reflecting in *The Hope of the Gospel* on the story of Jesus found in the temple as a child (Luke 2:48-50), MacDonald discusses Christ as the paradigm for the childlike, for, because of his relationship with God the Father, "the child-relation is the one eternal, ever enduring, never changing relation."[116] This relationship is above all rooted in absolute trust and love: "confidence in God [is] the one principle by which men shall live."[117] Jesus' perfect trust in the Father means that he is also perfectly at home in the world and can move about it with a sort of light mobility, for the world is the Father's. Humans, however, are not at home in the world because we lack this perfect trust in the Father:

> This reveals Jesus more than man, by revealing him more man than we. We are not complete men, we are not anything near it, and are therefore out of harmony, more or less, with everything in the house of our birth and habitation. [. . .] When we are true children, if not the world, then the universe will be our home, felt and known as such, the house we are satisfied with and would not change. Hence, until then, the hard struggle, the constant strife we hold with *Nature*.[118]

Because of his complete trust in the Father, the true child is in harmony with all of God's creation. Rather than a heavy struggling with nature to provide for one's needs, the child has a sense of supreme liberty and lightness and can play and delight in all of the Father's works—he exists in a state of "divine carelessness."[119] The corollary is that "the world has for him no chamber of terror."[120] Perfect love drives out fear, liberates the child from weighty concerns and anxieties, and turns the universe into a playground. More precisely, this feeling of being "at home" means that the child does not attempt to cling to things: "only by knowing them the things of our Father, can we escape enslaving ourselves to them. Through the false, the infernal idea of *having*, of *possessing* them, we make them our tyrants, make the relation between them and us an evil thing."¹²¹ All things are there for the child to play with, but the child owns nothing, for the child holds all things lightly. The childlike mind is insatiably curious and is at the "fullest liberty to ask questions." And while the child is "at home" with all things, this does not lead to a sense of familiar dullness:

> In the Perfect, would familiarity ever destroy wonder at things essentially wonderful because essentially divine? To cease to wonder is to fall plumbdown from the childlike to the commonplace—the most undivine of all moods intellectual. Our nature can never be at home among things that are not wonderful to us.¹²²

True children never experience boredom because like Jesus they see into the reality of things as they are—ever and always full of wonder. Common things thus do not appear common to the childlike; the child is just as delighted in the simple and lowly as with the high and complex.

Clearly, MacDonald has an exalted view of the childlike, and so when he claims that he writes fairytales not for children but for the childlike, we are left to wonder how large an audience he expects to find. MacDonald recognizes the loftiness of this ideal and that "the childlike are not yet the many," but instead of compromising the standards, he chooses to help construct his own audience, somewhat like Wordsworth's statement that "every Author, as far as he is great and at the same time *original*, has had the task of *creating* the taste by which he is to be enjoyed."¹²³ Since God, according to MacDonald, "can be revealed only to the child; perfectly, to the pure child only," then "all the discipline of the world is to make men children, that God may be revealed to them."¹²⁴ MacDonald speaks to the childlike, then, much in the same way that parents speak to their children—with language and expectations that are beyond their present abilities. By inviting the child into a more expansive world, the grown-up awakens the aspirations of the child and allows him to pretend and play at being grownup; though through mimesis, the child does then grow, progress, and learn. In the same way, MacDonald offers his fairytales to all those who will enter into the discipline of becoming childlike; he claims that his fairytales are exercise for the childlike imagination, and he sets out to help people progress beyond the small, fragmented understanding of reality offered by the typical Victorian attitude toward seriousness and discover the truly spacious playground of the "real." (And the larger one's reality is, the more one needs to be light, nimble, and quick in order to traverse it.) Hence in writing fairytales "for the childlike," MacDonald's desire is to wake the hope for a lighter and more expansive mode of being.

Exploring this claim within the fairytales will require a light and nimble touch, but perhaps, following MacDonald's lead, the best way to catch a glimpse of fairytale levity is to expand the traditional critical playgrounds. Rolland Hein expresses the typical view of MacDonald's fairytales when he says that "because the tales contain more of the absurd and the tone is more light and playful, fresh breakthroughs into the transcendent are more rare" and that "the adult mind" is more compelled by the longer fantasies.[125] By contrast, I want to suggest that MacDonald's fairytale levity is not opposed to the religious and may in fact offer its own "fresh breakthrough into the transcendent," or even more boldly that in his fairytales MacDonald problematizes simple binaries like child/adult and serious/frivolous by inviting his readers into more capacious realms where these heavy, categorical distinctions are shown to be aspects of a light and agile whole. Rather than focus on the *content* (psychological, religious, social, historical, or otherwise), therefore, we will instead discuss MacDonald's fairytale *mode* in relation to three expansive metaphysical concepts—time, space, and transformation.[126]

6

Time
Fairyland's Festive Sabbath

"If you knew time as well as I do," said the Hatter, "you wouldn't talk about wasting *it*. It's *him*."

—Lewis Carroll, *Alice's Adventures in Wonderland*

Fairytales love to manipulate time. Tolkien says that part of the "magic of Faerie" is in the "satisfaction of certain primordial human desires," among which is the desire "to survey the depths of space and time."[1] Fairytales are metaphysically curious; they ask and play with the most fundamental questions of existence. This, perhaps, is a further reason why fairy stories are associated with childhood—since children, as MacDonald argues in *Robert Falconer*, are born metaphysicians: "I believe that even the new-born infant is, in some of his moods, already grappling with the deepest metaphysical problems, in forms infinitely too rudimentary for the understanding of the grown philosopher."[2] The child constantly questions and explores the boundaries of time, space, and being.[3] Mythic stories, says Tolkien, "open a door on Other Time, and if we pass through, though only for a moment, we stand outside our own time, outside Time itself, maybe."[4] In addition to this outside-of-time perspective, MacDonald's fairyland also plays with different chronological modalities, exploring the possibilities of life in a place where the rules of everyday time are not ironclad and where creatures can subvert the laws of death and decay.

"Once Upon a Time"
The Festive Setting of MacDonald's Fairytales

The traditional narrative doorway into the fairyland realm of "Other Time" is the simple phrase "once upon a time." "It produces at a stroke," writes Tolkien, "the sense of a great uncharted world of time."[5] Inviting the reader to step out of quotidian time, this formulation acts as a frame or boundary marker to set the narrative within its own special sphere where different rules apply. Like the whistle blow that begins a sporting event or the liturgical formula that opens a religious ceremony ("lift up your hearts"), "once upon a time" is both a proclamation and an invitation. It proclaims the inauguration of a sphere where time operates differently, and it invites playful participation in this new chronological reality.[6]

Before it even begins, however, the audience encounters the fairytale in a specific setting that signals something about the promised narrative experience. If "once upon a time" is like the opening whistle or liturgical exhortation, then the setting is like the sporting culture (baseball—caps and hotdogs; cricket—whites and tea) or the liturgical atmosphere (Lent, Easter).[7] In addition to the obvious setting of the traditional European folktale, MacDonald also placed his fairytales within the festive atmosphere of Christmas—the festival that celebrates when God became a child.

MacDonald set most of his earliest fairytales within the frame novel *Adela Cathcart* (1864), which takes place during Christmastide.[8] The book tells the story of Adela, a young woman suffering from a psychological and spiritual malaise. To restore her spirits, her "uncle" (the first-person narrator) and her doctor (who is also romantically attracted to her) start a storytelling club in a manner similar to *The Decameron* or *The Canterbury Tales*.[9] This dialogical setting was more than just a gimmick to sell fairytales to publishers reluctant to print anything except novels; it was also a way for MacDonald to show the importance and impact of fairytales on audiences, and was another stylistic experiment by the young nonconformist writer. In 1864 MacDonald was still a relatively fledgling author struggling to provide for his burgeoning family, despite having published *Within and Without* (1855), a long dramatic poem that drew the attention of Lady Byron; *Phantastes* (1858), his adult fantasy read by the young Charles Dodgson;

and *David Elginbrod* (1863), the first of his many "realistic" novels.[10] The minor success of *David Elginbrod* prompted MacDonald to rework several short stories—including his first fairytales, which publishers seemed hesitant to print in the pre-*Alice* atmosphere—into the familiar Victorian form of the three-volume novel.[11] MacDonald's own summary shows that while he did not consider it to be his best work, the book was not without significance: "although slight, I don't think you will find it careless."[12] Critics, however, were not kind,[13] nor has the novel received much attention since.[14]

The novel begins in twilight on "the afternoon of Christmas Eve, sinking towards the night" with the narrator, John Smith, in the midst of a journey to visit his friend Colonel Cathcart and the Colonel's daughter Adela.[15] The description of the journey is punctuated by Smith's reflections on Christmas:

> Every year, as Christmas approaches, I begin to grow young again. At least I judge so from the fact that a strange, mysterious pleasure, well known to me by this time, though little understood and very varied, begins to glow in my mind with the first hint, come from what quarter it may [. . .] that the day of all the year is at hand—is climbing up from the under-world. I enjoy it like a child.[16]

Smith, who has "formed the Swedenborgian resolution of never growing old" and serves as a virtual mouthpiece for MacDonald, is an old bachelor of fifty who nevertheless finds himself "a welcome nobody [. . .] amongst young people" due to his childlike nature.[17] He has a playful spirit, is a bit of a trickster, and being from a different part of the country is more detached and disinterested than the other characters. The common name "John Smith" emphasizes his non-identity and therefore his suitability as a narrator. He tells himself, "please to remember a resolution you came to once upon a time, that, as you were nobody, so you would be nobody; and see if you can make yourself useful."[18] Not surprisingly, he is also the teller of the novel's three fairytales and thus MacDonald's representative on the use and significance of fairytales.

What is more, Smith's two primary interests throughout the novel are stories and Christmas. After describing his joy in Christmas traditions and rituals, Smith adds, "above all things [at Christmas], I delight in listening to stories, and sometimes in telling them."[19] Passing by houses with "happy fires," Smith ponders the festive nature of Christmas:

> Is it vulgar, this feasting at Christmas? No. It is the Christmas feast that justifies all feasts, as the bread and wine of the Communion are the essence of all bread and wine, of all strength and rejoicing. [. . .] Certain I am, that but for the love which, ever revealing itself, came out brightest at that first Christmas time, there would be no feasting—nay no smiling; no world to go careering in joy about its central fire; no men and women upon it, to look up and rejoice.[20]

Christmas festivities participate in the eternal joy of the divine. The events of the first Christmas Day, "the day of all the year," interpenetrate all of time with joy and revelry and out of this abundance give rise and warrant to all other stories of jollity.[21]

Smith arrives at his friend's house and finds his "niece" Adela suffering from a general sort of depression, which seems to have no physical causes. On Christmas Day, the family attends the local church, where Smith has a mystical reflection on the nature of doors: "All the doors that lead inwards to the secret place of the Most High are doors outwards—out of self—out of smallness—out of wrong." Spiritual journeys, in other words, are ecstatic—a principle continually exhibited in MacDonald's fairytales. It is through a stripping of the self that one is led into larger and more spacious realms (as we shall see in the next chapter). Smith's reverie is interrupted by the sermon, which just happens to be on the relationship of Christmas to the childlike:

> The winter is the childhood of the year. Into this childhood of the year came the child Jesus; and into this childhood of the year must we all descend. It is as if God spoke to each of us according to our need: My son, my daughter, you are growing old and cunning; you must grow a child again, with my son, this blessed birth-time. You are growing old and selfish; you must become a child.[22]

The structure of time itself changes on Christmas such that instead of growing older, people can actually grow younger so that they can regain the freshness and vitality of children. As the sermon continues, the preacher claims that because Jesus became a child, childhood is therefore in the "deepest nature" of God himself. Three years after *Adela*

Cathcart, MacDonald expanded upon this homily in his most famous unspoken sermon "Child in the Midst" (1867). But here in his first—and arguably most lucid—exposition of the "childlike," MacDonald highlights the connection of Christmas and the childlike almost as a preface to his first fairytales. The sermon concludes with a jubilant enjoinder partially taken from Ecclesiastes: "Then be happy this Christmas Day; for to you a child is born. [. . .] Eat and drink, and be merry and kind, for the love of God is the source of all joy and all good things, and this love is present in the child Jesus."[23] Past, present, and future collide in an excess of joy on Christmas Day as worshippers commemorate Christ's historical birth, proclaim his present lordship, and anticipate his future return. The liberating power of this festival allows people to rejoice and enter into the goodness of God without being burdened by the past or worried about the future. This is because festivals interrupt normal temporal patterns (how the present relates to memory and expectation) and usher in a chronological modality best described, according to Hans Gadamer, as "celebration."[24] Celebration is wholly participatory. It distances the individual from mere historical sequentiality by connecting him or her to transcendent moments of cosmic or communal significance, helping an individual to forget small temporal worries and regrets.

In *Sir Gibbie*, MacDonald describes this condition as the bliss of those "who do not 'look before and after, and pine for what is not,' but live in the holy carelessness of the eternal *now*."[25] And for MacDonald, no other time shows the eternal entering temporality like Christmas. In this moment, God himself embraces lowliness, vulnerability, and foolishness in a wild display of "holy carelessness." The way to celebrate this ultimate spectacle of God's foolishness is, therefore, to reverse the progress of time and "grow a child again," to forget the strictures of grown-up decorum and embrace the seemingly low and light joys of childhood.

Such is the setting into which MacDonald places his first fairytales. After it becomes clear that Adela is not responding to normal treatment of her "illness," Smith and the doctor suggest that a prescription of stories be given in order to "furnish a better mental table" for her.[26] Smith justifies his suggestion to Adela by arguing, "this is Christmas-tide, you know, and that is just the time for story-telling."[27]

For Smith, as for MacDonald, there is something about the joyous nature of Christmas which makes it particularly suitable for telling stories—and not just any stories. When Adela's pesky aunt asks if the story is "suitable to the season," Smith responds, "Yes, very [. . .] for it is a child's story—a fairy tale, namely; though I confess I think it fitter for grown than for young children. I hope it is funny, though. I think it is."[28] Here MacDonald recalls all that has previously been said about Christmas and the childlike and specifically places his fairytales within that festive context. Not only does Smith anticipate MacDonald's famous assertion in "The Fantastic Imagination" that he does not write for children but for "the childlike, whether of five, or fifty, or seventy-five," he also justifies the playful levity of his fairytales by appealing to Christ himself. When Mrs. Cathcart calls the propriety of fairytales into question "at a sacred time like this," Smith has a ready reply: "If I thought God did not approve of fairytales, I would never read, not to say write one, Sunday or Saturday."[29] But Smith's (and MacDonald's) claim is not simply that God tolerates fairytales; rather, God becoming a child and Christ's injunction to become little children (Mark 10:15) gives special license to all stories that enliven the childlike spirit, for such stories participate in the reality of the Christmas festival—they emulate the pattern of Jesus' "holy carelessness," forsaking the weightiness and safety of dignity for the ludicrousness and vulnerability of levity.

Smith begins "The Light Princess" with "once upon a time," but the curate immediately interrupts, asks to play "Master of the Ceremonies," and proceeds to rearrange the party in a circle around the fire for optimum listening pleasure. In addition, he lays down the ground rule that "anybody may speak that likes," encouraging a dialogical encounter with the fairy story.[30] As with festivals setting themselves apart from everyday time, there is a demarcation of story space and time that prepares the audience for the ludic experience. Similar instances of story preparation occur before "The Giant's Heart" and MacDonald's later story "Little Daylight," which he sets within the narrative of *At the Back of the North Wind.* Before the telling of "Little Daylight," MacDonald explicitly describes the internal preparation. Being ill, the children in the hospital are unable to have the "same busy gathering, and bustling, and shifting to and fro with which children generally prepare themselves to hear a story; but their faces, and the turning of their heads, and many feeble exclamations of expected pleasure, showed that all such preparations were making within them."[31] In addition to and more important than the physical preparations, hearers of fairytales must prepare an imaginative space and ready themselves to enter into the festive chronological experience.

Having prepared his audience, Smith begins "The Light Princess" with a revealing opening line: "once upon a time, so long ago, that I have quite forgotten the date, there lived a king and queen who had no children."[32] Just as the formula "once upon a time" shifts the characters of *Adela Cathcart* from the cozy circle by the fire to another realm, so too it shifts the reader of the novel from the homely, mundane scene into a fantastic world.[33] MacDonald gently parodies the fairytale convention with his digressive comment "so long ago that I have quite forgotten the date" but also thereby accentuates the dilation of time that occurs within the fairytale. Time in the fairytale is not aligned with the particularities of history but neither is it unreal—it dwells within a celebratory space akin to that of festivals.

After the christening scene in "The Light Princess," in which the evil witch Makemnoit chants a nonsensical incantation to rob the princess of her gravity, Mrs. Cathcart—who seems to represent the typical views of Victorian seriousness[34]—interrupts the story to question the propriety of putting church ceremonies into a fairytale. The curate answers that the Church is not "a cross-grained old lady" and that "a few gentle liberties" are perfectly acceptable. Smith then adds, "if both church and fairytale belong to humanity, they may occasionally cross circles [. . .]. They must have something in common."[35] Religious rites are acceptable in fairytales because both the church and the fairytale encompass the whole of human experience.[36] Nor is this the only church ritual that Smith sneaks into the fairytale. As the prince stands sacrificially in the hole in the lake, the princess feeds him "bits of biscuits, and sips of wine."[37] Read aloud in the midst of Christmastide, "The Light Princess" thus begins with a christening and ends with a kind of Eucharist, encapsulating symbolically the entire scope of the Christ-mass.

In addition to the Christmas setting of the frame novel, two of the stories explicitly reflect on the festival of God becoming a child: "My Uncle Peter" and "The Shadows." Whereas "My Uncle Peter" is blatant about its connection to Christmas—Peter is born on Christmas Day and hopes to die on Christmas Day, and the story concludes with the line "Christmas-day makes all the days of the year as sacred as itself"—"The Shadows," narrated by John Smith, is more subtle but no less a reflection on the nature of Christmas.[38] This fairytale is one of only two in which MacDonald does not begin with either "once upon a time" or the equally formulaic "there was once."[39] It opens, "Old Ralph Rinkelmann made his living by comic sketches, and all but lost it again by tragic poems."[40] In this, MacDonald's first fairytale, written (or told) initially during his first Christmas as a pastor in 1857,[41] the central character is, unusually, not a child but an old man. Yet it is precisely his childlike love of comedy and his "holy carelessness" of worldly wealth that make Ralph the ideal candidate to be the king of the fairies.

The fairies crown Rinkelmann while he is in the liminal time "between life and death" (another moment outside conventional chronology), and after he is seemingly safely back in his cramped apartment, some even stranger creatures approach him. The Shadows—grotesque creatures who appear "only in the twilight of the fire"—take him to Iceland to their "Shadow-church" to teach him their ways. His second trip to the Shadow-church is during the Shadows' "grand annual assembly, in which [they] report to [their] chiefs the deeds [they] have attempted, and the good or bad success [they] have had," and it just so happens that this is the night of Christmas Eve.[42] At this point, the story turns into another frame narrative as Rinkelmann listens to the Shadows telling stories about the pranks and jokes that they have played upon humans, most of which occur on Christmas Day. Taking the frames into account then, MacDonald is telling the story of John Smith, who during Christmastide is telling the story of Ralph Rinkelmann, who on Christmas Eve is listening to Shadows tell stories about jolly Christmas japes. It is difficult to imagine a narrative structure more interpenetrated by the day "the world was saved by a child."[43] "The Shadows" also seems to draw upon MacDonald's defense of Browning's "Christmas Eve" in the "mingling of the humorous, even the ridiculous, with the serious."[44] Christmas itself justifies the proximity of high and low, light and serious, in part by liberating people from a narrow, constricted experience of time. Indeed, if the Shadows are in some sense manifestations of the Christmas impulse to "jest in earnest"—they partake in "the salamandrine essence of all the Christmas fires over the world"[45]—then they also gesture to the alliance of mundane temporality with social respectability and self-dignity and the connection of festival celebration with self-forgetfulness. "Happy Shades!" says a shadow preacher, "for we only remember our tales until we have told them here, and then they vanish in the shadow-churchyard, where we bury only our dead selves."[46] Though they do not die permanently, the Shadows, in an echo of Jesus' injunction to his disciples (Luke 9:23), die daily to themselves and thus "have no gathered weight of years." They are always light enough to gambol and jest. Meanwhile, time in some way torments most of the humans they visit, who seem trapped in themselves because of their circumstances. One shadow "[whiles] away the time" for a little boy waiting for his mother, and another mimes a shadow dance for a musician to help him forget his poverty and troubles. When the shadows succeed, their subjects often find that the joy of forgetting their small chronological worries and living in the festive "eternal now" also brings a levity that is harmonized with gravity.

In addition to the three fairytales in *Adela Cathcart*, another five of MacDonald's fairytales first appeared either in Christmas editions of periodicals or during the Christmas season.[47] While this fact probably says something about the rise of consumerism in the Victorian era—Lewis Carroll also often produced new editions of *Alice* just in time for Christmas—it was for MacDonald nevertheless most fitting as it highlighted the festive modality of both Christmas and fairytales.

We can see this principle at play in MacDonald's own Christmas celebrations as well. One of the only detailed accounts of a MacDonald family Christmas comes, intriguingly, from the 1857 Christmas season, during which MacDonald wrote both "The Shadows" and *Phantastes*. Louisa records how after an early dinner, thirteen poor children joined their small family and George told them Hans Christian Anderson's story "The Ugly Duckling." The MacDonald family then gave each of the children presents, and while they were eating small cakes, MacDonald told them another tale: "the true story of the day—about the good Christ-child." Oranges were distributed to all, then games, plum pudding, and more gifts. MacDonald himself received "a history of Punch and Judy [. . .] and great glee was there over the display of his elocutionary talents in giving it to [the] party."⁴⁸ It is a day of festive storytelling. For MacDonald, the festival celebrating when God became child melds seamlessly with fairytales, play, feasting, and revelry. Christ, as the infinite dwelling in finitude, guarantees and redeems time and brings the highest heights into contact with the lowest depths. The past has an "infinite future" in him, and he saves the present from the worries of everyday time. And, as our reading of *Adela Cathcart* has shown, MacDonald set his fairytales lightly yet earnestly in this other festive temporality.

Twilight
Sabbath Time

The stories told in *Adela Cathcart* are not, like Scheherazade's in *The Thousand and One Nights*, told to delay death "by borrowing time from narrative" but to restore life and to expand celebration.⁴⁹ They literally distend the time experience of Christmas by adding narrative time to this sphere of celebration. MacDonald suspends readers in two moments with every new story, and in this way he stretches the frame story of a not overly eventful Christmastide into a three-volume novel (much to the chagrin of some critics). Nor is this, for MacDonald, escapist overindulgence. Despite acknowledging the problem of evil and the suffering of others, Smith defends the celebration: "[Those suffering] are in God's hands. Take from me my rejoicing, and I am powerless to help them."⁵⁰ Fairytales are not escapist but rejuvenating and restorative. They help supply the motive power to fight suffering by participating proleptically in God's ultimate victory. In other words, they provide rest and therefore find kinship with another unusual chronological modality: Sabbath.

Time—as the venerable Bede observes in *The Reckoning of Time*—is measurement, the measurement of rhythms, whether natural rhythms such as earth rotations (days) and solar cycles (years), or customary rhythms such as market/cultic schedules (weeks), or divisions of the day (hours).⁵¹ On the natural level, the binary opposition of certain phenomena allows us to count and thereby measure existence: day/night, summer/winter, new moon/full moon. This repetition in turn provides the basis for understanding the beauty of created order (in symmetry, harmony, and balance), but only, according to Catherine Pickstock, if one observes the "rests": "it is when human creatures fail to confess this nothingness, when their lives in time are without pauses, that this order is denied and a greater nothingness of disharmony ensues."[52] In other words, Sabbath does not only enable the very concept of time but it also keeps time and creation in proper order.[53] Sabbath in Jewish and Christian tradition is not auxiliary to everyday time but is itself fundamental. Gerhard von Rad comments on ancient Israel, "The Sabbath was an objectively hallowed day, that is to say, a day set apart for Jahweh, on which the community shared in the divine rest and, in so doing, was conscious that this rest upon which it entered was as it were an ontological reality."[54] Sabbath is not the reward at the end of the week (the dessert one gets for eating one's vegetables) but the joyful foundation that makes any time possible, for though it is God's seventh day in the creation story, it is man's first.[55]

Time in Genesis, moreover, is not measured by "day" and "night" but by "morning" and "evening," by the times between the times. Evening, according to Pickstock, is the "in-between time of angelic visitation, and the descent of God's heavenly fire," which is why "whatever the literal clock-time at which a Mass is celebrated, it occupies the prefatory time of evening, but not in the sense of a moment before the next moment, but of the distended moment before the eschaton."[56] Just as the Sabbath in Christian tradition begins rather than culminates the new week, so evening in Jewish tradition begins the new day.[57] The Old Testament primarily discusses twilight as the moment for slaughtering the Passover lamb—"the whole assembly shall kill their lambs at twilight" (Exod 12:6)—the symbolic death that brings new life and escape from temporal bondage. Twilight (literally "between lights") and Sabbath are thus in some sense "the gateway to time itself"—the liminal moments when past, present, and future touch.[58]

Perhaps it is not surprising, therefore, that twilight fills MacDonald's fairytales. "The Golden Key" opens, "There was a boy who used to sit in the twilight and listen to his great-aunt's stories."[59] In consonance with Pickstock's argument that the mass always occupies the evening "whatever the literal clock-time," MacDonald seems to say that no matter what time it is in the everyday world, the reader experiences the tale in twilight temporality. His great-aunt tells the boy (Mossy) stories of the golden key—that is, the same story that MacDonald is telling the reader. Moreover, "The Golden Key" narrates the quest to find "the country whence the shadows fell," and twilight is the period when shadows are most prevalent.[60] Fairyland itself wholly exists within twilight, as MacDonald describes in "Cross Purposes":

> Alice was the daughter of the squire, a pretty, good-natured girl, whom her friends called fairy-like, and others called silly.—One rosy summer evening when the wall opposite her window was flaked all over with rosiness, she threw herself on her bed, and lay gazing at the wall. The rose-colour sank through her eyes and eyed her brain, and she began to feel as if she were reading a story-book. She thought she was looking at a western sea, with the waves all red with sunset. But when the colour died out, Alice gave a sigh to see how commonplace the wall grew. "I wish it was always sunset!" she said, half aloud. "I don't like gray things."
>
> "I will take you where the sun is always setting, if you like, Alice," said a sweet, tiny voice near her. She looked down on the coverlet of the bed, and there, looking up at her, stood a lovely little creature. It seemed quite natural that the little lady should be there; for many things we never could believe, have only to happen, and then there is nothing strange about them. She was dressed in white, with a cloak of sunset-red—the colours of the sweetest of sweet-peas. [. . .]
>
> Are you a fairy?" said Alice
>
> "Yes. Will you go with me to the sunset?"[61]

Peaseblossom—a descendant of one of Titania's attendants from *A Midsummer Night's Dream*—tempts Alice to follow her into the sunset lands of Faerie, where time stretches eternally between night and day. MacDonald again connects twilight with stories, but here he links it explicitly with the reading encounter, as if confirming that reading fairytales is somehow analogous to "rosy summer evenings."

In *The Secret Commonwealth of Elves, Fauns and Fairies*—a "serious" treatise written in the seventeenth century but first published by Sir Walter Scott in 1815—Robert Kirk describes fairies as "of a middle nature betwixt man and angel [. . .], of intelligent studious spirits, and light, changeable bodies (like those called astral) somewhat of the nature of a condensed cloud and best seen in twilight."[62] Whether or not MacDonald knew this particular work, he was certainly familiar with the Celtic lore of his native Scotland and knew that twilight was the time when fairyland and the human world touched (the "in-between time of angelic visitation"). In the earlier *Phantastes*, for example, "the golden stream of the sunrise with many interchanging lights" transforms Anodos' room into a fairy forest while Alice's male partner in "Cross Purposes," Richard, enters fairyland during a "bright summer evening."[63]

The significance of MacDonald's twilight imagery clearly emerges when compared to Lewis Carroll's famous narrative. Laying to one side the question of which Alice[64] came first, the opening of *Alice's Adventures in Wonderland* has an odd mixture of harmony and discord with the beginning of "Cross Purposes":

> Alice was beginning to get very tired of sitting by her sister on the bank and of having nothing to do: once or twice she had peeped into the book her sister was reading, but it had no pictures or conversations in it, "and what is the use of a book," thought Alice, "without pictures or conversations?"
>
> So she was considering, in her own mind (as well as she could, for the hot day made her feel very sleepy and stupid), whether the pleasure of making a daisy-chain would be worth the trouble of getting up and picking the daisies, when suddenly a White Rabbit with pink eyes ran close by her.
>
> There was nothing so *very* remarkable in that; nor did Alice think it so *very* much out of the way to hear the Rabbit say to itself "Oh dear! Oh dear! I shall be too late!" [. . .] The Rabbit actually *took a watch out of its waistcoat-pocket*, and looked at it.

Both Alices become absorbed in their own minds (and thus experience an altered time state)—Carroll's because she is bored, MacDonald's because the rosy light enraptures her. Carroll's Alice finds the experience of reading books without pictures or conversations useless, whereas MacDonald's finds her moment of ecstasy analogous to her experience of reading stories. Carroll's story begins during "the hot day," while MacDonald's starts "one rosy summer evening." Carroll's Alice chases an oblivious, "late," pocketwatch-carrying white rabbit, whereas MacDonald's willingly accepts the invitation of a white and sunset-red-clad fairy to go to the place where the sun is always setting. The portrayals of time could hardly contrast more starkly.

At the end of Carroll's book, Alice's sister wakes her from the dream-sleep with the last spoken words of the book: "It was a curious dream, dear, certainly; but now run in to your tea: it's getting late." *Alice's Adventures in Wonderland* begins and ends with lateness (the Rabbit's "I shall be too late" are the first spoken words). Lateness highlights the sovereignty of clock-time independent of our activity—time advances at the same steady pace whether or not we are aware of it. Alice may, like the Mad Hatter, momentarily stop time in the fantastic world of Wonderland, but she returns only to find that she is actually late. The Mad Hatter may mock and jest at time, and the whole world may suspend time momentarily; in the end, however, time has his revenge.[65] Carroll does not, like MacDonald, think that his stories in some way participate in the reality of Sabbath time. In his Christmas poem of 1867, included in most subsequent editions, Carroll distances *Alice* from the Christmas event, saying that fairies lay aside "cunning tricks and elfish play" during Christmastide. Rather than participating in the festive jollity, playful fairy stories need an apology at Christmas—the grave solemnity of the moment does not mix with "tricks and play." While most of the time Carroll is happy to join "innocent merriment" with the "graver cadences of Life," when it comes to religious ceremonies he is more typically Victorian in his anxiety that levity somehow lessens reality whereas solemnity solidifies it.[66] In the end, what Alice's story has to offer, as the book's last line tells us, is the memory of "child-life, and the happy summer days."[67]

Meanwhile, MacDonald's fairytales do not linger in nostalgic memory but adventure toward the reality of the "eternal now."[68] His Alice does not just have a dream experience. A fundamental difference between the stories is how "Cross Purposes" complements Alice with a male companion, Richard. Among other things, their mutual experience suggests that fairyland is not a solipsistic dream but a surprising manifestation of reality that harmonizes apparent opposites. Both Alice and Richard have the same dilated experience of time within fairyland (arriving back in the mundane world shortly after their departures despite lengthy adventures), but they have more than just a memory of "happy summer days": they have "permission to visit Fairy-land as often as they pleased" and, MacDonald hints, a future life together.[69] MacDonald's Alice thus achieves her desire of it always being sunset, and her real adventures in fairyland mean she can always enjoy a Sabbath rest in the twilight realms with someone she loves.

Entering into this restful twilight realm is not, for MacDonald, a retreat into self-indulgent fantasy; rather it reflects one of the fundamental experiences of time. In the chapter following "The Shadows" in *Adela Cathcart*, the characters assemble at the curate's house for an evening of songs and poetry. After one dream poem, the conversation turns to the validity of nonrealistic literature with the curate providing the authorial view:

> They seem to me to hold the same place in literature that our dreams do in life. If so much of our life is actually spent in dreaming, there must be some place in our literature for what corresponds to dreaming. Even in this region, we cannot step beyond the boundaries of our nature. I delight in reading Lord Bacon now; but one of Jean Paul's dreams will often give me more delight than one of Bacon's best paragraphs. It depends upon the mood. Some dreams like these, in poetry or in sleep, arouse individual states of consciousness altogether different from any of our waking moods, and not to be recalled by any mere effort of the will. All our being, for the moment, has a new and strange colouring. We have another kind of life. I think myself, our life would be much poorer without our dreams; a thousand rainbow tints and combinations would be gone; music and poetry would lose many an indescribable exquisiteness and tenderness. You see I like to take our dreams seriously, as I would even our fun. For I believe that those new mysterious feelings that come to us in sleep, if they be only from dreams of a richer grass and a softer wind than we have known awake, are indications of wells of feeling and delight which have not yet broken out of their hiding-places in our souls, and are only to be suspected from these rings of fairy green that spring up in the high places of our sleep.[70]

Like twilight, fantastic dream literature bathes the world in "a new and strange colouring" and thereby awakes truths that lie dormant in the psyche. It functions more lightly than even the best discursive prose to "arouse individual states of consciousness" that cannot "be recalled by any mere effort of the will." For all of its intellectual prowess, the rational mind remains powerless to evoke certain moods. Here, however, the weakness of levity displays its real force, for where the thunderous march of reason frightens away shy sensibilities, the delicate mobility of lightness coaxes them from their "hiding-places in our souls." This is why MacDonald takes both dreams and fun so "seriously," because they call forth "new mysterious feelings" and open us up to "many an indescribable exquisiteness and tenderness" that would otherwise remain inaccessible. In this way, fairytales or "these rings of fairy green" teach about reality in the same light way that dreams unveil hidden truths. Entering the twilight of fairyland does Adela, for example, "a great deal of good." "It seems like magic," she says. "I sleep very well indeed now. And somehow life seems a much more possible thing than it looked a week or two ago."[71] Where more rational methods have failed, stories succeed in "somehow" rejuvenating Adela and making life seem more possible.[72] Her Sabbath time in fairyland lifts her spirits with hope and a sense of adventure such that her father's sudden poverty does not scare her but awakens her dormant energy.

Grotesque Revelry

The Christmas setting within which MacDonald placed his fairytales signals the separation from everyday temporality, while the dilated moment of twilight provides a Sabbath within which individuals can rest. This festive twilight atmosphere permeates the fairytales, allowing the marvellous to become the norm. Interlopers in a fairyland must become "like a child, who, being in a chronic condition of wonder, is surprised at nothing."[73] Chronic wonder is essential in fairyland because time operates in a radically different way. Change and transformation of outward form can happen in an instant and do not require the passage of lengthy time spans, whereas the solidity of inner reality cannot be weakened by the inexorable march of time. Like the feast of carnival, the fairytale also participates in "the feast of time, the feast of becoming, change and renewal."[74] This festive time rebels against self-important seriousness, revels in the joys of play, and reveals the truths obscured by the "degrading spirit of commonplace."[75]

While all the fairytales abide in festive time, none is more carnivalesque than "The Shadows," MacDonald's first attempt at the genre.[76] Possibly on account of its extremely subversive form and plot, this story has received very little critical attention.[77] The opening line, as already noted, is not the typical "once upon a time," and it immediately introduces the inversion and play which dominates the tale: "Old Ralph Rinkelmann made his living by comic sketches, and all but lost it again by tragic poems."[78] MacDonald inverts the normal child protagonist and gives his fairytale an unusual hero—an old man on his deathbed. Moreover, comedy and tragedy are united in Rinkelmann, which is why "he was just the man to be chosen king of the fairies." This is the only explanation for why the fairies want Rinkelmann as their king. From a human perspective, it does not make sense to elect as king ("in Fairy-land the sovereignty is elective"[79]) an ill old man who is careless with money. But the fairies, being unbound by time or economics, do not care about these shortcomings. They had to wait, however, until Ralph was "hovering between life and death" before "they carried him off, and crowned him king of Fairy-land" because "it is only between life and death that the fairies have power over grown-up mortals."[80] In the twilight between the worlds, fairies have authority, and they transform what should be a sad and solemn occasion into a carnival celebration—though one laced with seriousness. Imminent death, the ultimate victory of time, turns topsy-turvy into a revelatory opportunity. The gnomes and goblins "run quite wild, playing him, king as he was, all sorts of tricks" before returning him to his bed, where he encounters the anarchic shadows.

Anarchic is the best word to describe the shadows because they refuse to fit neatly into any category. They are not angels, evil spirits, or ghosts but "human shadows" (Smith says that they are "shadows of the mind") that only appear "in the twilight of the fire, or when one man or woman is alone with a single candle."[81] They have "remarkable traits of grotesqueness" combined with a "solemnity of mien," and this lawless combination is characteristic of all their appearance and behavior. When the new king, having seen their wild game-playing and acrobatics, insists they "do nothing but jest," they respond, "when we do jest, sire, we always jest in earnest."[82] Their desire is "to make people silent and thoughtful; to awe them a little," but they do this through violent gambols and grotesque masquerades.[83] This description accords with Ruskin's in *The Stones of Venice*—which MacDonald had likely read—in which he says that the grotesque has "two elements, one ludicrous, the other fearful."[84] After the Shadows say they want to reveal "the truth of things," the king responds:

> "Can that be true that loves the night?" said the king
> "The darkness is the nurse of light," answered the Shadow.

> "Can that be true which mocks at forms?" said the king.
> "Truth rides abroad in shapeless storms," answered the Shadow.[85]

The formless shadow ironically responds in poetic form, speaking of truth and "shapeless storms" in the playful shape of a couplet. The Shadows are thus continuously playing in a wild grotesque manner but always with a revelatory goal in mind. According to Ruskin in *Modern Painters*, the noble grotesque sets forth "in a moment, by a series of symbols thrown together in bold and fearless connection, truths which it would have taken a long time to express."[86] There is, therefore, a definite method in the Shadows' madness, or rather a method of madness. The king sees how they "rejoice" in an "insane lawlessness of form" and how "the wildest gambols" of goblins, gnomes, and kobolds are "orderly dances of ceremony beside the apparently aimless and wilful contortions of figure, and metamorphoses of shape" of the shadows.[87] "Madness is inherent to all grotesque forms," says Bakhtin, "because madness makes men look at the world with different eyes, not dimmed by 'normal,' that is commonplace ideas and judgments."[88] This is precisely the effect that Rinkelman notices when he returns from his mad journey to the "normal" world of his sickbed:

> The dancing shadows in his room seemed to him odder and more inexplicable than ever. The whole chamber was full of mystery. So it generally was, but now it was more mysterious than ever. After all that he had seen in the Shadow-church, his own room and its shadows were yet more wonderful and unintelligible than those. This made it more likely that he had seen a true vision; for instead of making common things look common place, as a false vision would have done, it made common things disclose the wonderful that was in them.[89]

The apparently rebellious nature of the shadows' mad revelry turns out to be a revelatory vision of the mystery and wonder of the commonplace. What mundane time limits and obscures, festive time frees and unveils.[90]

This transformative, liberating moment is the only time in which the shadows are interested. Because they do not remember a story once they tell it, the Shadows "have no gathered weight of years."[91] The Shadows reserve Christmas Eve for telling all the stories of the past year—again showing how MacDonald viewed the Christmas story as the ground and continual reason for all stories. This moment is the

Shadow Sabbath and festival, intended to rejuvenate them for their "work." The king asks, "Do they always go to church before they go to work?" and the answer is, "always." This Sabbath time includes dancing, frolicking, and telling stories—stories of revelatory moments in human lives. The stories include making a murderer confess his crime, inspiring a musician, shaming a vain clergyman, comforting a child, entertaining orphans, preventing a murder, and reconciling a father to two lovers, all of which occurs in twilight moments through grotesque antics. The last of these shadow stories has a brief description which interestingly unites many of the themes of this chapter: "When the blazing plum-pudding was carried in, we made a perfect shadow-carnival about it, dancing and mumming in the blue flames, like mad demons. And how the children screamed with delight!"[92] Christmas institutes a carnivalesque chronology, characterized by twilight feasting, grotesque dancing, and childlike joy.

MacDonald mentions "carnival" only a handful of times in his works, but most instances occur in three of his earliest works—once in *Within and Without* (1855), once in *Phantastes* (1858), and three times in *Adela Cathcart* (1864).[93] MacDonald probably had not seen a carnival by this time, but it is likely—given his devotion to German Romantic literature—that he had read Goethe's description of carnival in *Italian Journey* or another of his works. At the very least, MacDonald translated Goethe's "Legend: After the Manner of Hans Sachs," which narrates in rhyming couplets the comical story of Jesus sneaking cherries into his sleeves and then dropping them on the path to teach the proud St. Peter a lesson in humility.[94] Hans Sachs was attractive to Goethe, according to Bakhtin, because of his "comic, carnivalesque spirit."[95] Whatever the source of influence, the transformative interval of carnival plays an overt role not only in "The Shadows" but also in "The Light Princess."

Structurally, "The Light Princess" breaks into two main narratives: the initial description of the princess' affliction and the ridiculous situations that result (chaps.1–7), and the story of how the prince meets the princess and saves her by his loving self-sacrifice (chaps. 9–15). The first part becomes increasingly more humorous and lighthearted (culminating with "she was a fifth imponderable body, sharing all the other properties of the ponderable"), whereas the second becomes increasingly more "serious" (culminating with the death of the prince). In the middle is the pivotal chapter 8, which occurs "one summer evening, during the carnival of the country."[96] The silly king, who "rarely condescended to make light of his misfortune," was—probably on account of the carnival—"in a particularly good humour" and after losing his balance throws the princess into the lake.[97] The carnivalesque moment discloses the key revelation of the story that the princess becomes more human in water and thus that her ultimate cure is "water from a deeper source." The playful and surprising nature of this revelation—it did not occur through the careful philosophical reflection of Hum-Drum and Kopy-Keck but through a bit of light-hearted fun—also gestures toward the final carnival reversal of expectations. The "deeper source" of the princess' tears is not sadness or an awareness of suffering—all the attempts of the king and philosophers to make her cry through pain, fear, or distress for others fail—but joy and delight, as John Milbank argues: "the princess's tears fall first *through joy* when the prince is resurrected from his sacrificial death."[98] In an odd sense, therefore, her weight is restored not through a crude awareness of gravity but through an experience of true lightness. She forsakes her physical lightness only upon finding a better, more holistic levity, one that holds gravity lightly within itself.

The other dominant moment of transformation in the fairytales (as in much of MacDonald's writing) is the apparently anti-festive death. Tolkien's comment that "death is the theme that most inspired George MacDonald" is, of course, slightly misleading.[99] It would be truer to say that "life is the theme that most inspired MacDonald" but that he believed death to be the doorway to more life:

> "In the midst of life we are in death," said one; it is more true that in the midst of death we are in life. Life is the only reality; what men call death is but a shadow—a word for that which cannot be—a negation, owing the very idea of itself to that which it would deny. But for life there could be no death. If God were not, there would not even be nothing.[100]

Death is not the victory of time over life—it is at worst an illusion. Nevertheless, in the fairytales death and life are frequently bound together in an ambivalent image. Mossy in "The Golden Key" meets the Old Man of the Sea looking "much older than the Old Man of the Sea, and his feet were very weary."¹⁰¹ This weariness, however, is not with life: "low-sunk life imagines itself weary of life, but it is death, not life it is weary of."¹⁰² The Old Man of the Sea then leads him to a bath where he rests and discusses the golden key and his quest to find the country whence the shadows fall. When he rises, there is "not a grey hair on his head or a wrinkle on his skin," and the Old Man asks him:

> "You have tasted of death now," said the Old Man. "Is it good?"
>
> "It is good," said Mossy. "It is better than life."
>
> "No," said the Old Man: "it is only more life."¹⁰³

For MacDonald, death always leads to life. The only exception to this in the fairytales is the death of evil, as with the giant in "The Giant's Heart" or the witches Makemnoit ("The Light Princess") or Watho ("The Day Boy and the Night Girl"). The death of evil is always permanent. Such a view of death as wedded to life is directly in tune with the carnival spirit according to Bakhtin: "moments of death and revival, of change and renewal always [lead] to a festive perception of the world."¹⁰⁴ Such a perception transforms the very notion of time from the static quotidian to "the flux of becoming."¹⁰⁵

Death, in any case, is not a cause for mourning but for rejoicing. It is not the end of life but the beginning of greater life. Virtually all of MacDonald's protagonists must pass through some form of metaphorical death in order to come into a greater fullness of life. The princess Rosamond, for example, in "The Wise Woman" undergoes repeated deaths to her "Somebody" in order that she might have true life herself (a theme that MacDonald later vividly portrayed in *Lilith* with the Raven's house of death). This process climaxes in a vision of a lovely little girl whose eyes "were as full as they could hold of the laughter of the spirit—a laughter which in this world is never heard, only sets the eyes alight with a liquid shining." This little girl (actually the wise woman) plays with flowers in her lap before throwing them away to the ground where they spring to life again. Rosamond tries to touch the flowers, but they wither in her hands. The little girl then tells her why this happens:

> "If, to call them yours, you must kill them, then they are not yours, and never, never can be yours. They are nobody's when they are dead."

"But you don't kill them."

"I don't pull them; I throw them away. I live them."[106]

The little girl demonstrates "divine carelessness," loving the beautiful creations but then carelessly (without desire for possession or control) casting them aside to live on their own. So full of life and love herself, she is able to bestow life on other creatures. After a flying pony refuses her touch, Rosamond is on the brink of despair: "What sort of creature am I that the flowers wither when I touch them. [. . .] There is that lovely child giving life instead of death to the flowers, and a moment ago I was hating her!" As the pony approaches at terrible speed, she finally dies to herself: "I don't care. They may trample me under their feet if they like. I am tired and sick of myself—a creature at whose touch the flowers wither!"[107] She then confesses to the little girl that she is just "glad that there is such a you and such a pony" and that she has no desire to possess or control either, but that "[she does] wish the flowers would not die when [she touches] them."[108] This death leads to the life she desires. The girl then tells Rosamond to touch the flower—and it doesn't wither. She touches it again, and it changes color. She touches it a final time, and "it opened and grew until it was as large as a narcissus, and changed and deepened in colour till it was a red glowing gold."[109] Unlike the mythical Narcissus, who refused to die to self-love and was transformed by Echo into a solitary flower, Rosamond's death to self renews true life, both in her and in another creation. Death leads to life and celebration: "when the transfiguration of the flower was perfected, she sprang to her feet with clasped hands, but for very ecstasy of joy stood speechless, gazing at the child."[110] Finally escaping from the deathly prison of the self, she finds the ecstatic joy which is the nature of real love—and real life. It is this joyous revelatory time that is both the *telos* of MacDonald's tales and the air "that blows in that country."

"I Have No Time to Grow Old"

Shortly after transfiguring the flower, Rosamond looks at the lovely child and witnesses another transformation: "the child began, like the flower, to grow larger. Quickly through every gradation of growth she passed, until she stood before her a woman perfectly beautiful, neither old nor young; for hers was the old age of everlasting youth."[111] The fullness of life in the wise woman is such that age and time have no effect upon her. Or rather fairyland seems to purify and redeem time. No longer does time inevitably bring death; rather, time perfects life and forges true beauty. Within the festive carnival atmosphere of fairyland, the true function of time is to facilitate change and renewal.

In fairyland, therefore, time only afflicts those creatures that refuse to relinquish self-interest. The wise woman character in "The Golden Key" (one of MacDonald's most ubiquitous tropes[112]) discusses this idea with Tangle after asking how old she is:

> "Ten," answered Tangle.
>
> "You don't look like it," said the lady.
>
> "How old are you, please?" returned Tangle.
>
> "Thousands of years old," answered the lady.
>
> "You don't look like it," said Tangle.
>
> "Don't I? I think I do. Don't you see how beautiful I am?" And her great blue eyes looked down on the little Tangle, as if all the stars in the sky were melted in them to make their brightness.
>
> "Ah! But," said Tangle, "when people live long they grow old. At least I always thought so."
>
> "I have no time to grow old," said the lady. "I am too busy for that. It is very idle to grow old."[113]

Age has a different meaning in fairyland. Its carnivalesque mode completely inverts the normal expectations of decomposition with the passage of time, such that the longer the lady lives, the more she expects her beauty to increase. "Growing old" is an idle activity, a sign in fairyland that a creature lacks life, that one is not progressing toward perfection. Since the "outcome of life" is "righteousness, love, grace, truth," a lack of such activity signifies a lessening of life. "Life itself," says MacDonald, "is a thing that will not be defined, even as God will not be defined: it is a power, the formless cause of form."[114] A being that has God's eternal life is "a being beyond the attack of decay or death, a being so essential that it has no relation whatever to nothingness."[115] Such are MacDonald's fairy helpers and senders—they already have eternal life within them and thus are able to love and give life to those who need help.

Because of fairyland's reversal of the logic of time, it might at first appear that MacDonald's fairy helpers are leftovers from the Garden of Eden and the early parts of Genesis.[116] While the biblical patriarchs (Adam, Seth, Noah) do live extended life spans, they still die (except Enoch), whereas MacDonald's fairy helpers do not.[117] As Tangle continues her journey to find the land whence the shadows fall, she encounters the Old Man of the Sea, the Old Man of the Earth, and the Old Man of the Fire—each of whom is older than the next but also younger looking. Before she can see the beauty of the Old Man of the Sea, though, she must die and be resurrected in the same bath that Mossy will later use. As she bathes, Tangle receives "all the good of sleep without undergoing its forgetfulness"; she feels "the good coming all the time," and becomes "whole, and strong and well as if she had slept for seven days."[118] Death is the ultimate Sabbath for renewing life. She is then surprised to find "the form of a grand man, with a majestic and beautiful face, waiting for her," who turns out to be the Old Man of the Sea—death (or rather more life) has purified her vision and allowed her to see true reality.[119] She then descends to the Old Man of the Earth, who initially appears "bent double with age," but then Tangle sees that he is "a youth of marvellous beauty" who sits "entranced with the delight of what he beheld in a mirror of something like silver."[120] Ecstatically gazing into this mirror is his "work"—duty and delight are seamlessly blended—and this work keeps him from knowing the way to the land whence the shadows fall, so he sends her on to the Old Man of the Fire: the oldest man of all. Here is his description:

> A little naked child [was] sitting on the moss. He was playing with balls of various colours and sizes, which he disposed in strange figures upon the floor beside him. [. . .] He went on busily, tirelessly, playing his solitary game, without looking up, or seeming to know that there was a stranger in his deep-withdrawn cell. Diligently as a lace-maker shifts her bobbins, he shifted and arranged his balls. [. . .] For seven years she had stood there watching the naked child with his coloured balls, and it seemed to her like seven hours.[121]

The oldest man of all is the most childlike and the most Christlike. His "occupation" is playing with multicolored balls infinitely, "tirelessly." "Because children have abounding vitality," observes Chesterton, "because they are in spirit fierce and free, therefore they want things repeated and unchanged."[122] The oldest man of all is so full of life that his energy never flags, and he is able to "exult in monotony."[123]

On his face "there was such an awfulness of absolute repose." Perfect rest manifests itself in furious playful activity because it roots itself in the source of power. To Tangle's question, "Where is the Old Man of the Fire?" the child responds with perfect readiness the biblical formula, "Here I am" (cf. Gen 22:1; 1 Sam 3:4; Isa 6:8), and says with the utter assurance of humility: "I am very, very old. I am able to help you, I know. I can help everybody." Age, via time, has brought wisdom, joy, and vitality. Life overflows in him to such an extent that he can help anyone. Of all the characters in the story, he alone knows the way to the country whence the shadows fall: "I know the way quite well. I go there myself sometimes. But you could not go my way; you are not old enough."[124] Unlike the Old Man of the Earth, who must mind his work, the Old Man of the Fire perfectly harmonizes play with work and as a result has the time to go where he wants when he wants with no worries about time. Age has nurtured his divine childhood and brought with it knowledge, wisdom, power, peace, love, and joy.

Nor is this topsy-turvy functioning of time restricted to fairy creatures. Both Mossy and Tangle undergo the same experience of aging throughout the tale so that when they finally reunite, Tangle is as beautiful as her grandmother and "as still and peaceful as the Old Man of the Fire," while Mossy is like all the Old Men in Tangle's journey but still himself. They are "younger and better, and stronger and wiser, than they had ever been before."[125]

Since time in the fairyland does not lead to the end of life, characters encounter it more playfully. Time does not compress or speed up—though it seems this way to the reader—rather the characters experience it without boredom. Tangle watches the Old Man of the Fire for seven years but thinks that it is only seven hours because her interest never wanes. Just as boredom appears as the expansion of meaningless time, so play and interest result in the swift passage of meaningful time. In "The Carasoyn" the old blind woman tells Colin that he must "dream three days without sleeping," then "work three days without dreaming," and finally "work and dream three days together."[126] To accomplish the dreaming without sleeping, the old woman keeps "telling Colin one story after another, till he thought he could sit there all his life and listen." Here again we see MacDonald's association of stories with dreaming and the significant place that dreaming and stories have in the development of an individual—his quest must begin with an imaginative act that helps him to "lose himself" and be caught up in another time sequence. In part two of the same story, when Colin has only nine days to save his son, he again must begin by listening to a story. The old woman says, "There is no time to be lost. Sit down and listen to my story."[127] By the time Colin thinks "it must be midnight," the story (only one this time) has ended and seven days have passed, but he is rested and prepared, responding immediately with "I am ready." Narrative for MacDonald is a necessary precursor to any undertaking; it is an imaginative Sabbath renewing life and enabling action.

To work without dreaming, Colin goes to the goblin blacksmith where he alternates hammer blows with the mischievous goblin. Again he discovers with surprise that he has worked "three whole days and nights" without dreaming. As with listening to stories, the complete engagement of his body and the purposefulness of work allow Colin to "lose himself." His interest never lessens, and he is thus unaware of time's passing. To recall our earlier discussion of *A Midsummer Night's Dream*, he has beguiled "lazy time" with the delight of manual labor. Arriving at a mossy vineyard, he then works and dreams for three days—the pinnacle of the three experiences. The intermingling of dream and work grant perfect illumination:

> Those three days were the happiest he had ever known. For he understood everything he did himself, and all that everything was doing round about him. He saw what the rushes were, and why the blossom came out at the side, and why it was russet-coloured, and why the pith was white, and the skin green. [. . .] And all the time he seemed at home, tending the cow, or making his father's supper, or reading a fairy tale as he sat waiting for him to come home.[128]

The final sentence echoes what MacDonald says at the beginning of the story about Colin: "all the time that he was busiest working, he was busiest building castles in the air. I think the two ought always to go together."[129] Indeed, MacDonald presents the combination of dreaming and working as the highest ideal (as he also did in the image of the Old Man of the Fire playing at his work). Revelation into the heart of creation results when one perfectly unites play and work. The vital life of fairyland bestows the gift of understanding on the child who discovers the secret of playing while working, playing through working. Granted an abundance of life, Colin does not need to renew his strength and can wholly focus on the story, work, or creation before him. Lightened of the fears and worries so dominant in everyday temporality, he experiences time as a swift and delightful journey. When it loses the pallor of death, MacDonald suggests, time's levity shines forth.

Before Ever After
Time's Intensest Now

While we have seen that MacDonald almost exclusively employs the fairytale opening "once upon a time" to invoke fairyland, he never writes "happily ever after" to conclude his stories. The nearest he comes is in the playful ending of the Light Princess:

> So the prince and princess lived and were happy; and had crowns of gold, and clothes of cloth, and shoes of leather, and children of boys and girls, not one of whom was ever known, on the most critical occasion, to lose the smallest atom of his or her due proportion of gravity.[130]

But even this is not the unequivocal bliss of "they lived happily ever after." The parody lightly floats near tautology ("clothes of cloth," "children of boys and girls") implying that though they are happy it is not the joy of eternal bliss, which is of a wholly different order.

Comparing MacDonald's endings with Oscar Wilde's "The Young King" illuminates MacDonald's distinctiveness. Wilde's story of the coronation of a child king also ends with tautologies ("the trumpeters blew upon their trumpets and the singing boys sang"), but Wilde uses this device to intensify the artificial ending rather than as a self-reflexive parody. Wilde's tale ends in divine vindication for the idealistic king as the people fall down in awe before him and "no man dared look upon his face, for it was the face of an angel."[131] Where the fairytale brings out the light and playful in MacDonald, it tends to reveal the sentimental and nostalgic in Wilde. Unlike Wilde's fairytales, which seem to exist in a wholly aestheticized, ahistorical realm, MacDonald's fairytales appear to take place within the same salvation-historical dimension that human history currently inhabits—namely, the "already but not yet," the twilight time between creation and redemption.[132]

In the Christmas poem "An Old Story," MacDonald describes how "the son and heir eternal" of "the ancient house of ages" "leaves the all-world hearth, / Seeks the out-air, frosty-cold, / Of the twilight earth."[133] Elsewhere, MacDonald speaks of the "twilighted hearts" of humanity as compared to God's noon.[134] Earth and humanity are "twilighted" between Eden and eternity, but the birth of Jesus marks something new in the twilight age:

> Babe and mother, coming mage,
> Shepherd, ass, and cow!
> Angels watching the new age,
> Time's intensest Now!
> Heaven down-brooding, Earth upstraining,
> Far ends closing in!
> Sure the eternal tide is gaining
> On the strand of sin!
> [. . .]
> Hark the torrent-joy let slip!
> Hark the great throats ring!
> Glory! Peace! Good-fellowship!
> And a Child for king![135]

Christ's birth is within history, but nevertheless it initiates a "new age" and is "time's intensest Now." MacDonald describes what biblical scholars refer to as "inaugurated eschatology." The incarnation was the beginning of the end of the age (thus a "new age" but still before the *eschaton*) in that Jesus announced, "the time is now fulfilled, and the kingdom of God is at hand" (Mark 1:15). The birth of the Messiah was the fulfilment of time ("time's intensest Now") and the inauguration of a new era, but, though Jesus achieved the victory over sin and death on the cross and in the resurrection, the ultimate redemption is yet to come. Human history is, therefore, in the paradoxical period of "already but not yet": Christ has already redeemed humanity, but this redemption is not yet fully manifested. Karl Barth comments: "The day of His death was revealed on Easter Day to be the day of their life. And they now stand in the grey twilight before the dawn. They now advance into this day, which will eventually be theirs, but for the moment is only His."[136]

Given the Christmas setting of MacDonald's fairytales and their festive, Sabbath atmosphere, it is not surprising that his fairyland also participates in this "already but not yet" temporality.

Evil is thus still operative within fairyland, though it has no ultimate efficacy. In the manner of "Sleeping Beauty" and "The Light Princess," an evil witch sneaks into the christening of Little Daylight, and MacDonald interrupts the narrative to muse on the nature of evil:

> It is difficult to understand how they should be able to do [unkind things], for you would fancy that all wicked creatures would be powerless on such an occasion. But I never knew of any interference on the part of a wicked fairy that did not turn out a good thing in the end. What a good thing, for instance, it was that one princess should sleep for a hundred years![137]

The power of Christ should be sufficient to ward off the charms of evil during a child's baptism, so the only explanation is that the wicked fairies are actually doing the work of divine goodness without knowing it. MacDonald makes this explicit later in the story when the wicked fairy again intervenes to prevent the prince from meeting Little Daylight:

> Now wicked fairies will not be bound by the laws which the good fairies obey, and this always seems to give the bad the advantage over the good, for they use means to gain their ends which the others will not. But it is all of no consequence, for what they do never succeeds; nay, in the end it brings about the very thing they are trying to prevent. So you see that somehow, for all their cleverness, wicked fairies are dreadfully stupid, for, although from the beginning of the world they have really helped instead of thwarting the good fairies, not one of them is a bit the wiser for it.[138]

Wicked fairies appear "clever," but their inability or refusal to understand the ultimate victory of goodness causes them to become the dupes of the divine—unwitting tools like Pilate and Pharaoh.

Most of MacDonald's antagonists display this trait of cleverness. Makemnoit, whose very name implies the arrogance of knowledge ("make them know it"), is "awfully clever," and she "beat all the wicked fairies in wickedness, and all the clever ones in cleverness."[139] The fairy queen in "The Carasoyn" cleverly tricks Colin into fetching her the exotic Carasoyn wine while the goblins in *The Princess and the Goblin* have "grown in knowledge and cleverness," even as their bodies have grown more misshapen.[140] But this trait is most clearly articulated in describing Watho, MacDonald's last fairytale witch:[141]

> There was once a witch who desired to know everything. But the wiser a witch is, the harder she knocks her head against the wall when she comes to it. Her name was Watho, and she had a wolf in her mind. She cared for nothing in itself—only for knowing it. She was not naturally cruel, but the wolf had made her cruel.[142]

Preposterously, the end appears in the opening lines. Evil, MacDonald promises, in the form of selfish knowledge will ultimately knock its head against the wall of goodness—the only solid, lasting reality. The reader receives a foretaste of the promised ending in the second sentence, and hope suffuses fairyland. Hope lightens the typical narrative worries about endings, allowing readers and characters to rest and play in fairyland. While evil may play despicable tricks on innocent and good characters (e.g., Watho's demented experimentation with Photogen and Nycteris, raising the former to only know the day and the latter to only know the night), this only leads to greater good and the destruction of evil, for evil has a tendency to "self-destructiveness."[143] Upon seeing the two lovers united in marriage, Aurora (Photogen's mother) wonders "how even the wicked themselves may be a link to join together the good."[144]

A sort of holy nonchalance undermines the weightiness of evil. "To live carelessly-divine," says MacDonald in *Annals of a Quiet Neighbourhood* (1867), "duty-doing, fearless, loving, self-forgetting lives—is not that more than to know both good and evil—lives in which the good, like Aaron's rod, has swallowed up the evil, and turned it into good?"[145] This is what Photogen and Nycteris do—they take what was intended as evil and, by living "carelessly-divine," lightly turn it into a greater good. MacDonald's fairyland does not reverse the effects of knowing both good and evil as if it were a reconstituted Eden; instead it displays the power of levity to subvert the seriousness of evil in this "twilighted" era between the fall and redemption. Moreover, not even Watho—arguably MacDonald's most straightforwardly wicked fictional creation—is "naturally cruel"; rather the "wolf in her mind" has made her cruel. Evil is always privational in fairyland—it twists and distorts created goodness but has no reality of its own.

MacDonald's fairies are thus much in the same condition as humanity. They are not a specially preserved race of edenic beings, perfect in innocence, goodness, and purity, but ones who similarly must choose goodness over selfishness and repent when they have been wicked. "Cross Purposes," for example, instead of ending "happily ever after," concludes with the punishment of Peaseblossom and Toadstool for their cruelty to Alice and Richard: "they were both banished from court, and compelled to live together, for seven years, in an old tree that had just one green leaf upon it. Toadstool did not mind it much, but Peaseblossom did."[146] MacDonald makes explicit the shared situation of fairies and humans in "The Carasoyn" when describing the wickedness of the Scottish fairy queen: "She, no more than if she had been a daughter of Adam, could be happy while going on in that way."[147] And at the end of the tale, there are even signs that the queen is moving toward repentance, as when she tiredly says, "Look here, Colin, I wish you well."[148] Fairies may live longer and more playfully, but they still exist within the same salvation-historical dimension as humanity. MacDonald's fairytales thus simultaneously partake in a festive Sabbath chronology and the "in-between," twilight moment in salvation history when evil is still operative. This "two-time" condition is not contradictory but analogous to the paradox of Christ's relationship to history. In Christian tradition, Jesus is at the same time the present lord and the coming king.[149] And one of the main results of this two-time experience of reality is hope, as one has foretastes of the joy that will one day triumph over evil. In this way, hope lifts individuals out of the heaviness of present circumstances and lightens them so that they can take tangible steps toward the desired future.

Through the character of Colin in "The Carasoyn," MacDonald self-reflexively comments on the hope that leavens his fairytales: "People in fairy stories always find what they want. Why should not I find this Carasoyn? It does not seem likely. But the world doesn't go round by *likely*. So I will try."[150] Finding himself in the midst of one of his own fairytales, Colin decides to act based not on mundane probability but on divine hope. In this, he behaves like a holy fool, not pursuing tame self-interest but embracing the wild uncertainty of hope. Virtually all of MacDonald's protagonists are in this sense fools, wagering their very lives with little knowledge or certainty on the hope of something better. In addition to Colin (a forerunner to MacDonald's more famous holy fools Diamond from *At the Back of the North Wind* and Sir Gibbie), Nycteris overcomes her fear of Watho by her hope of finding a greater lamp; the prince in "Little Daylight" lives in hope of glimpsing the beautiful Daylight, and the prince in "The Light Princess" takes the ultimate step and offers his life with the selfless hope of improving the princess' life: "She will die if I don't do it, and life would be nothing to me without her; so I shall lose nothing by doing it. [. . .] And there will be so much more beauty and happiness in the world!"[151] Protecting one's own life—that most sensible of goals—is folly to the heart full of hope for greater life. Hope is the very essence of fairyland. And, as Jürgen Moltmann points out, hope is also the crux of Christianity:

> From first to last, and not merely in epilogue, Christianity is eschatology, is hope, forward looking and forward moving, and therefore also revolutionizing and transforming the present. The eschatological is not one element of Christianity, but it is the medium of Christian faith as such, the key in which everything in it is set, the glow that suffuses everything here in the dawn of an expected new day.[152]

One is tempted in the case of MacDonald to rewrite the above quotation by substituting "fairytale" and "faerie" for "Christianity" and "Christian." Indeed, Moltmann's images of "the key" and the glowing "dawn of an expected new day" cannot help but conjure MacDonald's fairytales, especially his most lauded tale, "The Golden Key."

After the tale's opening sentence, in which the reader hears of a "boy who used to sit in the twilight and listen to his great-aunt's stories," MacDonald immediately introduces the golden key and hope: "She told him that if he could reach the place where the end of the rainbow stands he would find there a golden key."[153] The key is in some sense the offspring or incarnation of the rainbow. In the Bible, rainbows signify the promise of God's covenant with humanity (Gen 9:12-16) and God's sovereign beauty in his throne room (Rev 4:3). Dante, whom MacDonald admired and quoted from profusely, draws on this biblical imagery in the final canto of the *Paradiso* to describe the Trinity:

> I saw the Great Light shine into three circles
> In three clear colors bound in one same space;
>
> The first seemed to reflect the next like rainbow
> On rainbow, and the third was like a flame
> Equally breathed forth by the other two.[154]

In his poem "Light," MacDonald borrows Dante's image and makes it the source of humanity's existence: "Thy living light's eternal fountain-play / In ceaseless rainbow pulse bestows our being."[155] The play of God constitutes humanity. Rainbows thus represent the hope of humanity for continued existence and ultimate perfection.

Mossy then speculates that the golden key is "the rainbow's egg" or that "it comes tumbling down the rainbow from the sky." The image of an egg is also pregnant with hope—an egg is a promise of new life, an "already but not yet" creation. Indeed, according to MacDonald's short allegorical poem "Hope and Patience," an egg consists of an unborn bird "a-dreaming of the world" and a shell that guards it. "*Hope* is the bird," says MacDonald, and "the shell that keeps it alive is *Patience*."[156] Hope has wings with which to defy gravity.

Furthermore, the golden key is a gift that inspires hope because of its suggestive incompleteness. The beauty of the key hints at a treasure of even greater worth—keys are less valuable than that which they open. Throughout the story, the key acts as an impetus which drives Mossy and Tangle onward in their journey, keeps them forward-looking and ever pressing on toward the goal. Though they are parted in the shadowlands, neither turns back to search for the other, but both forge on with hope and trust in their eventual reunion. MacDonald then ends the story when Mossy and Tangle finally find the rainbow hole in which the key fits. Hope has done its work and the promise has been fulfilled; the time of the "already but not yet" has ended and a new more glorious age has begun.

If the key does in some sense represent hope, then we might see MacDonald himself as the boy with the golden key, as a letter from 1893 suggests: "I always had a large gift of hope. It has been the one constitutional power of life in me—none of my making surely!"[157] Hope levitated MacDonald's life and stories and perhaps brought him more swiftly and effortlessly than others to the rainbow staircase.

Yet MacDonald's narrator does not follow Mossy and Tangle up to the land whence the shadows fall. He even is uncertain about the outcome: "and by this time I think they must have got there."[158] Like Dante coming face to face with the vision of God, "power [fails] high fantasy" when it attempts to leave the twilight time of humanity, and MacDonald's "own wings could not take [him] so high."[159] Words and language break down; story transfigures to a blinding glory, and we who are trapped "in-between" can only fall silent and wonder.

Such wondering speculation is MacDonald's favorite way of ending his fairytales. Little Daylight ends her tale in twilight with the wondering question, "Is that the sun coming?" Meanwhile Nycteris asks hopefully, "but who knows that, when we go out, we shall not go into a day as much greater than your day as your day is greater than my night?"[160] Fairytale endings are not themselves the ends but only foreshadowings of the greater bliss to come—a theme that C. S. Lewis drew upon in his conclusion to his Narnia stories.[161]

This, I think, underlies MacDonald's famous "endless endings."[162] In the time before the second coming, there is no ultimate consummation, as is most clear in the ending to *The Princess and Curdie*:

> Irene and Curdie were married. The old king died, and they were king and queen. As long as they lived Gwyntystorm was a better city, and good people grew in it. But they had no children, and when they died the people chose a king. And the new king went mining and mining in the rock under the city, and grew more and more eager after gold, and paid less and less heed to his people. Rapidly they sunk towards their old wickedness.[163]

MacDonald reverses the joyous fairytale conclusion almost instantly, and the reader is left with the reminder that the hold of goodness in this age is tenuous. We must battle evil and champion goodness until the blissful end. In this way, MacDonald extends the fairytale into the everyday, hinting that fairyland temporality verges upon the lives of his audience. You must take up Mossy's mantle, MacDonald seems to say, and adventure forth toward the rainbow; you must venture like Nycteris into the unexplored day.

Not surprisingly, the implicit exhortation in MacDonald's fairytale endings is closely akin to Christianity's call to hope:

> The hope of resurrection must bring about a new understanding of the world. This world is not the heaven of self-realization, [. . . nor] the hell of self-estrangement [. . .]. The world is not yet finished, but is understood as engaged in history. It is therefore the world of possibilities, the world in which we can serve the future. This is an age of diaspora, of sowing in hope, of self-surrender and sacrifice, for it is an age which stands within the horizon of a new future.[164]

Like the present state of the world from a Christian perspective, MacDonald's fairytales also dwell within the twilight chronology of hope, tasting in advance the ultimate victory of goodness but still living within the time of evil. While they participate in the festive time-logic of Christmas—the carnivalesque celebration of God becoming a child—and thereby experience time and death differently, fairytales still share the shadowy, in-between state of humanity. Bathed like Christianity in the "rainbow pulses" of the "living light's eternal fountain play," however, MacDonald's fairyland radiates the chronological lightness of hope, ever seeking to inspire new adventures in lighthearted ascent.

7

SPACE
Fairyland's Ecstatic Cosmology

> Dome up, O heaven, yet higher o'er my head!
> Back, Back horizon; widen out my world!
>
> —"A Story of the Sea-Shore"

Tolkien defines a fairy story as anything which deals with "the nature of Faerie: the Perilous Realm itself, and the air that blows in that country," but, with the humility of an anchorite, he warns against speaking directly about this realm: "I will not attempt to define [Faerie], nor to describe it directly. It cannot be done. Faerie cannot be caught in a net of words; for it is one of its qualities to be indescribable, though not imperceptible. It has many ingredients, but analysis will not necessarily discover the secret of the whole."[1] Tolkien here indulges in a little occultism: Faerie is a "secret" for the initiated who can only gesture toward its qualities.[2] Perhaps, then, a discussion of this world is doomed from the outset.[3] However, even if one of the qualities of *Faerie* is ineffability, Chesterton would be quick to rebut:

> It is perfectly true that there is something in all good things that is beyond all speech or figure of speech. But it is also true that there is in all good things a perpetual desire for expression and concrete embodiment; and though the attempt to embody it is always inadequate, the attempt is always made. If the idea does not seek to be the word, the chances are that it is an evil idea. If the word is not made flesh it is a bad word.[4]

It is thus with boldness and humility that this chapter embarks upon a journey into the fairy cosmos of George MacDonald.

The Quest for the Home-Centre

Between the two smaller stories that make up "The Carasoyn" (the first telling how Colin rescues and then marries the girl Fairy, and the second how Colin rescues their son), MacDonald describes the fate of the fairies after their queen's unfortunate decision to drink the Carasoyn. Being only "for really good people," the magic wine—which seems to be a kind of true-form-revealing potion—instantly changes the fairies into "old men and women fairies" and drives them out of their native country. MacDonald explains:

> For when the wickedness of any fairy tribe reaches its climax, the punishment that falls upon them is, that they are compelled to leave that part of the country where they and their ancestors have lived for more years than they can count, and wander away, driven by an inward restlessness, ever longing after the country they have left.[5]

MacDonald then compares this agony with our human situation: "a torture quite analogous to which many human beings undergo from their birth to their death, and some of them longer, for anything I can tell."[6] Fairies, unlike humans, are naturally "at home" within their environment, but these fairies through their wickedness have entered into a condition analogous to humanity: they restlessly long for their home.

Homeward desire is for MacDonald essential to human existence on earth. In his aforementioned essay "Browning's 'Christmas Eve,'" MacDonald, translating Novalis, goes so far as to equate the impulse to philosophize with the longing for home: "Philosophy is really homesickness, an impulse to be at home everywhere." He continues:

> The life of a man here, if life it be, and not the vain image of what might be a life, is a continual attempt to find his place, his centre of recipiency, and active agency. [. . .] It is a climbing and striving to reach that point of vision where the multiplex crossings and apparent intertwistings of the lines of fact and feeling and duty shall manifest themselves as a regular and symmetrical design. A contradiction, or a thing unrelated, is foreign and painful to him, even as the rocky particle in the gelatinous substance of the oyster; and, like the latter, he can only rid himself of it by encasing it in the pearl-like

> enclosure of faith; believing that hidden there lies the necessity for a higher theory of the universe than has yet been generated in his soul. The quest for this home-centre, in the man who has faith, is calm and ceaseless [. . .] In all relations of life, in all the parts of the great whole of existence, the true man is ever seeking his home.[7]

"Home" is emblematic of peace, harmony, and fullness. It is for MacDonald the perfection of what God intended and designed humanity to be, and the frustration of this completion or at least a consciousness of its lack is what propels an individual to quest after something better. If the entire drive of philosophy is the desire to be "at home" and children are natural metaphysicians (MacDonald says of Diamond that he was "a true child in this, that he was given to metaphysics"), then MacDonald's fairytales "for the childlike" would seem to be natural vehicles for reflecting this "quest for the home-centre."[8]

Indeed, given the predilection of fairytales for quests, journeys, and ceaseless strivings, it is no surprise that MacDonald would turn to this form to express his homeward longing. "The folktale hero," says the German folktale scholar Max Lüthi, "is essentially a wanderer." Using any excuse to turn its hero into a nomad, the fairytale "time and again sends its heroes out into the world."[9] Fairyland, therefore, is a questing realm where humans find wonders and adventures.

MacDonald's fairytales divide into two groups with regard to fairyland: those which begin in something akin to our everyday world and then journey into fairyland ("The Giant's Heart," "The Shadows," "Cross Purposes," "The Golden Key," and "The Carasoyn") and those which are set and take place entirely in a localized fairyland ("The Light Princess," "Little Daylight," "The Wise Woman," and "The History of Photogen and Nycteris"). All, however, have an element of wandering in an unknown land. The prince in "The Light Princess," for example, before he finds and courts the princess begins "his wanderings" by "setting out to look for the daughter of a queen" and then loses sight of his retinue and becomes lost in a great forest. MacDonald wryly comments: "these forests are very useful in delivering princes from their courtiers, like a sieve that keeps back the bran. In this they have the advantage of the princesses, who are forced to marry before they have had a bit of fun. I wish our princesses got lost in a forest sometimes."[10] The prince in "Little Daylight," meanwhile, is "compelled to flee for his life" because of a rebellion in his country and also ends up wandering in a fairy wood.[11] Watho steals Photogen and Nycteris from their mothers and traps them in their respective worlds of day and night. Both then must journey into their opposites in order to be completed. The title character in "The Wise Woman" similarly abducts Rosamond and Agnes from their natural homes, but unlike Watho the wise woman has benevolent intentions, only hoping to create within the girls a desire for their true home.

For those stories which begin in the everyday world, however, the journey into fairyland is even more explicitly a "quest for the home-centre." Colin in "The Carasoyn" must enter into fairyland in order to retrieve the abducted human girl "Fairy" from the cruel fairy queen (and later to regain his son). "Fairy" then becomes his wife, so in essence Colin sets out to establish a home for himself (and later to make it whole again). Alice, as we have already seen, enters fairyland longing to be "where the sun is always setting," though upon entering the unknown of fairyland she immediately declares that she wants "to go home."[12] After journeying a bit farther, she again asks Peaseblossom, "How far am I from home?" To which the fairy answers mystically, "The farther you go, the nearer home you are."[13] This seems to be one of the laws of MacDonald's fairyland—there is no turning back; to get home you must journey farther away. Richard, in the same story, following the grotesque Toadstool in order to get an umbrella for his mother, also becomes homesick and declares, "I will go home again," but he finds that he must go deeper into fairyland before he can return.[14] When the two children lose their fairy guides, they must continue this logic of journeying away, as they learn that "any honest plan will do in Fairyland, if you only stick to it."[15] Much like MacDonald's belief that there is no return to the Eden of childhood except by pressing on to the eternity of the childlike, Alice and Richard learn the paradoxical rule that the only way to return home is to press relentlessly forward.

Even more puzzling, however, is the border crossing in "The Giant's Heart":

> One day Tricksey-Wee, as they called her, teased her brother Buffy-Bob, till he could not bear it any longer, and gave her a box on the ear. Tricksey-Wee cried; and Buffy-Bob was so sorry and so ashamed of himself that he cried

too, and ran off into the wood. He was so long gone that Tricksey-Wee began to be frightened, for she was very fond of her brother; and she was so distressed that she had first teased him and then cried, that at last she ran into the wood to look for him, though there was more chance of losing herself than of finding him. And, indeed, so it seemed likely to turn out; for, running on without looking, she at length found herself in a valley she knew nothing about.[16]

"The Giant's Heart" is undoubtedly MacDonald's most disliked fairytale, having been called "repellent," "nauseous," and "sadistic."[17] The children—whose comical names echo their maladies in a Dickensian fashion (Tricksey-Wee is clever and cunning while Buffy-Bob is something of a brute)—do not, like every other fairytale, enter "Fairyland" but "Giantland."[18] Given the Rabelaisian landscape and creatures of Giantland (huge birds and Murkwood-like spiders) as opposed to MacDonald's usual fairyland, it seems that giantland represents something distinct, probably related to the "monstrous" behavior of both children just before their entrance.[19] In order to escape the selfish giant, the children must journey through giantland by working together and learning to use their personal proclivities for good and not for evil. Thus, in the end, Tricksey-Wee uses her knowledge of tricks to keep the giant from snaring them by deceit, and Buffy-Bob uses his physical strength to stab the giant's heart before the treacherous giant can kill them. The story is oddly at one and the same time MacDonald's most moralistic and his most grotesque, but the carnivalesque play obscures the moral and seems to mock Victorian conventionality.[20] Giantland may not be as subtle a place as fairyland, but it is still thoroughly polyvalent. Even so, MacDonald does make one thing clear in the frame of *Adela Cathcart* when a little girl comes up to Smith after his tale:

> "Thank you, dear Mr. Smith. I will be good. It was a very nice story. If I was a man, I would kill all the wicked people in the world. But I am only a little girl, you know; so I can only be good."
>
> The darling did not know how much more one good woman can do to kill evil than all the swords of the world in the hands of righteous heroes.[21]

MacDonald here subverts the apparent moral of his story (as interpreted by the girl that physical strength overcomes evil) by asserting the superior power of apparently subservient women. Paralleling the logic of 1 Corinthians 1:25, in which "the foolishness of God is wiser than men, and the weakness of God is stronger than men," MacDonald asserts the Christian principle that humility and apparent weakness are true power in the kingdom of God. Yet however one goes about it, the real moral is still to fight passionately for goodness and to strive ceaselessly against evil, to "quest for the home-centre."

Awful in Its Singleness
Fairyland and the Numinous

MacDonald's protagonists begin with a kind of nominal home, but it is shadowy and quickly forgotten in the grand home-quest. This home is almost always broken or incomplete: Richard's mother is a widow; Colin's father is a widower, as is Tangle's; Mossy does not seem to have any immediate family and lives with his great-aunt; Nycteris is an orphan, whereas Photogen only finds his parents after Watho's death; the prince's father in "Little Daylight" dies sparking a rebellion in his native land. And while they have both parents, Rosamond, Agnes, and the Light Princess cannot be said to come from loving families. The only true exceptions seem to be the prince in "The Light Princess" and Little Daylight (two of MacDonald's kindest and most joyful characters) who nevertheless distance themselves from their homes. This dissolution of home is necessary for the fairytale as it allows the children, who should otherwise be with their parents, to journey off into the unknown without compunction for those they have left behind.

In this, MacDonald is drawing on the great European folktale tradition. Max Lüthi observes, "the fairy tale sees man as one who is essentially isolated but who, for just this reason—because he is not rigidly committed, not tied down—can establish relationships with anything in the world. And the world of the fairy tale includes not just the earth, but the entire cosmos."[22] Elsewhere, Lüthi calls this the principle of "isolation" and "universal interconnection" because it first of all frees characters from all that binds them to a particular place or community, thereby allowing them to make links with anything in the cosmos.[23] The world becomes their playground.

The parallels with the gospels would not have escaped the eyes of a man who spent so much time reading both folktales and the New Testament.[24] Indeed, the gospels say very little about the past lives and families of the disciples. The first and last mention of Zebedee, the father of St. James and St. John, shows him mending nets as both of his sons leave him (Matt 4:21-22). Even Jesus' family virtually vanishes after the birth narratives. When they do come to take him home because they think he is foolishly "out of his mind," Jesus denies their claim upon him and asserts his universal connection with all who do the will of God (cf. Mark 3:32-35). Moreover, Jesus demands from his followers a radical denial of the claims of this world—including family. When a man desiring to be a disciple says, "I will follow you Lord, but let me first say farewell to those at home," Jesus responds, "No one who puts his hand to the plough and looks back is fit for the kingdom of God" (Luke 9:61-62). MacDonald understood these passages to be calls for absolute self-denial, given in order to liberate us from self, the great enslaver.[25] Much in the same way that Qoheleth speaks of the vanity of being, this radical demand dissolves the connections and claims of this world and frees the individual to orient toward the divine. God then deals with each person individually: "Before him stands each, as much an individual child as if there were no one but him. The relation is awful in its singleness."[26] The "as if" of the relationship with God shatters the fetters of selfishness, which bind people slavishly to things and people, and frees them to play with creation and their neighbors rather than possessing or worshipping them.

This principle of isolation explains, I think, why MacDonald's characters always enter fairyland in "awful singleness" (unlike Lewis' Narnia children, for example, who enter the fantastic land as part of a community). In every instance, the protagonist first has an experience of the numinous before connecting with another human. For Mossy in "The Golden Key," this is a vision of the beautiful rainbow with its "shade after shade beyond the violet" and "a colour more gorgeous and mysterious still" beyond the red, and in whose church-like columns he sees "beautiful forms slowly ascending as if by the steps of a winding stair."[27] Tangle's experience, on the other hand, is terrifying because a tree traps her in its branches (much like the hobbits in Bombadil's forest) and then a flying, feathered fish frees her and leads her to the benevolent grandmother. So, too, the titanic landscape of Giantland terrifies Tricksey-Wee and Buffy-Bob, and they have separate experiences of giantness before reuniting. In "Cross Purposes," Alice enters a delightful "dreamland" where she sinks into the poppies, while Richard takes a thrilling leaf-boat ride up hills and through storm and wave. And, though they do not enter into fairyland, both Photogen and Nycteris have profound encounters with sublime otherness before they even set eyes upon each other.

The princes in the two "Sleeping Beauty" parodies show an interesting variation on this theme as they experience the numinous in the future beloved. Both stories actually frame the initial romantic encounters in the language of religious ecstasy. In "Little Daylight," MacDonald establishes the mystical theme of "unknowing" from the outset when, after the witch curses Daylight to sleep all day, a good fairy provides the saving stipulation: "until a prince comes who shall kiss her without knowing it."[28] The poor king complains, "I don't know what that means"; to which the fairy responds, "the meaning will come with the thing itself."[29] When the prince enters the fairy forest, he stays with this same cryptic fairy and has a peculiar conversation with her when she encourages him to remain in the vicinity:

> "Thank you much, good mother," answered the prince, "but there is little chance of that. The sooner I get out of this wood the better."
> "I don't know that," said the fairy.
> "What do you mean?" asked the prince.
> "Why how *should* I know?" returned she.
> "I can't tell," said the prince.
> "Very well," said the fairy.
> "How strangely you talk!" said the prince.[30]

The fairy undermines the prince's blithe confidence in his ability to "know" what is best for himself. But the prince is just beginning his mystic lessons in "unknowing." Of course, the fairy is also prophetic, for when he leaves he "wanders and wanders" but "gets nowhere," and then goes "he knew not whither."[31] Thoroughly lost in the realm of the unknown, he comes upon a glade, and the narrator comments, "he had not seen so much room for several days."[32] This wandering through the unknown opens a space for the entrance of something entirely new and wonderful—Little Daylight, dressed in white and dancing like a nymph by the moonlight. The beauty of this vision enraptures the prince such that he questions its reality:

Perhaps she was but a vision of his own fancy. Or was she a spirit of the wood, after all? If so, he too would haunt the wood, glad to have lost kingdom and everything for the hope of being near her. He would build him a hut in the forest, and there he would live for the pure chance of seeing her again. Upon nights like this at least she would come out and bask in the moonlight, and make his soul blessed.[33]

Romantic love here speaks with the voice of divine self-denial. Jean-Luc Marion observes how "vanity follows and redoubles love as its shadow" so that when the beloved is in sight everything else seems indifferent.[34] Love places the world momentarily under the sign of vanity, freeing the prince to stay and devote his life to these moments of bliss. In the face of beauty, he forgets his own needs and desires—the prince even loses his hunger after one of his ecstatic encounters. This self-forgetting is not a condemnation of the bodily aspect of existence; rather it is a liberation from self that rightly orders things by placing the needs of others ahead of the self. Thus, when the prince, looking for Daylight, enters a part of the forest of which he "knew nothing," he does not spurn the poor old woman that he finds in order to continue his romantic search. Instead, he performs a very humble and Christ-like service: "he laid her down as comfortably as he could, chafed her hands, put a little cordial from a bottle, also the gift of the fairy, into her mouth; took off his coat and wrapped it about her, and in short did the best he could."[35] The almost exact correlation with Matthew 25:35-36 is not accidental: "For I was hungry and you gave me food, I was thirsty and you gave me drink, I was a stranger and you welcomed me, I was naked and you clothed me, I was sick and you visited me." The people in Jesus' parable also do not "know" whom they love, and it is exactly for this reason that Jesus invites them into the kingdom. Likewise, in a moment of profound sympathy with the old woman and mystical unknowing, the prince kisses her on the withered lips, and, of course, she transforms into the object of his desire, Daylight. Perfect revelation (i.e., transformation into the ideal) occurs in the instant that the prince most truly denies himself. His experience of the vanity of being, "awful in its singleness," liberates him to love without any hint of selfishness—without possessive knowledge or expectation of reciprocity—and as a result he receives his *eros* back as a gift.

The meeting of the prince and princess in "The Light Princess," meanwhile, is closer to the ridiculous than the sublime, yet it still portrays a numinous experience that opens a space for ecstatic love:

> The prince pursued his path through the gathering darkness. Suddenly he paused, and listened. Strange sounds came across the water. It was, in fact, the princess laughing. Now there was something odd in her laugh, as I have already hinted; for the hatching of a real hearty laugh requires the incubation of gravity; and perhaps this was how the prince mistook the laughter for screaming.[36]

The prince proceeds to "rescue" the princess by forcibly removing her from the water, which infuriates her either because "he frightened her, or caught her so as to embarrass her." As she floats "down" into the air she screams: "You naughty, *naughty*, NAUGHTY, NAUGHTY man!" This outburst is an unprecedented show of emotion, for "no one had ever succeeded in putting her into a passion before."[37] It may not be as awe-inspiring as the visions of St. Teresa, but as they experience the numinous in the other, both characters forget themselves somewhat and find themselves outside their normal order. Having been violently removed from the lake—the place where she is most "at home"—we might even say that the princess experiences a sort of rapture as defined by Aquinas: "rapture adds something to ecstasy. For ecstasy means simply a going out of oneself by being placed outside one's proper order; while rapture denotes a certain violence in addition."[38] For the first time, the princess experiences being dislocated from her selfish desires. Though small, this first step begins the process of liberating the princess from the tyranny of her "demoniac self."[39] MacDonald makes this clear when explaining the prince's attraction to the princess: "he had fallen in love with her almost, already; for her anger made her more charming than any one else had ever beheld her."[40] Anger is at least an awareness that there is such a thing as a "self" and therefore such a thing as an "other."

The prince, meanwhile, "falls" (both literally and metaphorically) in love: "he had really fallen in love when he fell in the lake."[41] His self-denial is already far more advanced than that of the princess, and, like the prince in "Little Daylight," he abandons everything to spend his nights with the princess. Their second meeting repeats the ecstatic formula as the prince calls down to the princess from the top of a cliff:

> "Come up then, princess."
>
> "Fetch me, prince."
>
> The prince took off his scarf, then his sword-belt, then his tunic, and tied them all together, and let them down. [. . .] The princess just managed to lay hold of the knot of money, and was beside him in a moment. This rock was much higher than the other, and the splash and the dive were tremendous. The princess was in ecstasies of delight.[42]

The prince again pulls the princess out of her "natural" sphere (this time with her permission), but then he leaves his "natural" sphere and falls into "her" lake, so that both are in "ecstasies of delight." They repeat this pattern night after night as both receive ecstatic training in being outside their accustomed spheres, metaphorically as well as physically. The princess even begins to see a glimmer of what the prince means by love: "after a while she began to look puzzled, as if she were trying to understand what he meant, but could not—revealing a notion that he meant something."[43] But struggle as she might, the reality of love can only break through to the princess in its purest, most divine form—the form of perfect self-denial:

> Death alone from death can save.
> Love is death, and so is brave
> Love can fill the deepest grave.
> Love loves on beneath the wave.[44]

Found on the plate of gold at the bottom of the draining lake (and reminiscent of the laws written on Narnia's stone table), this poem establishes the need for a Christ figure in the story, but it also highlights the fairytale principle of isolation and universal interconnection. Like Jesus' command to "deny yourself and take up your cross daily" (Luke 9:23), the line "love is death" speaks of how love is a kenotic and foolish self-emptying (like Jesus' incarnation, cf. Phil 2:1-11) that places the needs of others and the will of God before the self.[45] This isolation liberates a person for bold action on behalf of others: "and so is brave."

The prince's love moves him to offer his life bravely for the restoration of the lake and the princess. He resolves "to carry off the whole affair with nonchalance." In an act of "divine carelessness," he chooses to play the fool and give away the only thing that this world values. Ecstatic love here makes a smooth transition into folly, confounding the small-minded king in a hilarious parody of Jesus before Pilate. The prince's folly fortifies his courage and helps him to make light of that which he is about to sacrifice. Though his nonchalance eventually wears thin, it enables him to overcome the self-preservation drive and selflessly love the princess.

As in "Little Daylight," the moment of revelation is the moment of perfect love, though, unlike in "Little Daylight," transformation hesitates for a few agonizing moments. Having received his last supper of "wine and biscuits," the prince asks for a dying kiss, and MacDonald comments, "the nonchalance was all gone now."[46] Nevertheless, his last words are of the joy of self-denial: "I die happy." As the water slowly creeps up his face, the princess becomes increasingly disturbed:

> The water rose and rose. It touched his chin. It touched his lower lip. It touched between his lips. He shut them hard to keep it out. The princess began to feel strange. It touched his upper lip. He breathed through his nostrils. The princess looked wild. It covered his nostrils. Her eyes looked scared, and shone strange in the moonlight. His head fell back; the water closed over it, and the bubbles of his last breath bubbled up through the water. The princess gave a shriek, and sprang into the lake.[47]

The short, simple sentences in this climactic paragraph mimic the princess' experience as her focus finally becomes wholly riveted on something other than her own pleasure, and her world begins to feel "strange." The prince's love is perfected in death, a revelation so radiant and resplendent that the princess at last understands what he means by "love" and finds herself reciprocating. Hints or foretastes of gravity allow the weightless princess to pull the prince out of the water, row him back to the castle, and bring him to her room, but her final transformation delays until the prince's resurrection. Thus, gravity returns to her through tears of joy, and MacDonald avoids "a Gnostic or Hegelian message that all spiritual reality must suffer in order to develop."[48] The experience is for the princess "awful in its singleness" and one of MacDonald's most vividly portrayed moments of numinous encounter.

Significantly though, this awful instant does not lead the princess onto a path of solipsistic inwardness but into bodily existence and into the most physical of all human relationships—marriage. MacDonald's fairyland does isolate characters and force them to encounter something akin to the transcendent in utter singleness, but this experience frees them from the heavy tyranny of self, making them light enough to connect fully with (i.e., love) other creatures.

Going Out into Room Enough
Ecstatic Ascent and Fairyland

Fairyland, as we have seen, is a questing realm that awakens desire for the "home-centre," though it is a numinous world as well where characters experience the "wholly other," which liberates them from all that binds and entraps them. More precisely, the ecstatic moment of going out of oneself makes possible the Dantesque ascent to the "home-centre." Not only does ecstasy empower ascent, however, it also opens up new realms, new possibilities, and new relations—it gives the soul the room for which it has always longed.

When Ralph Rinkelmann, "the king of the Shadows," agrees to leave his cramped sick-room, the Shadows bear him on a litter up through England and Scotland and then over the ocean toward Iceland:

> The sea was not frozen; for all the stars shone as clear out of the deeps below as they shone out of the deeps above; and as the bearers slid along the blue-gray surface, with never a furrow in their track, so pure was the water beneath, that the king saw neither surface, bottom, nor substance to it, and seemed to be gliding only through the blue sphere of heaven, with the stars above him, and the stars below him, and between the stars and him nothing but an emptiness, where, for the first time in his life, his soul felt that it had room enough.[49]

The ecstatic movement out of the small, dingy room into the grand sublimity of the cosmos reveals to Rinkelmann not his smallness but his largeness—he feels that his soul has always previously been cramped. This revelation is a call to ecstatic ascent: one must get out of the small worlds that constrict life and find the open spaces where there is "room enough." As MacDonald observes in *What's Mine's Mine* (1886), a sense of the great expanse of space teaches us how to interpret smaller things:

> One of the first elements in human education is the sense of space—of which sense, probably, the star-dwelt heaven is the first awakener. He believed that without the heavens we could not have learned the largeness in things below

them, could not, for instance, have felt the mystery of the high-ascending gothic roof—for without the greater we cannot interpret the less; and he thought that to have the sense of largeness developed might be to come a little nearer to the truth of things, to the recognition of spiritual relations.[50]

Moreover, Rinkelmann sees that he must reconsider prosaic truths, rethinking them in the light of his enlarged world. His mind reopens, and he is able to contemplate cosmic relationships without the hindrance of commonplace assumptions. Like the "chronic condition of wonder" experienced by Anodos in *Phantastes*, Rinkelmann "soon found that amongst the Shadows a man must learn never to be surprised at anything; for if he does not, he will soon grow quite stupid, in consequence of the endless recurrence of surprises."[51] His ecstasy frees him to see reality in a new and more eerie light. Crucially, one of the things he discovers is that large, wonderful worlds already surround him, so that when he returns to his little home, he sees how "his own room and its shadows were yet more wonderful and unintelligible than those [in the shadow church]."[52] MacDonald here complicates traditional Platonism, for though Rinkelmann's journey does echo Plato's "Allegory of the Cave" in that he begins in a shadowy room, journeys into a larger reality, and then returns to his shadowy room, it is vitally different in that the Shadows function, as Frank Riga argues, "to enhance, not dismiss, material reality."[53]

Indeed, MacDonald seems to offer a direct criticism of Plato's allegorical vision when he says, "This made it the more likely that he had seen a true vision; for instead of making common things look commonplace, as a false vision would have done, it had made common things disclose the wonderful that was in them."[54] Ecstasy opens up paths for ascending toward our divine home, including seeing the beautiful in the common. In his essay "The Imagination: Its Function and Its Culture," MacDonald speaks of the ecstatic imagination:

> Seek not that your sons and your daughters should not see visions, should not dream dreams; seek that they should see true visions, that they should dream noble dreams. Such out-going of the imagination is one with aspiration, and will do more to elevate above what is low and vile than all possible inculcations of morality. Nor can religion herself ever rise up into her own calm home, her crystal shrine, when one of her wings, one of the twain with which she flies, is thus broken or paralyzed.[55]

Only when the imagination is "out-going" toward the divine and toward the neighbor does it help to safeguard against vice and to lift the individual toward "her own calm home, her crystal shrine."[56] Ecstasy is the motive power of ascent, much more so than teaching the laws of morality.

MacDonald fascinatingly invokes the Holy Spirit with great subtlety in this passage, reworking Joel 2:28 ("I will pour out my Spirit on all flesh; your sons and your daughters shall prophesy, your old men shall dream dreams, and your young men shall see visions")—which is quoted by Peter in Acts 2 when the Holy Spirit descends—and then immediately equating the ecstatic imagination with "aspiration" and levity ("elevate," "rise up," "wings," "flies"). From the same root as "inspire" and "expire," aspiration literally means the act of breathing or being filled with spirit. The analogy should not be pressed too far, yet Pentecost is the moment when the Spirit liberates the selfish, frightened disciples from their fears and petty worries and gives them the power to "go out" to the ends of the earth (Acts 1:8: "you will receive power when the Holy Spirit has come upon you, and you will be my witnesses in Jerusalem and in all Judea and Samaria, and to the end of the earth"). The Holy Spirit drives the disciples out into the world (in an inversion of his driving Jesus into the desert, cf. Matt 4:1). Likewise, the ecstatic imagination propels the individual outward and upward toward the divine. It fuels ascent and leads to even greater experiences of ecstasy.

The fairytale in which this principle is clearest is MacDonald's last, "The History of Photogen and Nycteris" (1879). As we have seen, Watho locks Nycteris in an underground cave (much like Plato's cave) as a kind of intellectual experiment in darkness. The result, however, is not a twisted monster or a dull ignoramus but a highly sensitive girl (another slight criticism of Plato). With only the lamplight, "her whole apparatus for seeing, grew both larger and more sensitive," and she is able to see "much better than Watho imagined."[57] Furthermore, not knowing any better, she is relatively happy, except for a ticklish longing for something greater:

> She knew nothing of the world except the tomb in which she dwelt, and had some pleasure in everything she did. But she desired, nevertheless, something more or different. She did not know what it was, and the nearest she could come to expressing it to herself was—that she wanted more room.

> Watho and Falca would go from her beyond the shine of the lamp, and come again; therefore surely there must be more room somewhere.⁵⁸

In a reversal of Rinkelmann's experience of "room enough," Nycteris senses that the feeling of her room's smallness is evidence both that there is "more room" somewhere and that she herself was made for greater spaces. But it is only when a far-off rumbling—"a new sign of something beyond these chambers"—breaks her lamp that Nycteris' vague longing changes to urgent desire: "her lamp gone, the desire at once awoke to get out of her prison."⁵⁹ This small incident is a moment of incipient ecstasy in that Nycteris had never before experienced the terror of utter darkness and because it sparks her imagination for "going out" in the same way that the lamp "went out." Ecstasy leads to greater ecstasy as "the desire to go out grew irresistible." After groping around in darkness, she finally "tumbles out of the cavern" only to discover that "*out* was very much like *in*, for the same enemy, the darkness, was here also."⁶⁰ Soon, however, she espies a firefly, which was "of the same spirit as her lamp—and had wings," also "seeking the way out." It flies higher and leads Nycteris up "an ascending stair." MacDonald observes that having "never seen a stair before, [she] found going-up a curious sensation."⁶¹ Going out and going up unite in the image of the staircase.

Staircases are one of MacDonald's most frequent symbols—"I have a passion for stairs," he wrote in a letter to a friend and, despite his asthma and other numerous ailments, he always insisted on climbing towers and mountains.⁶² He writes to his wife after a visit to the Weissenburg cathedral:

> Then I did what the others declared themselves unable for—I went up the tower and up the spire. Oh, my dear, what would you think of such climbing and such visions like out of a balloon! I went up as far as they would let me without an order from the Mayor, and all my weariness and fatigue was gone. And, darling, I am sure the only cure for you and me and all of us is getting up, up—into the divine air. I for my part choose the steeple-cure for my weariness.⁶³

Rest and restoration accompany the extreme exertion of ascension. MacDonald's ecstatic ascent vivifies him much in the same way that it quickens Nycteris.

Like MacDonald ascending his cathedral spire, Nycteris climbs the stair until she reaches a door that opens to the "outside," and seeing the enormity of it all, she levitates in a moment of confused bliss:

> [She] stood in a maze of wondering perplexity, awe, and delight. What was it? Was it outside her, or something taking place in her head? Before her was a very long and very narrow passage, broken up she could not tell how, and spreading out above and on all sides to an infinite height and breadth and distance—as if space itself were growing out of a trough.[64]

Reminiscent of St. Paul's wondering "whether in the body or out of the body, I do not know" (1 Cor 12:2), Nycteris has no conceptual or sensual framework by which to understand her new experiences and so briefly questions the locus of her encounter. But though she questions the reality of her vision, she continues to lose herself in the ecstasy: "She was in a dream of pleasant perplexity, of delightful bewilderment. She could not tell whether she was upon her feet or drifting about like the firefly, driven by the pulses of an inward bliss." The scene then changes explicitly into one of religious ecstasy as Nycteris stands "in the ravishing glory of a southern night" and sees the moon for the first time:

> "It is my lamp," she said, and stood dumb with parted lips. She looked and felt as if she had been standing there in silent ecstasy from the beginning. "No, it is not my lamp," she said after a while; "it is the mother of all the lamps." And with that she fell on her knees, and spread out her hands to the moon. She could not in the least have told what was in her mind, but the action was in reality just a begging of the moon to be what she was—that precise incredible splendor hung in the far-off roof, that very glory to the being of poor girls born and bred in caverns. It was a resurrection—nay, a birth itself, to Nycteris.[65]

This is the pinnacle of ecstasy—a perfect out-going of the self, for the self only wants to express its gladness that something else is what it is. The feverish intensity of bliss culminates in a kind of death of self (much like the heavenly visions of Isaiah and John), thus guarding against solipsism. In this death of self, there is resurrection and new birth, a widening out of reality to include new and greater truths. As with Bernini's *The Ecstasy of St. Teresa*, in the "ravishing glory" Nycteris with lips parted feels lifted off her feet like a firefly, and time becomes for her a taste of eternity.

Even in this passage, though, MacDonald cannot avoid very lighthearted remarks about "the being of poor girls born and bred in caverns." Ecstasy may intensify language to convey the anarchic "beyond-ness" of its experience, but its whole thrust is toward levity and the making light of things—especially the self. Nycteris becomes as a little child in this grand new world, delighting in every star, every leaf, every breath of wind. She names the wind "Everywhere, for she goes through all the other creatures, and comforts them."[66] Her childlike vision reunites the divorced images of wind and spirit into a *pneuma* or *spiritus* to which she ascribes attributes typically associated with the Holy Spirit (omnipresence and comfort). While not knowing the science behind the movement of air, in her climactic moment of ecstasy she is keenly aware of pneumatic power:

> Still less did she know of the air alive with motion—of that thrice blessed thing, the wind of a summer night. It was like spiritual wine, filling her whole being with an intoxication of purest joy. To breathe was a perfect existence. It seemed to her the light itself she drew into her lungs. Possessed by the power of the gorgeous night, she seemed at one and the same moment annihilated and glorified.[67]

Much in the same way that some people in Acts thought the disciples were drunk at Pentecost, Nycteris experiences the wind as an intoxicating wine that suffuses her entire being with gladness. Breath, wind, and spirit meet in this perfect moment of joy, in an ecstasy that immediately draws her upward to a new ecstasy of ascent as her soul is "drawn to the vault above" with its "endless room." Importantly, however, "endless room" does not mean "empty room," as she discovers the following night when the moon is absent. The fairy cosmos may be one in which souls have "room enough," but it is not the vast impersonal emptiness of our contemporary understanding of outer space. The endless room teems with life and spirit, symbolized by the everpresent wind.

This experience of otherness in nature could still be seen as solipsistic, except for the fact that once again MacDonald shows how ecstasy leads into relationship and paradoxically brings self-knowledge in the escape from the self. Photogen experiences ecstasy as well, but his is an ecstasy of terror, which brings low his towering pride. He finds he is not a god and needs other people. Both receive necessary personal revelation that simultaneously prepares the way for their relationship with the other. MacDonald also—drawing on sources such as Novalis' *Hymns to the Night*, which he translated—avoids the exclusive emphasis on the goodness of light common in Gnosticism by showing how Photogen has important lessons to learn from the darkness. Both characters end the story loving their opposites best—Photogen the night and Nycteris the day—but Nycteris has the final word, and, not surprisingly, it is ecstasy: "But who knows that, when we go out, we shall not go into a day as much greater than your day as your day is greater than my night?" Ecstasy leads to ecstasy in MacDonald's fairyland as, drawn on by the power of desire and a love they do not fully understand, his characters continually ascend together toward the beyond.

The Dance of Prophetic Harmony
Sacramental Order in Nature

It is not accidental that this chapter on "cosmology" has focused thus far on the experiences and responses of MacDonald's characters to fairyland. No comprehensive account of the flora and fauna is possible, because human experience of this realm is necessarily limited and fragmented. Unlike Tolkien's Middle-earth, Philip Pullman's other Oxford, and J. K. Rowling's Hogwarts, with their historians, researchers, chemists, and wizards, MacDonald's fairyland does not have exhaustive chronicles or magical treatises. The long brooding over minutiae, which occupied Tolkien endlessly, is absent in MacDonald. Though he reused symbols and types regularly, MacDonald's fairytales each can be seen as exploring very different territory within fairyland. Thus small inconsistencies are not hard to spot: in "The Shadows," the fairies elect a human as king of fairyland, whereas in "Cross Purposes" one fairy queen apparently rules all of fairyland, while in "The Carasoyn" a fairy queen is just the ruler of a particular band of fairies. Clearly, no discussion of the political structures of MacDonald's fairyland would be very fruitful.

Yet MacDonald was not haphazard or inept in his composition. On the contrary, he was very aware of the importance of law and order in fantastical worlds:

> To be able to live a moment in an imagined world, we must see the laws of its existence obeyed. Those broken, we fall out of it. [. . .] The mind of man is the product of live Law; it thinks by law, it dwells in the midst of law, it gathers from law its growth; with law, therefore, can it alone work to any result. [. . .] Obeying laws, the maker works like his creator; not obeying laws, he is such a fool as heaps a pile of stones and calls it a church.[68]

The emphasis on law, however, seems to contradict another of MacDonald's fairytale principles—the unsettling strangeness of fairyland.[69] According to the long Novalis quotation that precedes *Phantastes*, fairytales usher readers into an anarchic modality:

> A fairytale is like a dream-vision without coherence. An ensemble of miraculous [*wunderbarer*] things and events [. . .] In a true fairytale everything must be miraculous [*wunderbar*], secret and coherent. Everything alive, each one in a different way. The whole of nature must be miraculously [*wunderlich*] merged with the whole spiritual realm; here enters the time of anarchy, of lawlessness, freedom, of the natural state of nature, the time before the world.[70]

How should we understand the apparent contradiction between fairytales being both "without coherence" and a "coherent ensemble"? How does "the time of anarchy" relate to MacDonald's other assertion about fairytales "obeying laws"? The answer for MacDonald as for Novalis seems to lie in nature being "miraculously merged with the whole spiritual realm." In the above passage, I have translated *wunderbar* and *wunderlich* with "miraculous" rather than "wonderful" or "wondrous" to highlight what is lucid in the original German—the association of fairytales with miracles.[71] Perhaps, then, exploring MacDonald's thoughts about miracles will also illuminate how fairyland paradoxically holds together anarchy with order and how it harmonizes nature with the spirit.[72]

The final chapter of MacDonald's *The Miracles of Our Lord* (1870) is not, as one might expect, on Christ's resurrection (the penultimate chapter) but on his transfiguration, for MacDonald believes this miracle to be "a window through which we gain a momentary glimpse of the region whence all miracles appear."[73] According to MacDonald, Jesus ascended the mountain with the heavy burden of imminent death pressing upon him, but then "in heaving off the weight of this awful shadow by prayer, he did not grow calm and resigned alone, but his faith broke forth so triumphant over the fear, that it shone from him in physical light."[74] Making light of his fear, Jesus physically manifests his inner joy. The transfiguration was a foretaste of the resurrection in which Jesus put on for a moment "his new glorified body" even though the shadow of death still lay before him. It was "the divine defiance of the coming darkness."[75] MacDonald then speculates on the relationship between the spiritual and the material that is exemplified in Christ's perfect inner harmony with the Father, which radiates out of Christ's physical body in visible light. He says that "the shining of the garments is a type of the glorification of everything human when brought into its true relations by and with the present God," and then asks, "what if this light were the healing agent of the bodies of men, as the deeper other light from which it sprung is the healing agent of themselves?" Might there not, in other words, be some more direct relationship between physical and spiritual than we normally acknowledge? There is no ultimate dichotomy between body and spirit for MacDonald, only an apparent disjunction as a result of not being wholly one with the Father:

> Where, when, or how the inner spiritual light passes into or generates outward physical light, who can tell? This border-land, this touching of what we call mind and matter, is the region of miracles—of material creation, I might have said, which is *the* great—I suspect, the *only* miracle. But if matter be the outcome of spirit, and body and soul be one man, then, if the soul be radiant of truth, what can the body do but shine?[76]

MacDonald hearkens back to the original miracle, God's creation of a physical cosmos, to emphasize the truly miraculous reality of bodily existence. That there is not nothing is *the* wonder of the universe. But he also points forward to the hoped-for future in which bodies will be directly and utterly responsive to the spirits within them. The transfiguration is a unique instant in which past, present, and future meet—the living power of the past is still operative (Moses and Elijah appear), and the ultimate victory over sin and death manifests itself. Yet the cross still lies before Jesus. It is a glimpse, a glimmer not fully understood by the disciples until after the resurrection. Like Christmas and the resurrection but in some ways even more oddly, the transfiguration is a moment of finitude particularly redolent with eternity.

MacDonald speaks of the transfiguration as a "border-land" and a "touching" of "mind and matter," much in the same way that he speaks of fairyland as a border region. Fairyland is, as we have seen, a twilight realm, but it is also a place where, like in the transfiguration, spirit more directly and immediately affects the physical (where nature "miraculously merges with the whole spiritual realm"). When the bickering Richard and Alice in "Cross Purposes" find themselves in complete darkness while wandering through the strange anarchic places of fairyland, Alice clings to Richard and murmers, "Dear Richard." MacDonald comments:

> It was strange that fear should speak like love; but it was in Fairyland. It was strange, too, that as soon as she spoke thus, Richard should fall in love with her all at once. But what was more curious still was, that, at the same moment, Richard saw her face. [. . .] The fact was, that the moment he began to love Alice, his eyes began to send forth light. What he thought came from Alice's face, really came from his eyes. All about her and her path he could see, and every minute saw better; but to his own path he was blind.[77]

Soon after this, Alice realizes her love for Richard, and she also sees his path so that "between the two sights they got on well." It might be tempting to treat this scene merely as a beautiful allegorical image of how romantic love creates sympathetic vision of the other,[78] but without excluding this reading, MacDonald is doing something more radical—he is suggesting that love in a perfected state might have physical manifestations. Material light coming from the eyes is miraculous, but miracles are not the abrogation of physical law but rather its higher fulfilment. "What can the body do but shine," MacDonald speculates, "if the soul be radiant of truth?"

It is ironic that critics frequently see MacDonald as a solipsistic mystic longing only after a spiritualized heaven, when he actually offers one of the most blatantly physical accounts of the transfiguration and the resurrection. He even admits in reference to his account of physical light radiating from inner truth, "some will object that this is a too material view of life and its facts."[79] One wonders if critics read MacDonald so allegorically because they have hardly dared to believe that he could have had such a radical—and yet wholly orthodox—vision of the ultimate harmony of the cosmos.

But harmony is precisely what miracles reveal, according to MacDonald—"the harmony of within and without" (to play with two of MacDonald's favorite images). Although miracles might appear to David Hume and other Enlightenment thinkers as "violations of the laws of nature" and therefore as anarchic rebels that need philosophical policing, their anarchic element only rebels against the tyranny of materialism. Miracles look like revolts to us because they reinstitute a higher, more fundamental law. They are not the rebels—we are. Speaking of Jesus' miracles of governing nature, MacDonald says:

> There is perfect submission to lower law for himself, but revelation of the Father to them by the introduction of higher laws operating in the upper regions bordering upon ours, not separated from ours by any impassible gulf—rather connected by gently ascending stairs, many of whose gradations he could blend in one descent. He revealed the Father as being *under* no law, but as law itself, and the cause of the laws we know—the cause of all harmony because himself *the* harmony. Men had to be delivered not only from the fear of suffering and death, but from the fear, which is a kind of worship, of nature.[80]

All of Jesus' miracles, whether of healing, creation, destruction, casting out devils, or resurrection, reveal the complete sovereignty of the Father, his care for his children, and the ultimate harmony of all things physical and spiritual in God. The miraculous momentarily unravels the apparent contradiction of the cosmos—what MacDonald calls "the knotted and twisted coil of the universe"—so that humanity can catch a glimpse of the divine harmony.[81] The above quotation also hints at another truth of MacDonald's fairyland cosmos—fearlessness toward nature.

One of the main distinctions between MacDonald's "adult" fantasies and his fairytales is the portrayal of nature. Whereas in *Lilith* and *Phantastes* malevolent trees lurk in dark forests and deadly leopardesses roam arid wastelands, MacDonald's fairytales present much more congenial landscapes and creatures. By far the scariest monster is the Watho-wolf (a precursor to the ferocious feline transformations in *Lilith*), but most of the even marginally frightening creatures—the gnomes, goblins, giants—are essentially harmless to the childlike protagonists. Twice in "The Carasoyn," for example, goblins threaten and assault Colin. When the old fairy woman sends Colin to the fairy cobbler to get a magic awl, the cobbler initially appears as a host of hideous goblins, and together they consider every portion of Colin's body as material for their trade:

> "Top of his head—good paste-bowl."
>
> "Coarse hair—good ends."
>
> "Sinews—good thread."
>
> "Bones and blood—good paste for seven-leaguers."
>
> "Ears—good loops to pull 'em on with. Pair short now."
>
> "Soles—same for queen's slippers."
>
> And so on they went, portioning out his body in the most irreverent fashion for the uses of their trade, till having come to his teeth and said—
>
> "Teeth—good brads,"—they all gave a shriek like the whisk of the waxed threads through the leather, and sprung upon him with their awls drawn back like daggers.[82]

But the sheer levity of its presentation empties the scene of fear. The grotesqueness is too much too fast, and MacDonald prompts laughter in his audience as they consider for one strange moment their bodies as material for shoemaking.

Moreover, when Colin reveals that "the old woman with the distaff" sent him, "they all scurr[y] back to their seats." His relationship with a higher authority immediately brings the rebellious creatures to order. Colin then steps out of the shop with one of the goblins and looking back sees "all the stools vacant, and the place as still as an old churchyard." The one remaining goblin is "a very respectable, not to say conventional, little man" who proceeds to give him all the information he requires and one of his awls. This transformation from many terrible, bloodthirsty monsters to one kind, ordinary man empties nature of its fear and frees Colin then to behave nonchalantly and decisively with the equally threatening fairies. Nature in MacDonald's fairyland is not a tyrant to be feared but a fellow playful creature also submissive to "higher laws." Perhaps this draining of fear from Nature is one of the reasons why Tolkien—for whom Faerie is "the perilous realm"—was somewhat ambiguous toward MacDonald.[83]

MacDonald's fairyland is only a terrifying place to those who are not in proper relationship to higher powers. When in "The Wise

Woman" the title character carries off Rosamond from her luxurious palace home and her pampering parents, Rosamond initially thinks of the wise woman as an ogress and starts violently resisting the abduction. In response, the wise woman leaves Rosamond alone in the darkened forest, and wolves surround her:

> She caught sight at last of [the wolf's] lamping eyes coming swiftly nearer and nearer. Terror silenced her. She stood with her mouth open, as if she were going to eat the wolf, but she had no breath to scream with, and her tongue curled up in her mouth like a withered and frozen leaf. She could do nothing but stare at the coming monster.[84]

But the wise woman catches the huge old wolf by the throat and kills him—perfect force contained in the form of fragility—and Rosamond leaps back into her arms. As long as Rosamond trusts the wise woman, nature—no matter how malevolent or potent—has no power over her. This is a lesson she must repeatedly learn. Fear reveals the weakness of the self and its need for something or someone beyond. With Rosamond back in her arms, the wise woman then passes through the horde of beasts:

> But now the huge army of wolves and hyenas had rushed like a sea around them, whose waves leaped with hoarse roar and hollow yell up against the wise woman. But she, like a strong stately vessel, moved unhurt through the midst of them. Even as they leaped against her cloak, they dropped and slunk away back through the crowd.[85]

The metaphors of "sea," "waves," and "vessel" and the stately calm of the wise woman find profound resonances in Jesus' miracles of calming the storm and walking on water. True power is the perfection of peace and rest, against which the darkest forces of nature are as evanescent breath.

Turning to *The Miracles of Our Lord* and MacDonald's commentary on the miracles over nature, we discover more of his daring speculation on the relation of body and spirit:

> We know nothing yet, or next to nothing, of the relation between a right soul and a healthy body. To some no doubt the notion of a healthy body implies chiefly a perfection of all the animal functions, which is, on the supposition, a matter of course; but what I should mean by an absolutely healthy body is, one entirely under the indwelling spirit, and responsive immediately to all

the laws of its supremacy, whatever those laws may be in the divine ideal of a man. As we are now, we find the diseased body tyrannizing over the almost helpless mind: the healthy body would be the absolutely obedient body.[86]

MacDonald admits this is "ignorant yet devout speculation" but cannot seem to stop himself from imagining "a higher condition of harmony with law" which might one day "enable us to do things which must now *appear* an interruption of law."[87] But since fairyland exists within the festive sphere of Sabbath and eschatological time, it is able to present these speculations as realities. Creatures like the wise woman demonstrate a perfect harmony of body and spirit. "Harmony, that is law, alone is power," MacDonald says and adds, "discord is weakness."[88] The power of the wise woman and other creatures in fairyland is the fruition of their inner and outer harmony.

By focusing on the "prophetic harmony" that exists in these characters (all the "grandmothers," the wise woman, the old men, the good fairies), another vital point of MacDonald's fairyland cosmology becomes clear. The wise woman is not "a personification of God's providence"; the grandmother figures are not MacDonald's depiction of a "Magnus Mater in the Trinity," nor is the Old Man of the Fire "a surrogate in the story for a high revelation of God," at least not directly.[89] Rather, they are human-like creatures who as a result of their perfect harmony represent MacDonald's ponderings about the nature of ultimate reality. In other words, they are not allegories for God but fantastical creations exploring the wide realm of "may be." Such an interpretation seems confirmed by the way in which human protagonists in several stories also begin taking on divine power when they experience moments of harmony. In "The Golden Key," after Mossy bathes himself in the Old Man of the Sea's pool and tastes death—which is "only more life"—the old man says, "your feet will make no holes in the water now," and Mossy is able to walk miraculously across the ocean to the foot of the rainbow staircase.[90] Other instances include Rosamond miraculously transfiguring a flower in "The Wise Woman" after she kills her terrible "Somebody," and the physical transformations of both princesses ("The Light Princess" and "Little Daylight") after the characters break the curses of the wicked fairies.

If this reading is correct and the powerful fairy creatures are not allegories for God, it also means that God is never directly present in any of MacDonald's fairytales, but always indirectly present through the mediation of a sacramental nature.[91] In *The Hope of the Gospel* (1892), MacDonald explains how evildoers are always thwarted by God's familial mediation:

> Against the heart-end of creation, against that for which the Son yielded himself utterly, the sowers of strife, the fomenters of discord, contend ceaseless. They do their part with all the other powers of evil to make the world which the love of God holds together—a world at least, though not yet a family—one heaving mass of dissolution. But they labour in vain. Through the mass and through it, that it may cohere, this way and that, guided in dance inexplicable of prophetic harmony, move the children of God, the lights of the world, the lovers of men, the fellow-workers with God, the peacemakers—ever weaving, after a pattern devised by, and known only to him who orders their ways, the web of the world's history. But for them the world would have no history; it would vanish, a cloud of windborne dust.[92]

God presents himself as one who chooses to operate through his children. He graciously guides them "in dance inexplicable of prophetic harmony" so that what appears to be chaos and dissolution is in reality the formation of an eternal family. Much like MacDonald's evil witches and ravenous wolves, all the powers of evil "labour in vain" and only end up aiding the harmonious conclusion they attempt to resist. But more than this, God also chooses to make creation and his children channels of grace—without them the world would reveal itself as the vanity it seems and vanish as "a cloud of windborne dust."

It is in this sense that nature is sacramental in MacDonald's fairyland. Commenting on how the outside of a book had a profound influence on him, Duncan in "The Portent" says, "it was a kind of sacrament—an outward and visible sign of an inward and spiritual grace; as, indeed, what on God's earth is not?"[93] The cosmos is full of grace: God gifts his glory to creation and therein guarantees continued existence, and everything is therefore a potential messenger of God's love—all things are incipient angels.[94]

For fairyland cosmology, then, nature behaves as a mediator of grace and revelation. It is not itself God, but it carries traces of his glory. The lake in "The Light Princess" reveals the ultimate cure for the princess' malady, but it is also the first thing for which the princess is passionate.

Before meeting the prince, she thinks, "Oh! If I had my gravity, I would flash off this balcony like a long white sea-bird, headlong into the darling wetness."[95] This is her first longing, her first contemplation that things are not what they ought to be, and also therefore the first glimmer that they might one day be different. The lake then becomes that which brings the prince and princess together, the medium for their blossoming love. Without the particular delights of swimming, falling, and sporting, love would not have taken root. It is thus not surprising that the crisis of the story involves not peril to the princess but peril to the lake. The lake is everything to the princess, as the prince and Makemnoit fully realize. Makemnoit cannot threaten the princess by direct violence, but the witch knows that by attacking the mediator of joy and revelation she is even more effectively attacking the princess' soul (and thereby her body, as the frame story of *Adela Cathcart* makes clear). Once sacrifice, love, and joy restore harmony *within* the prince and princess, nature *without* reflects the same harmony:

> The princess burst into a passion of tears, and *fell* on the floor. There she lay for an hour, and her tears never ceased. All the pent-up crying of her life was spent now. And a rain came on, such as had never been seen in that country. The sun shone all the time, and the great drops, which fell straight to the earth, shone likewise. The palace was in the heart of a rainbow. It was a rain of rubies, and sapphires, and emeralds, and topazes. The torrents poured from the mountains like molten gold; and if it had not been for its subterraneous outlet, the lake would have overflowed and inundated the country. It was full from shore to shore.[96]

Again, this may seem merely allegorical (the only *real* meaning is the inner spiritual one that all the world seems right when we love and are loved), but perhaps it is more accurate to call it symbolic or prophetic. MacDonald himself—much like Tolkien[97]—was insistent that his stories were not allegories: "A fairytale is not an allegory. There may be allegory in it, but it is not an allegory. He must be an artist indeed who can, in any mode, produce a strict allegory that is not a weariness to the spirit. An allegory must be Mastery or Moorditch."[98] A symbol, on the other hand, resists reduction and allows for multiple meanings:

> It is God's things, his embodied thoughts, which alone a man has to use, modified and adapted to his own purposes, for the expression of his thoughts;

therefore he cannot help his words and figures falling into such combinations in the mind of another as he had himself not foreseen, so many are the thoughts allied to every other thought, so many are the relations involved in every figure, so many the facts hinted in every symbol.[99]

If nature is symbolic, then both the spiritual and the physical elements are integral. Symbols on the one hand resist materialists saying that everything is merely physical, but symbols also resist gnostics saying that everything is really spiritual. MacDonald believes that we must approach a symbol as a thing in itself—not treat it as a slave to rational meaning nor worship it as a deity of mystical knowledge but love it as a fellow creature. In this light, the restoration of the princess' lake appears as a polyvalent miracle, revealing the harmony at the heart of creation: the interconnectedness of man and nature, inner and outer, spiritual and physical. It is, like the miracles of Jesus, prophetic of the harmony to come. As St. Paul indicates, the return of harmony to humanity will also signify the return of harmony to creation (Rom 8:21: "The creation itself will be set free from its bondage to decay and obtain the freedom of the glory of the children of God").[100]

Though the fairytales never mention God, let alone Christ, this cosmic harmony is for MacDonald not some vague pantheistic or agnostic belief in spiritual meaning but the specific revelation of the Christian faith:

> The bond of the universe, the chain that holds it together, the one active unity, the harmony of all things, the negation of difference, the reconciliation of all forms, all shows, all wandering desires, all returning loves; the fact at the root of every vision, revealing that "love is the only good in the world," and selfishness the one thing hateful, in the city of the living God unutterable, is the devotion of the Son to the Father. It is the life of the universe.[101]

MacDonald does not fret that fairyland does not make this Christian message explicit. He is content with the indirect mode of awaking truth, confident that the glimpse of harmony and a true longing after "the home-centre" will eventually lead to the more specific revelation of Jesus. God uses numerous forms and modes to spur his children on toward knowledge of himself. Nevertheless, there is no question that in MacDonald's mind, the love within the Godhead is the law and order that gives harmony and meaning to both our cosmos and fairyland.[102]

MacDonald's fairyland cosmology is therefore neither Deistic nor a form of gnostic inwardness but rather is relational and prophetic. More so than the quotidian world, fairyland shows lucid glimpses into the harmony of the cosmos. Fairyland is a questing realm that arouses a desire for a "home-centre" in individuals—a harmonious relationship with the entirety of the cosmos. It calls individuals in awful singleness out of weighty selfishness and into the great expanses of a harmonious universe where the soul lightened of its burden finally feels that it has room enough to play. As ecstasy leads to greater ecstasy, characters find themselves drawn into more real and embodied realms, but they also enter into relationships with other humans and creatures. Freed from the idolatry of self, they are at perfect liberty to establish new relationships even with apparently monstrous creatures. And as these characters achieve inner and outer harmony, they also find themselves more at home with nature and other creatures. MacDonald once wrote to a friend: "To what a bliss we are called—to be the heirs of God! I shall one day live in the universe as God lives in it, with a pure, potent, perfect existence, at home with every form of life, because one with the Heart of all life."[103] In his fairyland cosmology, MacDonald provides prophetic glimpses of what this unity might look like—of how spiritual and physical, outer and inner, nature and humanity might ultimately reflect the love eternally existent within God.

8

Transformation
"Shall not the Possible Become the Real?"

Despite the arguments of J. R. R. Tolkien and C. S. Lewis, most people still view fairytales as primarily for children.[1] While fantasy has become an acceptable (if slightly dubious) genre for adults, fairytales have yet to evade their association with children. Many adults have a difficult time "entering into" a fairytale. A common criticism is that a fairytale is a flight of fancy, an indulgent escape from the "real world." Because fairytales do not present a world directly correspondent to the one in which we customarily live, many would say, they are at best temporary vacations and at worst corrupting deceptions. Fairytales can make a person disregard present responsibilities or cause profound disappointment when the expectations they create are not fulfilled. In other words, fairytales aren't serious enough about reality.

According to the surrealist writer Pierre Mabille, however, this criticism is almost exactly opposite of the truth: "Beyond entertainment, beyond curiosity, beyond all the emotions such narratives and legends afford, beyond all need to divert, to forget, or to achieve delightful or terrifying sensations, the real goal of the marvellous journey is the total exploration of universal reality."[2] Far from abandoning the real, fairytales are acutely concerned with reality. They strive toward a more holistic conception of the world. The folktale scholar Max Lüthi concurs: "the folktale does not show us *a* world that is in order; it shows us *the* world that is in order. It shows us *that* the world is the way it should be. At one and the same time, the folktale depicts the world as it is and as it ought to be."³ Within the fairytale, there is a strange coming together of *is* and *ought*. Indeed, uniting disparate elements and synthesizing things that normally must remain separate (e.g., past and future or the possible and the real) are a defining fairytale characteristics. Reality, according to the fairytale, is larger, more diverse, and more mysterious than we commonly believe, but it is also more integrated and interconnected.

Such a conception of reality is difficult to accept for a modern Western adult accustomed to thinking through lenses of rationalism and materialism. One must have more than a "willing suspension of disbelief" to enter into the logic of a fairytale; one must exercise the kind of belief that is now most common to children.⁴ Like fairytales, children also connect things and ideas in surprising ways and bring together the realms of *is* and *ought*. Children hold infinite potential within themselves, and the telling of a story can wholly change their world. Unlike the adult who has relegated fiction to the strictly delimited category of entertainment, children allow stories to transform them. Unfamiliar with the laws and facts of the world, they use a fairytale precisely as Pierre Mabille indicates—as a means of exploring universal reality—and therefore as something that can alter what they desire and how they behave. Transformation, as children so readily sense, is not just a prevalent fairytale motif; it is the essential mode of the fairytale, and as I hope to show in this chapter, the mode is, as it were, the moral of the story.

We have already discussed many aspects of transformation within the fairytale in the two preceding chapters—how the different operations of time and space in fairyland engender transformations in characters, landscapes, and creatures. What has only been occasionally hinted at, though, is MacDonald's belief in the power of fairytales to transform readers in the world outside the text. When MacDonald claims that he writes "for the childlike, whether of five, or fifty, or seventy-five," he is not expanding his reading audience to boost sales or trying to make his stories seem more serious by saying they are for adults, too. Instead, among other things, MacDonald contends that he writes to transform his audience into childlike individuals, that to those who are willing his fantastic stories can actually shape and mold their reality toward his vision of the childlike (and therefore toward the divine). Fairytales can help to transform *ought* into *is* in the real lives of individuals. This chapter will delve into how MacDonald thought that fairytales could transcend the boundaries of literature to bring their transformative ways to readers.

Shadows, Shadows, Shadows All

With only two exceptions, all of MacDonald's fairytales self-reflexively portray the effects of reading stories, either inside the tale itself, as when "The Golden Key" begins with Mossy reading stories in twilight, or outside the tale, as in *Adela Cathcart* when other fictional characters respond to and comment upon the stories.[5] "The Shadows," however, uses both methods liberally and seems to play openly with the transformative power of storytelling.

The first step in the process of transformation, as "The Shadows" highlights, is to alter our mode of perception. One of the first things that the Shadows do to Ralph after he becomes their king is to "make strange" his vision:

> Lifting a dark forefinger, he drew it lightly but carefully across the ridge of his forehead, from temple to temple. The king felt the soft gliding touch go, like water, into every hollow, and over the top of every height of that mountain-chain of thought. He had involuntarily closed his eyes during the operation, and when he unclosed them again, as soon as the finger was withdrawn, he found that they were opened in more senses than one.[6]

Ralph is then able to see that the Shadows are "tall," "solemn," "rather awful," and "very *eerie* indeed to look at, dressed as they all were in funeral black." Here and throughout the story, the Shadows seem to initiate an "eerie" mode of vision—they unveil something of the vanity of being.

Vanity itself relates directly to vision. The key declaration of Qoheleth is "I have seen everything that is done under the sun, and behold, all is vanity" (Eccl 1:14). Creation is contingent and fleeting; only God is eternally self-generating. Qoheleth's vision transpierces all things and thereby reveals their ephemerality. The gaze of vanity, according to the philosopher Jean-Luc Marion, places all things "in suspension," revealing "not that all disappears or falls, but all *can* fall and disappear."[7]

Intriguingly, though the modern usage of the word "vanity" to mean the high value of one's appearance apparently conflicts with the older definition of "emptiness," the more recent definition also has strong associations with vision. Vanity in the modern sense relates closely with mirrors because mirrors allow the self to gaze endlessly upon itself like Narcissus. In these two divergent senses of the word, vanity reveals the polarized possibilities of vision—which can be the most outward- or the most inward-focused of the senses. Vision can draw us ecstatically out of ourselves to see "everything that is done under the sun," or on the other hand vision can aid the self in constructing an ever smaller mental prison. Jean-Luc Marion's discussion of the difference between idols and icons is helpful here. Whereas an idol is "the gaze's landing place," an icon "summons the gaze to surpass itself by never freezing on a visible."[8] The idol is thus a kind of mirror that reflects the gaze of the worshipper back upon the self so that the gaze becomes trapped within itself. An icon meanwhile calls the gaze of the worshipper beyond the self and brings the worshipper into contact with the wholly other. In a similar way, MacDonald believed—following the traditional Christian definition of sin—that people who focus inwardly upon the self are not just arrogant or obnoxious but spiritually degenerate.

Sin, as we saw in chapter 2, is a matter of spiritual orientation. Augustine says that the cause of the evil angels' misery is "the just result of their turning away from him who supremely is, and their turning towards themselves."[9] Since only God has existence in himself, turning away from the source of one's being actually lessens one's connection with reality. Thus, when Adam "turned toward himself his being was less real than when he adhered to him who exists in a supreme degree" and "so, to abandon God and to exist in oneself, that is to please oneself, is not immediately to lose all being; but it is to come nearer to nothingness."[10] Sin is not ultimately a list of things not to do; it is rather a question of direction—is the self turned inward or outward? Sin acts as a kind of gravity, a force that pulls us away from God and into ourselves—as we saw with Dante's depiction of Satan. Moreover, an inward orientation, as one scholar describes it, is "a venturing towards non-existence, towards the literal undoing of creation."[11] Hell, therefore, is literally the path to destruction—the final dissolution of being—and, *pace* Sartre, is an absence of other people.

MacDonald likewise believed the greatest spiritual danger was to be trapped in the self, to consider oneself to be a "Somebody." Thus the earnestly playful Shadows tell stories about self-absorbed people who are continually gazing upon the self and then about how they break people out of that vision. In one story, an old man sits alone in the dining room "gnawing the bone of his selfishness" until startled into tears by the loving approach of a child (brought by the Shadows), while in another a Shadow prevents a greedy nurse from killing a self-engrossed miser and then helps reconcile the miser to his daughter. One Shadow makes sport of a clergyman as he is practicing his sermons in the mirror, because the man is more interested in his image and reputation than his spiritual flock. The listening Shadows immediately respond, "he was fair game; fair shadow game."

The Shadows have a particular dislike for "the creatures that appear in mirrors," almost as if these other quasi-spectral beings are inimical to the Shadows' goals and desires.[12] Their near similarity as reflections or copies of humans creates a kind of sibling rivalry. Indeed, whereas the creatures in mirrors encourage individuals to turn ever more inward, the Shadows conversely strive to make individuals turn ever more outward. Continuing his story of the clergyman, the Shadow brags: "I made such fun of him one night on the wall! He had sense enough to see that it was himself, and very like an ape. So he got ashamed, turned the mirror with its face to the wall, and thought a little more about his people, and a little less about himself."[13] MacDonald frequently reserves his harshest criticism for the hypocrisy of religious people, especially church leaders (much like Jesus with the Pharisees, scribes, and Sadducees). The Shadows act as a different kind of mirror that breaks the gaze of the self and reveals vanity.[14] Like the gaze of vanity, which "renders the world strange, deranged, a stranger to itself," the Shadows unveil an "eerie" vision of the world, startling the clergyman out of his self-complacency.[15] Unlike the physical mirror that only reflects the expected outer illusion of respectability, the grotesque reflection of inner ugliness unsettles the preacher's pride and causes him to spend more time attending to others.

The Shadows are themselves reflections or imitations of things having bodily substance. They have an evanescent existence. They lack memory; their form fluctuates and is unstable. Since their nature requires a dynamic interplay of light and darkness, they only appear "in the twilight of the fire." Yet they claim that their purpose is to show "the truth of things."[16] What are we to make of these creatures? What "truth" do they reveal?

We can find some hints in the various structures and character responses to the story. As if to emphasize its flickering nature, MacDonald gave "The Shadows" two different endings. In *Adela Cathcart*, the story ends with Ralph returning to his bed, where one of his children is waiting to say goodnight so "that he might rise early too, and be very good and happy all Christmas-day." Then comes the tale's final words: "And Ralph Rinkelmann rejoiced that he was a man, and not a Shadow"—a line with echoes of the Pharisee's prayer in Luke 18:11: "God I thank you that I am not like other men, like this tax collector." It seems unlikely that MacDonald's primary intent with this line was to make his listeners entirely happy to be human. In the frame narration, for example, the response to the story is general confusion. Adela's reaction is halting uncertainty: "I must think. I don't know. I can't trust you." Adela's father, on the other hand, says that Smith has "the most confounded imagination I ever knew." The curate's response is silent musing, which receives Smith's approval: "I was glad to see the curate pondering over it."[17] This pondering seems to be the result that both Smith and the Shadows intend—for individuals to be roused out of narrow self-satisfaction and into a fuller contemplation of universal reality.

It would, however, preclude the desired effect to say directly that the intention of the story was to induce pondering. Thus, when MacDonald placed "The Shadows" in *Dealings With Fairies*, he extended the ending, but only to make it more enigmatic and unsettling. The passage, which continues immediately after Ralph rejoices that he is a man and not a shadow, is best read in full:

> But as the Shadows vanished they left the sense of song in the king's brain.
> And the words of their song must have been something like these:—
>
> Shadows, Shadows, Shadows all!
> Shadow birth and funeral!
> Shadow moons gleam overhead;
> Over shadow-graves we tread.

Transformation

> Shadow-hope lives, grows, and dies.
> Shadow-love from shadow-eyes
> Shadow-ward entices on
> To shadow-words on shadow-stone
> Closing up the shadow-tale
> With a shadow-shadow-wail.
>
>   Shadow-man, thou art a gloom
> Cast upon a shadow-tomb
> Through the endless shadow air,
> From the Shadow sitting there,
> On a moveless shadow-throne,
> Glooming through the ages gone
> North and south, and in and out,
> East and west, and all about,
> Flinging Shadows everywhere
> On the Shadow-painted air.
> Shadow-man, thou hast no story
> Nothing but a shadow-glory.
>
> But Ralph Rinkelmann said to himself,—
>   "They are but Shadows that sing thus; for a Shadow can see but Shadows. A man sees a man where a Shadow sees only a Shadow."
> And he was comforted in himself.[18]

A more self-deconstructive ending is hard to imagine. The shadows "vanish," leaving a little shadow remainder echoing in Ralph's brain, yet the words are not the actual ones but "something like" them. All of the narrative sentences begin with conjunctions ("but," "and"), as if to insinuate the incompleteness and contingency of even "complete" authorial constructions. The final line, "And he was comforted in himself," clashes with the destabilizing thrust of the Shadows and the story in general. Clearly the reader should not be at ease with Ralph's apparent comfort.

The poem similarly resists straightforward interpretation and remains one of the eeriest elements of the story. It is light and playful in manner but seemingly dark and nihilistic in content. The simple trochaic tetrameter evokes the gay fluidity of nursery rhymes but creates dissonance with the poem's theme—somewhat like the gamboling darkness of William Blake's poem "Tyger, Tyger." At the heart of the poem is a Shadow "on a moveless shadow-throne" who lamp-like casts the Shadow-men out into the shadow world. Is this a shadowy God? Or Satan, "the prince of the power of the air" (Eph 2:2)? No easy answers are available. What the poem seems to be doing, however, is reflecting the vanity of human existence. Indeed, the opening line "Shadows, Shadows, Shadows all!" echoes Qoheleth's cry, "Vanity, vanity, all is vanity!" especially when we recall that "vanity" translates *habbel* (meaning "vapor" or "mist). The apparent pessimism of this refrain vanishes, though, when we consider MacDonald's understanding of vanity:

> Corruption brings in vanity, causes empty aching gaps in vitality. This aching is what most people regard as evil: it is the unpleasant cure of evil. It takes all shapes of suffering—of the body, of the mind, of the heart, of the spirit. It is altogether beneficent: without this ever invading vanity, what hope would there be for the rich and powerful, accustomed to, and set upon their own way? What hope for the self-indulgent, the conceited, the greedy, the miserly? The more things men seek, the more varied the things they imagine they need, the more are they subject to vanity—all the forms of which may be summed in the word disappointment. He who would not house with disappointment, must seek the incorruptible, the true. He must break the bondage of havings and shows; of rumours, and praises, and pretences, and selfish pleasures. He must come out of the false and into the real; out of the darkness and into the light; out of the bondage of corruption into the glorious liberty of the children of God. To bring men to break with corruption, the gulf of the inane yawns before them. Aghast in soul, they cry, "Vanity of vanities! All is vanity!" and beyond the abyss begin to espy the eternal world of truth.[19]

Vanity is a sign of the self's catching sight of itself in a mirror and seeing that it is not self-generating. Significantly, vanity does not merely reveal the evanescence of all things; it also draws vision "beyond the abyss" of self and the fleeting demands of this passing age "to espy the eternal world of truth." Before humans can begin their "quest for the home-centre," they must encounter the awful expanse of dead emptiness that comprises much of what they consider reality. Far from pessimistic, therefore, for MacDonald the mirror of vanity is primarily liberating—it frees *from* illusory reality and *for* ultimate reality. The "observed facts" of materialistic vision are dethroned so that the individual can once again participate in the transformation of *is* into *ought*. Indeed, transformation has already begun when one has a vision of vanity, for in order to register a sense of distaste with the self there must already be a degree of detachment—one must have already in some way broken out of the enclosed inner circle.

This is the "truth of things" that the Shadows reveal to humanity and how they initiate transformation. Rinkelmann's shadows are a more positive and lighthearted version of the shadow that comes out of the ogress' cupboard and attaches itself to Anodos in *Phantastes*. Anodos' shadow unveils the "aching gaps in vitality" and causes him to long for the incorruptible by making his life dull and miserable, but Rinkelmann's shadows perform the same function playfully and simultaneously encourage their subjects to take themselves lightly. Unlike Anodos' shadow—which light cannot affect—Rinkelmann's shadows revel in the play of light and dark. They mingle contraries and unsettle rigid conceptions of reality. As "ghosts of the body," they are both material and immaterial, and they remind people that the world did not have to be the way it is. More than this, they show how existence is a gift that comes continually from outside the self; the self cannot possess existence without it slowly decaying into nothingness. If the self turns inward, it is the one truly in danger of becoming shadowy and losing its hold on reality. When two shadows once longed to make such an inward turn by holding on to the past, they "rebelled against their nature" and "thickened and thickened till they vanished out of [the shadow] world."[20] Memories and cares weigh things down, steadily increasing the gravity of the self.

To counteract this existential heaviness, the shadows try to provoke various forms of levity in their subjects and thereby move them to moral action, as if they are humanity's lighthearted consciences. They are moral mischief-makers. Although the conscience might seem to be a weighty and burdensome faculty ("he has a heavy conscience"), the Shadows draw attention to the light function of the conscience. It is not the conscience that is heavy but the soul; the conscience reveals the burdens and prods the individual to release them. Much in the same way that John Donne says confession produces a "blessed levity" and a "cheerefull lightnesse," the shadows induce a beneficent letting go of self.[21]

Interestingly, though they lack a weighty sense of the self, the Shadows nevertheless have individuality:

> They retained, however, all the time, to the surprise of the king, an identity, each of his own type, inexplicably perceptible through every change. Indeed, this perseveration of the primary idea of each form was more wonderful than the bewildering and ridiculous alterations to which the form itself was every moment subjected.[22]

It is as though they are nascent selves, containing all the possibilities and none of the actualities. The fact that each successive transformation does not erase the informing identity further suggests that one need not fear that the continuous process of transformation will obliterate the true self. In fact, taking the self lightly might be the only ultimate way of having a self at all. Through all of this, the effect of the shadows upon their audience is to remove illusory obstacles and to open up a space for the hearing of the question: Shall not the Possible become the Real?" In *Adela Cathcart*, this altered mode of vision is the first step in Adela's transformation—through the fairytales she begins to espy the vanity of her life and to wonder whether certain possibilities might become real for her.

While the Shadows seem to embody this revelatory vision specifically, it is also more generally the function of MacDonald's fairytales. With only slight exceptions, most of the tales have two children, a boy and a girl, on the border of crossing into adulthood.[23] This creates a mirror in which anyone can see their reflection—young children anticipate their transition into adulthood, while adults recall their childhood, finding their present identity in their past journey. Young and old, male and female, everyone can see their reflection in MacDonald's tales. Through viewing a "strange" mirrored reflection, readers can consider their lives from a distance, seeing life's fragility and its potential, and thereby—MacDonald appears to hope—freeing them from the vain trappings of commonplace worries and concerns. Even though a fairytale may not lead a person to "turn toward" God, in the simple act of "entering into" a story a person must at least slightly "turn away" from the self, and this is a vital first step. Every additional frame story creates more distance from the self, providing greater opportunity to see the vanity of the self and widening contemplation of the possible.

The distancing effect of narrative framing might also help explain MacDonald's penchant for interpolating stories and poems within other stories.[24] The reader needs a certain amount of levity in order to move farther and farther away from the everyday world and to switch rapidly from the logic of one story to another.

To make the gaze of vanity even more encompassing, MacDonald frequently gives his characters different social or economic places. Alice in "Cross Purposes" is the daughter of a squire, whereas Richard is "so poor that he did not find himself generally welcome."[25] In "The Golden Key," Mossy lives in a little cottage with his loving great-aunt, while Tangle is the daughter of a merchant and is mistreated by servants. Watho in "The History of Photogen and Nycteris" pampers Photogen as a prince but treats Nycteris as a prisoner (though both have noble parentage). Yet none of these distinctions ultimately make any difference in fairyland. Even gender roles are "queered" since female characters have just as much agency as male characters.[26] Without excluding a subversive element of social criticism, MacDonald seems to be mirroring as much of human experience as possible and then casting it all in the shadow-light of vanity.[27] There is no male nor female, rich nor poor, old nor young in fairyland. All that matters is whether or not an individual chooses to join the dance of being and becoming. By entering into this realm of "as if," the reader catches a mirrored glimpse of the vanity of his world and the possibility of a truer reality.

MacDonald makes this especially clear in "The Wise Woman," a story he subtitles "a parable." Critics have called this fairytale MacDonald's most "preachy," precisely because the mirror on the reader seems a little too clear.[28] Both Rosamond and Agnes are spoiled and proud little girls—one the daughter of a king and queen, the other a daughter of lowly shepherds. Initially, the impoverished Agnes is less morally repugnant—Rosamond beats her pet animals, whereas Agnes is merely "distorted to silliness by self-complacency"—but after the wise woman abducts both girls, Agnes is the one who refuses correction.[29] The wise woman shows both their "Somebody" in a mirror "so clear that nobody looking into it could tell what it was made of, or even see it at all—only the thing reflected in it."[30] This miraculous mirror shows the concealed ugliness within both girls—an ugliness which only the discipline of doing their duty can amend. Though neither girl enjoys the experience, it is ultimately the princess Rosamond who submits to the death of her "Somebody" and begins voluntarily following the path of duty and self-denial, whereas Agnes absconds and grows even more recalcitrant. Given Agnes' lower social status and her less blatantly offensive behavior, this is a reversal of fairytale expectations. Familiar with the stories of pig-hands marrying princesses and wicked kings receiving their just deserts, it is surprising to find MacDonald apparently upholding the status quo. But the point is that MacDonald is ultimately uninterested in the status quo or its reversal. He portrays social disparities not to promote the cause of the poor as such (though he always did) but to cast all experiences of life in the light of vanity and bring every individual face to face in the story's mirror with his own hideous "Somebody." Vanity, then, uses a true mirror to interrupt the gaze of the self from its solipsistic self-worship. Faced in vanity's mirror with an empty world and an ugly face, the viewer finds himself freed from the enclosed illusions of world and self and released to turn toward "reality" again for what seems the first time. But this is just the beginning of transformation.

The Fairy Palace
Sabbath Restoration and Twilight Vision

In an introductory letter to *The Portent*—written in the same year as *Adela Cathcart* (1864)—MacDonald defends the writing and reading of fantastic stories on the basis of their connection with real human experience: "seeing so much of our life must be spent in dreaming, may there not be a still nook, shadowy, but not miasmatic, in some lowly region of literature, where, in the pauses of labour, a man may sit down, and dream such a day-dream as I now offer to your acceptance."[31] Fantasy through dreams is a major element in everyone's life and therefore has just as great a claim to realism as fiction which only deals with the commonplace world. "Escapism" in literature is justified because escape itself is "realistic," for dreams are a natural and healthy part of life.

In the aforementioned quotation, MacDonald emphasizes how important different modes of vision are for a holistic understanding of reality. Fantasy is "shadowy" in that it dims the full force of the sun's light and stimulates creative imaginings, but this does not make it "miasmatic," that is, false or illusory. Instead, this lessening of the "hot noontide unideal" allows for a special mode of perception:[32]

> We have seldom real positive night in this world—so many provisions have been made against it. Every time we say, "What a lovely night!" we speak of a breach, a rift in the old night: there is light more or less, positive light, else were there no beauty. Many a night is but a low starry day, a day with a softened background, against which the far-off suns of millions of other days can show themselves. The near vision vanishes, the far hope awakes. It is not said of heaven there shall be no twilight there.[33]

Rather than ushering in the time of deception, the setting of the sun allows for a different type of optics. Freed from the distractions of the immediate, the eye can reach "millions of other days," and the shy distant stars can shine. The night of our world is really twilight. It is the time for resting from the labours of the day to renew one's strength and the time for dreaming, for seeing beyond the tyrannous clamour of the nearby and awaking the far hope. Similarly, reading or hearing the words "once upon a time" is like looking through "a rift in the old night." It ushers one into the twilit fairyland, where as we have already seen one can rest in a Sabbath realm, but where in addition "the near vision vanishes" so that in the twilight distance "the far hope awakes."

Thus far, I have consciously avoided in-depth discussion of either *Phantastes* or *Lilith* on the grounds that these two longer "adult" fantasies often overshadow the fairytales because they seem to display more characteristics of "seriousness." Critics by and large take the view of Rolland Hein that "because the tales contain more of the absurd and the tone is more light and playful, fresh breakthroughs into the transcendent are more rare" and that the longer fantasies compel the "adult mind," whereas "the fairy tales dilute and simplify these themes so that children can understand them."[34] Yet in interesting ways, *Phantastes* provides metacommentary on the experience of engaging with and being transformed by fairytales. Though they are "light and playful," fairytales are the primary agents of change that teach Anodos "breakthroughs into the transcendent" by enabling him to take himself lightly. By this line of topsy-turvy thinking, *Phantastes* becomes the derivative, secondary work and fairytales the vital, primary creations.

In a strange sense, *Phantastes* is MacDonald's laboratory for testing the effects of fairytales upon readers. Just after his twenty-first birthday, the first-person narrator, Anodos, awakes to find his room transforming into a magical forest, and the book then records his various adventures in fairyland. Here Anodos not only reads fairytales on several occasions and records his reactions but he also enacts them in different episodic encounters (visiting an ogress' cottage, slaying giants, escaping from a tower prison). The epicenter of this engagement with fairytales is the fairy palace and its enchanted library. Stephen Prickett, in a passing comment, draws attention to how "when Anodos is reading in the magic library, his reading seems to be pointing to *our* experience of reading about him."[35] The fairy palace and its library thus become symbols of the experience of reading fairytales in an ideal state.

Before arriving at the fairy palace, Anodos has several encounters that reveal the vanity of being to him, many of which his newly found shadow initiates. Though there are moments of respite, as when Anodos visits the two human huts and the willow tree, most of his adventures in fairyland up until he reaches the fairy palace are wearisome, so that just before being led to the palace by the river, he is walking "listlessly and almost hopelessly along" with the shadow "in [his] heart as well as at [his] heels."[36] Yet the time that Anodos spends at the fairy palace is a kind of pause in the action—a Sabbath "breach in the old night."

The palace is "the home of wonder itself" in which Anodos finds an exact "copy" of his own room where his attendant shadow "dares not come."[37] He feasts and drinks to his heart's content and then sleeps "dreamless" yet with "a sense of past blessedness."[38] "All the pleasures to be found in the most varied and artistic arrangement" are present in the palace, and Anodos has constant experiences of rest and refreshment. In short, the fairy palace participates fully in festive, Sabbath time—it brings Anodos into momentary contact with eternity. Whereas fairyland outside of the palace tends to be dangerous, dark, and just a little bit sinister—much closer to Tolkien's definition of "Faerie" as "the perilous realm"—inside everything is beautiful, light, and carefree. The fairy palace thus seems to be located within the same festive, Sabbath temporality as MacDonald's fairytales.

Further examination reveals that it is also a place of twilight. Everything is silver rather than gold. Anodos calls it the "palace of marble and silver, and fountains and moonshine," and he records how after bathing in a bath of "the purest, most liquid and radiant water" he begins "to discern faint, gracious forms," which are most visible in moonlight and when he is in the shade.[39] In premodern cosmology, silver is the metal of the moon (just as gold is for the sun). Symbolically, therefore, MacDonald establishes the palace as a twilight place, a "shadowy," "still nook" of literature "where in the pauses of labour a man may sit down, and dream such a day-dream." Both the moon and silver have associations with mirrors as well. Just before arriving at the fairy palace, Anodos calls the moon "the lovelier memory or reflex of the down-gone sun, the joyous day seen in the faint mirror of the brooding night."[40] Mirrors in this case do not trap the vision of the self as with the creatures in the mirrors in "The Shadows"; rather they function like twilight, allowing a person to see beyond the horizon of the immediate. "All mirrors are magic mirrors," says Anodos, because in them "the commonest room is a room in a poem."[41] Twilight likewise has the same power of unveiling the wonder hidden in the commonplace, as can be seen from MacDonald's poem "My Room" (1857):

> [Twilight] stains the air with power estranging
> Known with unknown clouding, changing.
> See in ruddy atmosphere
> Commonplaceness disappear!
> Look around on either hand—
> Are we not in fairyland?[42]

While the effect of both mirrors and twilight might be described as "magical," this magic is not deceptive but revelatory. It removes the dullness that accrues as a result of habit and familiarity. What disappears is the room's "commonplaceness" not the things themselves. The items lose a certain manner of their appearing, a manner which is itself a distortion or limited way of looking at things. Mirrors lift things "out of the region of fact into the realm of art" such that the "very representing of it" clothes "that which was otherwise hard and bare" "with interest."[43] The problem lies not in *what* we see but in *how* we see. In this way, the twilight mirror of art is not less true than reality, as it is in a strict Platonic sense, but potentially more true:

> Art rescues nature from the weary and sated regards of our senses, and the degrading injustice of our anxious everyday life, and, appealing to the imagination, which dwells apart, reveals Nature in some degree as she really is, and as she represents herself to the eye of the child, whose every-day life, fearless and unambitious, meets the true import of the wonder-teeming world around him, and rejoices therein without questioning.[44]

MacDonald likely borrows this understanding of art from the Romantics, in particular Coleridge's *Biographia Literaria*:

> [Wordsworth was] to give the charm of novelty to things of every day, and to excite a feeling analogous to the supernatural, by awakening the mind's attention from the lethargy of custom, and directing it to the loveliness and the wonders of the world before us; an inexhaustible treasure, but for which in consequence of the film of familiarity and selfish solicitude we have eyes, yet see not.[45]

And, of course, both writers draw upon the biblical tradition in which people often "have eyes, yet see not." Jesus, for example, claims that he teaches in parables "because seeing they do not see, and hearing they do not hear, nor do they understand" (Matt 13:13). Parables awaken "the mind's attention from the lethargy of custom"; they startle and provoke thought, thereby allowing people to see past the "film of familiarity" and into things as they really are. As Oscar Wilde says, "to look at a thing is very different from seeing a thing. One does not see anything until one sees its beauty."[46] When, therefore, MacDonald depicts the fairy palace as the domain of silver, the moon, pools, and reflections, he intends to affiliate it with the power of twilight and mirrors to transform one's vision from looking to seeing.

In addition to resting and restoring his spirits through feasting and playing in the fairy palace, Anodos renews his fairy vision as well. When he finds his shadow, Anodos' vision becomes "disenchanted." Instead of beautiful fairy creatures, he only sees common peasants. But after one deeply refreshing bath in the palace's rainbow pool, he once again begins "to discern faint, gracious forms" moving all about him, and these forms he can see especially well "when they [come] between [him] and the moon; and yet more especially when [he himself is] in the shade."[47] Like the delicate light of stars, there are some things which can only be seen when the harsh light of day wanes and one is still and restful enough to progress beyond looking at a thing and into seeing its beauty. In this restorative environment, Anodos' far-off hope awakens. He begins to wonder if he might find "a magic word of power to banish the demon [shadow]" or "a shadow of light" to "devour" his shadow of darkness.[48] And, of course, his hope reawakens that he might find his "ideal," the marble lady whom he awoke with his song of love. Hope, as we have already seen, was "the one constitutional power of life" in MacDonald; it was the force that lightened the load of his financial difficulties and lifted him up when so many of his family and friends died before him.[49] Hope is thus, we might say, the fuel of transformation. Without hope, even if a person espies the possibility of *ought* becoming *is*, they do not have the energy to strive toward this transformation.

Even more than this, hope helps figure forth the ideal; it creates a playful link or bridge between *is* and *ought* that aids in actualizing metamorphosis. As Shelley says in *Prometheus Unbound*, "to hope till Hope creates / From its own wreck the thing it contemplates" (4, 570). Thus MacDonald calls twilight "a concentrated tumult of undetermined possibilities" because in it "the germs of infinite adventure and result are floating around you like a snow storm."[50] By entering into a fairytale, a reader must let go of himself, all that he rigidly holds on to as "reality," and see the "germs of infinite adventure" that are floating all around him. Like Shelley's description of hope creating "from its own wreck the thing it contemplates," these "germs of infinite adventure" are the intermediaries between *is* and *ought* that make transformation possible.

From Glory to Glory
Mirrors and Metamorphosis

The effects of fairytales upon readers described so far in this chapter are all prior to the culmination of transformation. Vanity breaks an individual out of the enclosed self, Sabbath revitalizes the weary soul, and twilight both reveals the beauty in the commonplace and awakens hope. These are necessary elements of transformation, but they are not its consummation. While transformation for MacDonald never finally finishes until we are perfectly in the image of the Son, he does suggest that fairytales might even have the power to transform readers at an ontological level. Anodos' reading in the fairy library reflects this idea most clearly.

The fairy palace is the structural center of *Phantastes*, and the library is the center of the palace. There is a sort of chiasm (following the pattern A B C B A) in how Anodos arrives at the palace in chapter 10 of the 25 chapter work, departs in chapter 16, and in chapters 12 and 13—the exact middle of the palace episode and the book as a whole—reads fairytales. Fernando Soto observes how Cosmo's "magic mirror intellectually and physically bisects the story" of Anodos and provides the key to understanding the overarching structure of the apparently chaotic narrative.[51] The whole of the romance pivots upon these two little stories—stories that just happen to have eerie echoes of fairytales.

The first story describes a planet that orbits the sun at a greater distance than the earth and where babies are born without erotic love. When the inhabitants hear about love, their longing and hope for something greater leads them—much like Nycteris—to seek a way out of their world and into ours through MacDonald's favorite gateway, death and rebirth. Cosmo's story, meanwhile, parallels almost exactly the episodes and themes of "The Light Princess" and "Little Daylight"—a young man falls in love with a woman enchanted by an evil witch, and the enchantment both brings them together and keeps them apart. Ultimately, Cosmo's self-sacrifice breaks the spell (as with the princes). Both stories from the fairy library, however, take place outside of fairyland—fairies apparently like telling stories of other worlds, too—on a distant planet and in Prague.[52] Yet an even more important contrast with fairytales in terms of genre is that the stories in *Phantastes* elicit strong, weighty emotions, and both end in tragic death. It is as though to holiday from their levity, fairies tell stories of pathos. Like a mirror retaining form and figure but inverting direction, these stories are the uncanny doubles of MacDonald's fairytales.

Within the ludic landscape of the fairy library—a playful mixture of gothic grandeur and baroque excess—Anodos spends from "noon till twilight" reading on "sumptuous eastern carpets" until "weary; if that can be designated as weariness, which was rather the faintness of rapturous delight."[53] His reading magically transports him into the books. If he reads metaphysics, he instantly ponders the truth and begins "constructing the intellectual machine whereby to communicate the discovery," whereas if it is a book of travels he finds himself the traveler.[54] In fictional stories, he becomes "the chief actor therein," experiencing intimately all the fears and joys of the protagonist. Summarizing these reading encounters, Anodos says:

> I did sit in that grand hall, buried and risen again in these old books. And I trust that I have carried away in my soul some of the exhalations of their undying leaves. In after hours of deserved or needful sorrow, portions of what I read there have often come to me again, with an unexpected comforting; which was not fruitless, even though the comfort might seem in itself groundless and vain.[55]

Anodos is like Wordsworth in "Tintern Abbey," who "oft, in lonely rooms, and 'mid the din / of towns and cities" receives "in hours of weariness, sensations sweet" (26–28) from his recollection of beautiful landscapes, though, unlike Wordsworth, for Anodos it is the memory of reading fairytales and not an experience of nature that produces

> That blessed mood,
> In which the burthen of the mystery,
> In which the heavy and weary weight
> Of all this unintelligible world
> Is lighten'd. (38–42)

Oblique allusions to Christ (death and resurrection) and the Holy Spirit ("exhalation," "comfort") meanwhile charge Anodos' assertion with theological force. Reading fairytales in the magic library has soteriological resonances. These salvific undertones may seem excessive, but the structural positioning of these chapters within the narrative suggests even greater import for the reading of fairytales: they effect some fundamental change in the character of Anodos such that instead of spiralling downward as he does in the first half of the book, in the second half he begins to learn from his errors and slowly ascends until his final triumph of self-sacrifice.[56] Furthermore, this final act perfectly mirrors the two interpolated stories: Anodos gives his life for the freedom of others (like Cosmo), and dies only to rise again in a higher world (like the children of the distant planet). In other words, the reading of these stories actualizes some definite change within Anodos. How does MacDonald think this transformation occurs?

A clue can be found in the sermon "The Mirrors of the Lord" (1889), in which MacDonald comments on 2 Corinthians 3:18 ("But we all, with open face beholding as in a glass the glory of the Lord, are changed into the same image from glory to glory, even as by the spirit of the Lord").[57] MacDonald insists on retranslating "beholding as in a glass" with "mirroring" because Paul, like a poet, utilizes the "outer show of things, which outer show is infinitely deeper in its relation to truth, as well as more practically useful, than the analysis of the man of science."[58] Surface is depth, as Oscar Wilde might say (and as "camp" does say). The surface show of a mirror is not "throwing back the rays of light" but "receiving, taking into itself, the things presented to it." The mirror surrounds "the visage with its liquid embrace." MacDonald cites Dante as support (*Inferno*, XXIII, 25–27) before explaining the theological ramifications:

> Our mirroring of Christ, then, is one with the presence of his spirit in us. The idea, you see, is not the reflection, the radiating of the light of Christ on others, though that were a figure lawful enough; but the taking into, and having in us, him working to the changing of us.[59]

Something ontological occurs when a person reflects upon Jesus—the image of Christ that is held in the mirror of an individual's mind begins to transform that person into the same likeness through the power of the Holy Spirit. Undoubtedly, MacDonald would make a distinction between Jesus shaping a person's soul and a story transforming that person—Jesus is the "sun-glory," the primal source of life and being, whereas all else is "moonlight."[60] Even so, we can easily make the interpretative leap from St. Paul's symbolism of mirrors in 1 Corinthians to MacDonald's symbolism of mirrors in *Phantastes*.

By opening his imagination to the fairytales, Anodos receives more than just a pleasant tale—he mirrors the stories in his mind (according to MacDonald's poetic understanding of mirrors), thereby initiating his own ontological transformation. Anodos narrates the story of the distant planet in the first person as he finds himself mirrored into the fantastic landscape. Then, though it is told in the third person, Anodos recalls Cosmo's story:

> While I read it, I was Cosmo, and his history was mine. Yet, all the time, I seemed to have a kind of double consciousness, and the story a double meaning. Sometimes it seemed only to represent a simple story of ordinary life, perhaps almost of universal life; wherein two souls, loving each other and longing to come nearer, do, after all, but behold each other as in a glass darkly.[61]

The story begins after this passage, but MacDonald significantly omits a discussion of what the story meant "at other times." The universality of Cosmo (not accidentally named) creates the potential for Anodos simultaneously to mirror himself into the story and to mirror the story within himself. There is thus a "double consciousness."[62] By participating in the story and allowing it to participate in him, Anodos undergoes real metamorphosis as he licenses the shaping of his self into the image of Cosmo. Like a "germ of infinite adventure" in the soil of his mind, the fairytale, held in the imagination's "liquid embrace," begins to take on a life of its own, leading finally to the good fruit of freely letting go of the self for the sake of others.

In this way, MacDonald seems to hope that his fairytales will be mirrors within which readers can see themselves so that they too can have a "double consciousness" and simultaneously mirror the fairytale in their mind. As we have already seen, MacDonald's fairytale characters are universal types that aid the functioning of the stories as mirrors, but MacDonald designs the symbolism of the stories to be polyvalent for the same reason. Thus in "The Fantastic Imagination," MacDonald refuses to offer any interpretations of his fairytales to the interlocutor who complains that a person could imagine "what he pleases" rather than what MacDonald meant: "If he be a true man, he will imagine true things; what matter whether I meant them or not."[63] Here MacDonald is not just posturing, attempting to maintain the mystery of his stories; rather he hopes that his fairytales will take on a transformative life of their own within the reader. They cannot do this, however, if an authorial interpretation were to finalize their meaning. Thus, he constantly compares his fairytales to living things such as butterflies, bees, fireflies, and roses, as if to emphasize their ability to grow, morph, and move independent of his will. "My tales may not be roses," he says, "but I will not boil them."⁶⁴ Much like Wordsworth's famous line "we murder to dissect," distilling the moral essence kills the ability of the fairytale to evolve independently within each reader. Alive within their readers, fairytales retain the power to transform "from glory to glory." As readers develop, the tales change their meaning and the reader can reapply them to new situations.

Significantly, though, MacDonald depicts the tales as light, defenseless creatures that require the reader's cooperation to live and flourish: "Let fairytale of mine go for a firefly that now flashes, now is dark, but may flash again. Caught in a hand which does not love its kind, it will turn an insignificant, ugly thing, that can neither flash nor fly."⁶⁵ But in the right hands, fairytales can foster the metamorphosis of their readers into similarly lighthearted, defenseless creatures, reminiscent of Dante's words:

> Do you not understand that we are worms,
>   Each born to form the angelic butterfly,
>   That flies defenseless to the Final Judge?
> Why do your souls' pretensions rise so high,
>   Since you are but defective insects still,
>   Worms as yet imperfectly evolved? (XI, 124–29)

Forming the Angelic Butterfly
Morals and Miracles

It seems ironic that the MacDonald who frequently disrupts his novels with moralizing monologues is the same writer who refused to assign morals to his fairytales. In almost all of his other works, MacDonald continually interrupts narratives to explain the importance of doing one's duty, loving God, and loving one's neighbor, so it seems strange that even when earnestly asked to explain the practical message of his fairytales he adamantly declined to do so. Did MacDonald's love of the fairytale genre overcome his normal religious drive toward moralizing? While this explanation is tempting psychologically, what this study has tried to show is that the mode and function of fairytales was more meaningful to MacDonald than any "message" he might have put in them. The mode, in other words, is the moral. There is not a hidden dichotomy in MacDonald's thinking and artistic practice; instead, fairytales are theologically significant for the levity they exhibit and for nurturing in their readers a similar light mode of engaging with the self and the world—they help to "form the angelic butterfly."

For MacDonald, a condition of entry into the world of the fairytale is the letting go of certain rigid ways of seeing and being: "We spoil countless precious things by intellectual greed. He who will be a man, and will not be child, must—he cannot help himself—become a little man, that is, a dwarf. He will, however, need no consolation, for he is sure to think himself a very large creature indeed."[66] Fairytales do not lend themselves to straightforward intellectual gain—their form frustrates such an activity. One must let go of seeing the world as something to be grasped, cataloged, and mastered, and instead participate in the fairytale with the wonder and delight of a child. MacDonald would have agreed with Karl Barth's statement that "one can walk before God in full seriousness only when one realizes that God alone is fully serious."[67] When a fairytale demands that a person release the seriousness of life as a condition of entry, it is therefore not just teaching one of the highest moral truths but inducing its practice. Moreover, readers of fairytales must participate more than readers of "realistic" stories. Unlike stories of everyday life that depict scenes that people need barely visualize and tell of objects with which everyone is familiar, fairytales cannot work without an imaginative performance by the audience. Readers cannot merely spectate from a distance; they must play.

Rather than being a mere marvel to stare at, fairytales become a sort of *praxis* in lighthearted engagement. Devoid of an active element, spectacles can actually begin to hinder transformation and to deaden one's perception, as MacDonald makes clear when discussing the miracles of Jesus:

> It was not good for men to see too many miracles. They would feast their eyes, and then cease to wonder or think. The miracle, which would be all, and quite dissociated from religion, with many of them, would cease to be wonderful, would become a common thing with most. [. . .] A wonder is a poor thing for faith after all; and the miracle could be only a wonder in the eyes of those who had not prayed for it, and could not give thanks for it; who did not feel that in it they were partakers of the love of God.[68]

The relative scarcity of MacDonald's fairytales thus can be seen as aiding in their proper functioning. Dear as the form was to him, MacDonald seems to have recognized that fairytales need to be quick, subtle, and rare if they are to be effective. Despite his large role in the development of the modern genre of fantasy, then, it seems likely that MacDonald would have had criticisms of how some fantasy has become a "feast for the eyes" that does more to dull people's senses than sharpen them.

In any event, what MacDonald reiterates throughout *The Miracles of Our Lord* is that miracles—counter to the prevailing opinion of Victorian times—are not "evidences" of Jesus' power but personal invitations to faith. Jesus did not allow people to receive miracles passively; rather he required them to participate in the work: "God gives a share to every one in what work He does for them. [. . .] Such active faith is the needful response in order that a man may be a child of God, and not the mere instrument upon which his power plays a soulless tune."[69] Thus MacDonald is adamant that the miracles were not for the spectators but for those on whom they passed. "The true mode in which [the miracles] reached others," says MacDonald, "was through the healed themselves."[70] Here MacDonald shifts the focus from the outward show of power for the masses to the transformation of individuals. Fairytales likewise in MacDonald's view should reach others not through a plot summary of the most exciting elements or a distillation of their important moral themes but through the transformation of individual readers.

There are striking parallels between MacDonald's understanding and treatment of miracles and fairytales. Miracles suffer from the same hermeneutical problem as fairytales—they dazzle the eye with unusual wonders from an unseen world, but it is not immediately apparent what they signify or how they function. Their brilliance hides their meaning—they are "by abundant clarity invisible."[71] Unlike sermons, with their straightforward, practical messages, the otherworldly miracles do not seem to speak directly to our circumstances. Both miracles and fairytales appear to be about display and ostentation, but for MacDonald they are actually about quietly transforming individuals. By further examining the functioning of miracles, therefore, we can also hopefully discover more about the moral modality of fairytales and how they transform their readers.

An important part of the functioning of miracles and fairytales is their style. According to Max Lüthi, both miracles and fairytales have "abstract style," a phrase he borrows from Wilhelm Worringer's work *Abstraction and Empathy: A Contribution to the Psychology of Style*. Worringer argues that style reflects volition, that instead of viewing primitive works of art as deficient in skill because they are not "naturalistic," we should consider "the psychic needs which they satisfy."[72] Style reflects a particular "psychic state," an inner experience of relating to the cosmos. Chesterton expresses a similar idea when he says, "the supreme and most practical value of poetry is this, that in poetry, as in music, a note is struck which expresses beyond the power of rational statement a condition of mind, and all actions arise from a condition of mind."[73] Sympathetically engaging with a style is therefore also to experience a particular psychic state of being or "condition of mind." What psychic state does the "abstract style" of miracles and fairytales engender?

MacDonald defines miracles as the Son doing "briefly and sharply" before the "very eyes" of humanity the works that the Father does "so widely, so grandly that they transcend the vision of men."[74] Miracles "epitomize" and "condense" the mysteries of the cosmos; they unravel "the knotted and twisted coil of the universe" so that humanity can, for a brief moment, see the divine source of all creation.[75] The wonder is not people healing, fish multiplying, or storms ceasing, for God is always doing these things; the wonder is the agility and clarity with which Jesus executes these normal things. It is as though Jesus lifts the weight of time and space so that people can see the levity at the heart of things.

There is, moreover, no complicated ritual involved in the performance of Jesus' miracles—he uses simple words ("be clean," "get up") and base materials (spittle and dirt) to enact the greatest of marvels. Christ treats power with "divine carelessness," for "power in itself is a poor thing."[76] In this, Jesus demonstrates the triumph of levity. Miracles have already shown that sickness, famine, storms, hunger, and even death are not ultimately serious, but in his treatment of power as something to be used on behalf of others, Jesus demonstrates that the only thing of true weightiness is divine love. "It is the love," says MacDonald, "that is at the root of power, the power of power, which alone can create."[77] In Philippians, St. Paul speaks of Jesus' humble lightness in how "he did not consider equality with God a thing to be grasped but made himself nothing" (2:6-7). This seems to be the "psychic state" that the style of miracles embodies and nurtures in others—a levity that does not grasp at poor things like power.

Similarly, lightness characterizes the style and "psychic state" of MacDonald's fairytales. Like miracles, fairytales perform wonders with nonchalance, as in "The Golden Key" after Mossy's baptism and rebirth:

> Across the waste of waters, against the bosom of a fierce black cloud, stood the foot of a rainbow, glowing in the dark.
>
> "This indeed is my way," said Mossy, as soon as he saw the rainbow, and stepped out upon the sea. His feet made no holes in the water. He fought the wind, and clomb the waves, and went on towards the rainbow.[78]

In contrast to the arduous wrestling with magic in fantasies like *The Lord of the Rings* or *Harry Potter*, fairytales accomplish the impossible with ease. Characters like Little Daylight experience magical transformation and respond with divine carelessness:

> She stood upright on her feet. Her hood had dropped, and her hair fell about her. The first gleam of the morning was caught on her face: that face was bright as the never-ageing Dawn, and her eyes were as lovely as the sky of darkest blue. [. . .]
>
> "You kissed me when I was an old woman: there! I kiss you when I am a young princess," murmured Daylight.—"Is that the sun coming?"[79]

There is no trace of modesty or shame in her response, nor even much dwelling upon her gratitude. She receives her lifelong desire with nonchalance, and instead of turning her gaze inward to consider herself, she opens it outward to the prince and the dawn. The reader who looks at the aforementioned passage and belittles it for being simple or not reflecting the complexity of life is thus missing the moral of the mode. It is not deficient skill or insufficient knowledge of human nature that leads a writer to use the form of the fairytale. Likely thinking of artistic forms such as ballet and the baroque, Max Lüthi writes that "lightness and masterly simplicity are the distinguishing characteristics of late forms," and MacDonald agrees: "simplicity is the end of all things—all manners, all morals, all religion. [. . .] Simplicity is art's perfection."[80] Like Ruskin's category of the playful grotesque (arising from "the healthful but irrational play of the imagination in times of rest" and extremely rare), the creation of a light style is one of the most difficult accomplishments in art.

If, then, we can say that the style of the fairytale is "pure and clear, with joyous, weightless mobility," it would follow that this lightness is the "psychic state" that the fairytale aims at communicating to its readers.[81] MacDonald supports this "psychic state" theory of style when he says that fairytales should be "mood-engendering" and "thought-provoking" rather than teach prosaic truths.[82] As the previous chapters have shown, the playful pattern of levity everywhere shapes the plot, characters, creatures, and landscape of the fairytale. But how would "engendering" even a lighthearted mood transform a reader?

It seems as if MacDonald tried to transform his readers into the "angelic butterfly" by getting them to play at being light. Here again miracles offer a useful analogy. MacDonald's method of approaching miracles could be described as a form of *lectio divina*—a tradition of "divine reading" in which readers often imaginatively place themselves inside biblical stories. MacDonald constantly exhorts the reader to "regard the miracle from the point of view of the person healed," or to "imagine" a scene, or to internalize the feelings of the disciples.[83] The method has much in common with Ignatius' *Spiritual Exercises* and the Catholic practice of divine reading. Like this tradition, reading in this way increases one's engagement with the text, heightens emotion, and stimulates response. Instead of viewing the miracles from a distance as "evidences" of Jesus' divinity, MacDonald invites the reader to experience them imaginatively, especially to feel how every miracle uniquely liberates and unburdens individuals to worship God with a light and carefree heart.

In addition, miracles are "loopholes to the infinite" because they occupy a "border-land" where there is a "touching of what we call mind and matter."[84] Beyond their revelation of Jesus' love for humanity, miracles stimulate speculation about the ultimate harmony of body and spirit, and this speculation actually helps to bring about the change:

"The man who will not speculate at all, can make no progress. The thinking about the possible is as genuine, as lawful, and perhaps as edifying exercise of the mind as the severest induction."[85] As with fairytales, miracles transform *ought* into *is*, and the bare act of speculating helps make this happen. "There is a wide *may be* around us," says MacDonald, "and every true speculation widens the probability of changing the *may be* into the *is*."[86] Playing with "the possible" is the only way that it will ever become "the real." The reader who plays in and with a fairytale thus initiates transformation.

Furthermore, as Jürgen Moltmann argues, "in playing we can anticipate our liberation and with laughing rid ourselves of the bonds which alienate us from real life."[87] Having playfully taken on the fairytale's light burden and its easy yoke, the reader finds that the psychological weightiness of the self and its alienating habit of turning in upon itself rather than making the outward movement of love toward God and the world cause many unnecessary difficulties in life. Fairytales loosen the shackles of the present and give glimmers of the future. "O happy they for whom the Possible opens its gates of madness, and becomes the Real around them," says MacDonald and then adds,

> Such madness may be but a formless faith—
> A chaos which the breath of God will blow
> Into an ordered world of seed and fruit.
> Shall not the Possible become the Real?[88]

The light playfulness of fairytales might appear to be foolish madness, but MacDonald viewed it paradoxically as "a formless faith," a playing with the "germs of infinite adventure" that are "floating all around us." Like the Old Man of the Fire in "The Golden Key" playing and working effortlessly with his colored balls, the levity of fairytales might just be the serious work of paradise. Indeed, it might be some of the most significant work of this life as well, as MacDonald, after quoting Francis Bacon and Ecclesiastes, indicates in his final words to "The Imagination: Its Function and Culture":

> Thus to be playfellows with God in this game, the little ones may gather their daisies and follow their painted moths; the child of the kingdom may pore

Transformation

upon the lilies of the field, and gather faith as the birds of the air their food from the leafless hawthorn, ruddy with the stores God has laid up for them.[89]

The fairytale's light mode engenders eschatological transformation in the here and now. Thus, to return to the beginning of the chapter, fairytales *are* "flights of fancy," but levity itself has one of the highest moral functions. Levity facilitates that most important of spiritual transformations—taking the self and the world lightly so that one can rise from being a "defective insect" to "form the angelic butterfly."

Conclusion
The Haunting Force of Levity

There is a strange irony in the way physical gravity operates through waves and particles that are massless and "pass unchanged through any material in their path and so [. . .] carry signals with absolute clarity across the vast reaches of space."[1] With an infinite host of heavenly angels (*angelos*, as we know, is Greek for "messenger") backing up gravity, levity would seem to be the true force in the universe. Despite being the most universal force in physics, gravity remains unseen—scientific instruments have never recorded gravity waves or particles. Even if scientists do find a way to observe these gravitons and gravitational waves, gravity will be the last and most elusive of the four physical forces in the cosmos to yield to human investigation.[2]

The metaphorical levity that we have been tracing in this book is similarly evasive and difficult to observe. I have tried on the one hand to show how lightness functions theologically to engender a mode of being that takes itself lightly and that delights in created existence, and on the other how George MacDonald subtly crafted his fairytales with this levity in the hope that it might transform others. But perhaps it is fitting to conclude this somewhat theoretical discussion with something a little more practical and visible. MacDonald's concept of fairytales subtly changing people into childlike individuals is intriguing, the reader might think, but does it work? What is the force of levity?

At least in the case of two monumental writers and thinkers—G. K. Chesterton and C. S. Lewis, with whom we began this inquiry—the answer seems to be that levity is a haunting force that can indeed have a life-altering influence. In Chesterton's introduction to Greveille MacDonald's biography of his father, he claims that MacDonald's fairytales (in particular *The Princess and the Goblin*) "made a difference to [his] whole existence" in that they "helped [him] to see things in a certain way from the start."[3] Here is his account of how particular images took root in his mind:

> Another recurrent image in his romances was a great white horse; the father of the princess had one, and there was another in *The Back of the North Wind*. To this day I can never see a big white horse in the street without a sudden sense of indescribable things. But for the moment I am speaking of what may emphatically be called the presence of household gods—and household goblins. [. . .] There is something not only imaginative but intimately true about the idea of the goblins being below the house and capable of besieging it from the cellars. [. . .] Anyhow, that simple image of a house that is our home, that is rightly loved as our home, but of which we hardly know the best or the worst, and must always wait for the one and watch against the other, has always remained in my mind as something singularly solid and unanswerable.[4]

The important thing to observe is not Chesterton's particular interpretation of *The Princess and the Goblin* but how the story lightly planted images like seeds in his mind that then blossomed into multiple meanings, which were perpetually able to blossom anew. On account of MacDonald's fictional white horses, Chesterton claims that real white horses give him "a sudden sense of indescribable things"—his expanded imagination dilating his sense of reality—a feeling that yielded literary fruit in his own *The Ballad of the White Horse*.[5] MacDonald's fairytales enlarge and unfold the meanings and associations of commonplace objects and experiences, and they open the unsettling possibility that our present existence might be small and cramped, whereas the expansiveness of the fairytale might more accurately reflect the eternal world.[6]

Meanwhile, Chesterton's interpretation of the princess' household geography—though fitting and insightful—is not definitive, finalizing, or even, possibly, what MacDonald intended. Though in a sense it is paradoxically exactly what MacDonald intended in that he created a spacious imaginative playground filled with beautiful things and invited the reader to participate in the meaning-making game. The thoughts that are lightly generated from this play are thus not wholly MacDonald's or Chesterton's but, being partially vitalized by both (and maybe others as well), quicken into a life of their own. For Chesterton, this new thing became "singularly solid and unanswerable" and shaped his view of life, giving him an imaginative stronghold within which he could resist the "five alternative philosophies of the universe that have come to our colleges out of Germany, blowing through the world like the east wind."[7]

Unlike Chesterton, who read MacDonald's fairytales as a child, Lewis discovered *Phantastes* in 1916 when he was seventeen and about to go to war. He immortalized this reading experience in *Surprised by Joy* in a passage worth quoting at length:

> It is as if I were carried across the frontier, or as if I had died in the old country and could never remember how I came alive in the new. [. . .] I did not yet know (and I was long in learning) the name of the new quality. I do now. It was holiness. For the first time the song of the sirens sounded like the voice of my mother or my nurse. Here were old wives' tales; there was nothing to be proud of in enjoying them. It was as though the voice which had called to me from the world's end were now speaking at my side. It was with me in the room, or in my own body, or behind me. If it had once eluded me by its distance, it now eluded me by proximity. [. . .] Now for the first time I felt that it was out of reach not because of something I could not do but because of something I could not stop doing. If I could only leave off, let go, unmake myself, it would be there. Meanwhile, in this new region all the confusions that had hitherto perplexed my search for Joy were disarmed. There was no temptation to confuse the scenes of the tale with the light that rested upon them, [. . . yet] at the same time, never had the wind of Joy blowing through any story been less separable from the story itself. [. . .] I now perceived that while the air of the new region made all my erotic and magical perversions of Joy look like sordid trumpery, it had no such disenchanting power over the bread upon the table or the coals in the grate. That was the marvel. Up till now each visitation of Joy had left the common world momentarily a desert. [. . .] But now I saw the bright shadow coming out of the book into the real world and resting there, transforming all common things and yet itself unchanged. [. . .] In the depth of my disgraces, in the

then invincible ignorance of my intellect, all this was given me without asking, even without consent.[8]

At both the beginning and the end of this extract, Lewis emphasizes his passivity in describing how he was "carried across the frontier" and "could never remember how [he] came alive" in that new land and that it happened "without asking, even without consent." Reading MacDonald's "old wives' tales," in which "there was nothing to be proud of in enjoying," lightly induced Lewis to let go of himself, to enter a state of "divine carelessness" in which he could release his arduous intellectual questing and receive the gifts of rest, goodness, and joy. "Without consent," however, does not mean that Lewis was entirely passive or that the transformation occurred wholly against his will. Rather, given the context of Lewis' longer conversion narrative and his wrestling with different philosophical positions, it would seem to mean "without consent of my rational mind," for of course what is readily apparent is that Lewis' own imagination immediately accepted MacDonald's invitation and began to play—and to delight exceedingly—in MacDonald's fairyland. By "holiness" Lewis means, according to Stephen Prickett, "the transformation of the mundane world into something new, set aside by divinity, and transcendent."[9] What is so powerful about MacDonald's fairytale levity, then, is that it refuses to remain within the bounds of the story; it "[comes] out of the book into the real world" and begins "transforming all common things."[10] It so intoxicates and catches Lewis up in its lighthearted approach that he cannot help carrying it into everyday life (or perhaps letting it carry him).

Lewis captures the paradox of this active passivity in his famous summation: "that night my imagination was, in a certain sense, baptised; the rest of me, not unnaturally, took longer."[11] There is a rich ambiguity in this image, for in baptism (assuming that the subject is not an infant) the self elects to let go of itself and to be passive as someone else submerges it in water (where one incidentally has the sensation of floating). Baptism is a passive cleansing that requires an active releasing of sin—in Lewis' case, he found himself freed from the lust for "erotic and magical perversions." Like John Donne's description of confession, the result is "blessed levity" and "cheerefull lightnesse of spirit" as the self, lightened of its allegiance to the weightiness of this world, can align itself with the joyous liberty of the divine.

Furthermore, what made this experience so powerful for Lewis was its haunting levity, not any specific intellectual "content." He describes an elusive "something" that hovers just out of view, which if he could only "let go, unmake [himself], it would be there." Had Lewis been able to reduce his reading experience to a set of moral principles or intellectual ideas, this ghostly presence likely would have dissipated. Instead, the adventitious indeterminacy of MacDonald's fairyland continued to cast its "bright shadow" of holiness into Lewis' life and thus became a sort of subterranean force that nimbly and imperceptibly began transforming him from within.

Chesterton speaks similarly of MacDonald's fairytale levity as a kind of spectral presence that floats in and out of everyday life:

> The great thought which Dr. Macdonald utters and leaves unuttered alike in a kind of fatalistic optimism will never wholly cease to haunt and attack us. At a hundred odd moments, in crooked streets, in twilight fields, in lamp-lit drawing-rooms, there will come upon us the confounding, and yet comforting, notion that we and all our nationalistic philosophies are all in the heart of a fairy tale and playing an uncommonly silly part in it.[12]

Gravity may have the strength of obviousness on its side, but levity, though it works in strange and elusive ways, may ultimately be the more potent force. We may one day discover that we have been "playing an uncommonly silly part" "in the heart of a fairy tale"; as Nycteris—to conclude this book with a fairytale ending—speculates, "But who knows that, when we go out, we shall not go into a day as much greater than your day as your day is greater than my night?"[13]

Notes

Introduction

1. C. S. Lewis, *The Great Divorce* (London: Bles, 1946), 59. [Throughout this book, if there is emphasis in a quotation it is original to the source unless otherwise noted.]
2. Lewis, *The Great Divorce*, 60.
3. Lewis, *George MacDonald: An Anthology* (London: Bles, 1946), 14, 18.
4. Lewis, *George MacDonald: An Anthology*, 14.
5. Lewis, *George MacDonald: An Anthology*, 17.
6. Lewis, *George MacDonald: An Anthology*, 21; J. R. R. Tolkien, *A Tolkien Miscellany* (New York: SFBC, 2002), 135.
7. Colin N. Manlove, "G. K. Chesterton and George MacDonald: Strangers and Brothers," *The Chesterton Review* 27, nos. 1–2 (2001): 64.
8. According to Colin Manlove, MacDonald is "steadily serious in his fantasy" and "his tone rarely shifts from spiritual earnestness," a sentiment echoed by Richard Reis when he describes *Phantastes* and *Lilith* as MacDonald's most excellent symbolic works because they have "adult readers in mind" and are "serious" (Manlove, "G. K. Chesterton and George MacDonald," 62; Richard Reis, *George MacDonald* [New York: Twayne, 1972], 86).
9. In his recent biography, Ian Ker argues that Chesterton is one of the best critics of Victorian literature to date. Ian Ker, *G. K. Chesterton: A Biography* (Oxford: Oxford University Press, 2011), 100, 123; G. K. Chesterton, "George MacDonald," *The Daily News*, September 23, 1905.
10. G. K. Chesterton, "George MacDonald and His Work," *The Daily*

News, June 11, 1901. All subsequent quotations in this section are taken from this source. This work cites MacDonald as "Macdonald," which is reflected in all the quotations. This essay is oddly not listed in any of the MacDonald bibliographies. For its discovery, I am indebted to William Oddie, *Chesterton and the Romance of Orthodoxy* (Oxford: Oxford University Press, 2008), 38.

11 In his *Autobiography*, Chesterton recounts the story of a man at a dinner party who asked him, "I suppose I'm right in thinking you don't really *believe* in those things you're defending against Blatchford?" When Chesterton affirmed that he did believe them the man began to behave "as if he were sitting next to a fabulous griffin" (*Autobiography* [London: Hutchinson, 1950], 179). Chesterton discusses this phenomenon more fully in a chapter of *Heretics* entitled "Mr. McCabe and a Divine Frivolity."

12 G. K. Chesterton, *The Everlasting Man* (San Francisco: Ignatius, 1993), 9.

13 Characters in MacDonald's fairytales, as we shall see, never enter fairyland directly by desiring the magical realm in particular but always indirectly by longing for something else or because they, in a Dantesque fashion, have lost their way.

Chapter 1

1 Charlton Lewis and Charles Short, *A Latin Dictionary* (Glasgow: Oxford University Press, 1951), 1054–55.

2 This usage was also present in the Latin. Levity seems to have always borne the weight of a predominantly negative connotation. Even before its eventual scientific victory, gravity was accorded greater respect.

3 "In pre-scientific physics, [levity was] regarded as a positive property inherent in bodies in different degrees, or varying proportions, in virtue of which they tend to rise, as bodies possessing gravity tend to sink" (*Oxford English Dictionary*, 2nd ed. [Oxford: Clarendon, 1989], "levity, n.1.").

4 In his preface to Newton's *Principia*, Roger Cotes in 1713 said, "it is now agreed by all philosophers that all circumterrestrial bodies gravitate towards the earth" and "that which is relative levity is not true levity, but apparent only, and arises from the preponderating gravity of the contiguous bodies" (Isaac Newton, *Principia*, trans. Andrew Motte and Florian Cajori [Berkeley: University of California Press, 1934], xxi).

5 *OED*, "levitate, v."

6 G. K. Chesterton, *Orthodoxy* (London: John Lane, 1927), 221.

7 All quotations from Dante are taken from *The Portable Dante*, trans. Mark Musa (London: Penguin, 2003).

8 Dante, *The Portable Dante*, 245.

9   Aristotle, *Physics*, trans. Robin Waterfield (Oxford: Oxford University Press, 1999), III, 5, 205b25. The Latin text has *gravitatem* and *levitatem* for "weight" and "lightness," respectively.
10 Unless otherwise indicated, all Scripture quotations are from *The Holy Bible, English Standard Version* (Wheaton, Ill.: Good News Publishers, 2001).
11 Chesterton, *Orthodoxy*, 222.
12 Recent popular treatments of physics interestingly challenge the supremacy of gravity. Frank Wilczek, e.g., in his book *The Lightness of Being* discusses how "gravity is ridiculously feebler than the other fundamental forces" and how in modern physics "there is only one thing, and it's more like the traditional idea of light than the traditional idea of matter" (*The Lightness of Being* [London: Penguin, 2010], 145, ix).
13 The *OED* uses "earnest" seven times in its entry on "serious" and then uses "serious" three times in its entry on "earnest." *OED*, "serious, adj."; *OED*, "earnest, adj."
14 C. S. Lewis, *Experiment in Criticism* (Cambridge: Cambridge University Press, 1961), 11.
15 For an excellent discussion of how camp refuses the demands of seriousness, see Susan Sontag, "Notes on 'Camp,'" in *Against Interpretation*, ed. Susan Sontag (London: Eyre & Spottiswoode, 1967), 275–92.
16 Andrews Stott, *Comedy* (London: Routledge, 2005), 22.
17 Pseudo-Dionysius, *Pseudo-Dionysius: The Complete Works*, trans. Colm Luibhéid and Paul Rorem (New York: Paulist Press, 1987), 170.
18 Chesterton, *Orthodoxy*, 221–22.
19 Pseudo-Dionysius, *Complete Works*, 182.
20 Pseudo-Dionysius, *Complete Works*, 187.
21 Pseudo-Dionysius, *Complete Works*, 187–88.
22 Pseudo-Dionysius, *Complete Works*, 184.
23 Michel Serres, *Angels: A Modern Myth*, trans. Francis Cowper (Paris: Flammarion, 1995), 44.
24 Pseudo-Dionysius, *Complete Works*, 186.
25 Quoted in Joad Raymond, *Milton's Angels* (Oxford: Oxford University Press, 2010), 289.

Chapter 2

1   Quoted in Robert Torsten Petersson, *The Art of Ecstasy: Teresa, Bernini, and Crashaw* (London: Routledge & Kegan Paul, 1970), 40.
2   Hans Urs von Balthasar, *The Glory of the Lord: A Theological Aesthetics*. Vol. 1: *Seeing the Form*, ed. Joseph Fessio and John Kenneth Riches, trans.

Erasmo Leiva-Merikakis, 7 vols. (New York: Ignatius Press, 1983), 33; David Bentley Hart, *The Beauty of the Infinite* (Grand Rapids: Eerdmans, 2003), 244.

3. Lennart Ryden, ed., *The Life of St Andrew the Fool*. Vol. 2: *Text, Translation and Notes* (Uppsala, Sweden: Uppsala University Press, 1995), 17.
4. Ryden, *The Life of St Andrew the Fool*, 41.
5. Alban Butler, *Butler's Lives of the Saints*, vol. 3, ed. Herbert Thurston and Donald Attwater (New York: P. J. Kennedy & Sons, 1956), 588.
6. Butler, *Butler's Lives of the Saints*, 589.
7. Desiderius Erasmus, *The Praise of Folly and Other Writings*, trans. Robert M. Adams (New York: W.W. Norton, 1989), 82.
8. Erasmus, *The Praise of Folly and Other Writings*, 85.
9. The Hebrew Scriptures obviously describe epiphanies in which individuals directly encounter the divine, but these experiences tend to emphasize terror and amazement rather than any experience of the soul's delight in being temporarily free from the normal physical constraints.
10. This is discussed most fully in the *Phaedrus*: "if it can help, it never quits the side of its beloved, nor hold any one of more account than him, but forgets mother, and brothers, and friends, and though its substance be wasting by neglect, it regards that as nothing, [. . .] and is read to be a slave and lie down as closely as may be allowed to the object of its yearnings" (252) (Plato, *The Phaedrus, Lysis, and Protagoras*, trans. J. Wright [London: Macmillan, 1925], 58).
11. Plato, *The Phaedrus, Lysis, and Protagoras*, 54.
12. Examining a wide selection of ecstasies across history and religions, Marghanita Laski observes that "up-feelings are the most common quasi-physical feelings" that one experiences during ecstasy. (*Ecstasy: A Study of Some Secular & Religious Experiences* [London: Cresset Press, 1961], 67.)
13. Because Plato talks about the body as a prison for the soul, many of his followers such as Philo and Plotinus saw physical existence as one of the key things that needed to be overcome before the soul could achieve unity with the One. Believing in the resurrection of the body, Christians could not agree with this view, and so took a more agnostic approach to the question of how ecstasy related to the body as in Paul's phrase "whether in the body or out of the body I do not know" (2 Cor 12:3). For a good discussion of how Christianity modified the Greek concept of ecstasy, see M. A. Screech, *Ecstasy and the Praise of Folly* (London: Duckworth, 1980), 48–61.
14. Augustine, *The Confessions of St. Augustine*, trans. E. B. Pusey (London: Dent, 1907), 194. IX.x.24.

15 Quoted in Screech, *Ecstasy and the Praise of Folly*, 57.
16 Plotinus' Neoplatonic description of his ecstasies highlights the key difference: "lifted out of the body into myself; becoming external to all other things and self-encentred." The problem is the body, not the self. In fact, once out of the body, the soul finds that it is truly "into itself" and "self-encentred." Christians reverse this and say that the problem is the self, not the body. (Plotinus, *The Enneads*, trans. Stephen MacKenna [London: Penguin, 1991], 334, IV.8.1.)
17 Augustine, *City of God*, trans. Henry Bettenson (London: Penguin, 2003), 572, book XIV, chap. 13.
18 Augustine, *City of God*, 572.
19 Matt Jenson, *The Gravity of Sin* (London: T&T Clark, 2006). Jenson traces the use of the phrase *homo incurvatus in se* from Augustine to Martin Luther to Karl Barth and shows that this image is at the heart of Western Christianity's conception of sin.
20 Augustine, *City of God*, 573.
21 Quoted in L. L. Welborn, *Paul, The Fool of Christ: A Study of 1 Corinthians 1–4 in the Comic-Philosophic Tradition* (London: T&T Clark, 2005), 70.
22 For a classic study of the fool's role in culture and literature, see Enid Welsford, *The Fool: His Social and Literary History* (London: Faber & Faber, 1968).
23 Plotinus says that God has no need of his derivatives, and "he ignores all that produced realm, never necessary to Him, and remains identically what He was before He brought it into being" (*Enneads*, 404, V.5.12).
24 Pseudo-Dionysius, *Complete Works*, 264.
25 Hart, *The Beauty of the Infinite*, 329.
26 M. A. Screech comments, "the incarnate Son of God acted in ways which made even his earthly brethren believe he was mad" (*Laughter at the Foot of the Cross* [London: Penguin Books, 1999], 101).
27 John Dominic Crossan, *Cliffs of Fall: Paradox and Polyvalence in the Parables of Jesus* (New York: Seabury Press, 1980), 65.
28 John Dominic Crossan, *The Dark Interval: Towards a Theology of Story* (Niles: Argus Communications, 1975), 123.
29 R. T. France, *The Gospel of Mark: A Commentary on the Greek Text* (Carlisle: Paternoster, 2002), 297.
30 Speaking of this story, Elton Trueblood argues, "one of the best evidences of Christ's wit is the way in which He responded to the wit of another" (*The Humor of Christ* [New York: Harper & Row, 1964], 124).
31 For an excellent history and exploration of the "holy fool," see John

Saward, *Perfect Fools: Folly for Christ's Sake in Catholic and Orthodox Spirituality* (Oxford: Oxford University Press, 1980).

32 Peter L. Berger, *Redeeming Laughter: The Comic Dimension of Human Experience* (Berlin: de Gruyter, 1997), 189.

33 Balthasar, *The Glory of the Lord*, 1:671.

34 St. Thomas Aquinas, *umma Theologiae*, trans. Fathers of the English Dominican Province (London: Burns, Oates & Washbourne, 1922), III, 45, 42.

35 Both Mark and Matthew emphasize the bodily element when they record how the disciples first think that Jesus is a disembodied ghost, only to have Jesus calm their fears.

36 Mark Allen McIntosh, *Mystical Theology: The Integrity of Spirituality and Theology* (Oxford: Blackwell, 1997), 53.

37 Most commentators believe there is only one experience and that "paradise" is just a chiastic repetition and reinforcement of "third heaven." Nevertheless, "paradise" originally referred to a walled garden, whereas "heaven" designated the airy regions in the skies above. See Ralph P. Martin, *2 Corinthians*, Word Biblical Commentary (Milton Keynes: Word Publishing, 1986), 401–4.

38 Victor Paul Furnish observes how the fact that Paul "does not really care [. . .] suggests that there are some in Corinth that really do" (*II Corinthians*, The Anchor Bible [London: Yale University Press, 2005], 545).

39 Aquinas quotes Augustine in Aquinas, *Summa Theologiae*, II-II, 175, 176.

40 Alan Jacobs, e.g., contends that the mysticism represented by Simone Weil and Fyodor Dostoevsky is characterized by "*kenosis*-as-self-evacuation," an eradication of the self that "leads also to the abdication of answerability and the refusal of self-activity" (*A Theology of Reading: The Hermeneutics of Love* [Oxford: Westview, 2001], 109, 105).

41 Rowan Williams, *The Wound of Knowledge: Christian Spirituality from the New Testament to St. John of the Cross*, 2nd rev. ed. (London: Darton, Longman & Todd, 1990), 138–39.

42 James Buchanan Wallace comments, "he knows that boasts in visions and revelations can create a disposition hostile to the meekness of Christ" (*Snatched Into Paradise [2 Cor 12:1-10]: Paul's Heavenly Journey in the Context of Early Christian Experience* [Berlin: de Gruyter, 2011], 282).

43 Quoted in Balthasar, *The Glory of the Lord*, 1:195.

44 Quoted in Balthasar, *The Glory of the Lord*, 1:143.

45 Quoted in W. H. Auden, *Forewords and Afterwords* (London: Faber & Faber, 1973), 73.

Chapter 3

1. Augustine, *Confessions*, 195–96. IX.x.26.
2. Augustine, *Confessions*, 195. IX.x.25.
3. Friedrich Schiller, *On the Aesthetic Education of Man*, trans. Reginald Snell (New York: Dover, 2004), 78.
4. Cf., Eccl 2:14; 11:10; 3:19; 1:9; 5:7; 5:10; 7:15-17; 1:10; 7:14; 11:3-4.
5. Jean-Luc Marion notes that "vanity aims at goods to the very extent that they remain present and possessed in full enjoyment" for "the gaze of boredom strikes with vanity presence as such" (*God Without Being*, trans. Thomas A. Carlson [Chicago: University of Chicago Press, 1991], 124).
6. Most recent treatments of Ecclesiastes have noted this parallel. For a thorough and systematic discussion of this connection, see David M. Clemens, "The Law of Sin and Death: Ecclesiastes and Genesis 1-3," *Themelios* 19, no. 3 (1994), 5-8.
7. These include sin and its consequences (Eccl 4:1-3; cf. Gen 3-4), work/toil (Eccl 2:4-8; cf. Gen 3:17-19), eating (Eccl 2:24; cf. Gen 2:9, 3:6), longing/desiring (Eccl 4:8; cf. Gen 3:6, 16), knowledge of good and evil (Eccl 6:8-12; cf. Gen 2:17), and the wicked prospering while the righteous perish (Eccl 7:15; cf. Gen 4).
8. Clemens, "The Law of Sin and Death," 5.
9. Milan Kundera, *The Unbearable Lightness of Being*, trans. Michael Henry Heim (New York: HarperPerennial, 1999), 223.
10. See B. Pick, "Ecclesiastes or the Sphinx of Hebrew Literature," *Open Court* 17 (1903): 361–71; A. Wright, "The Riddle of the Sphinx: The Structure of the Book of Qoheleth," *CBQ* 30 (1968): 313-34; idem, "The Riddle of the Sphinx Revisited: Numerical Patterns in the Book of Qoheleth," *CBQ* 42 (1980): 35-51.
11. Gary D. Salyer gathers from other commentators that "there are 27 *hapax legomena* in the book and 26 words or combinations of words that occur only here in the First Testament. There are also 42 grammatical *hapax* and 42 Aramaicisms" (*Vain Rhetoric: Private Insight and Public Debate in Ecclesiastes*, JSOTS [Sheffield: Sheffield Academic, 2001], 138).
12. Derrida, e.g., speaks of how "the absence of the transcendental signified extends the domain and the play of signification infinitely" ("Structure, Sign and Play in the Discourse of the Human Sciences," in *Writing & Difference*, trans. Alan Bass [London: Routledge, 1978], 280).
13. Cf. 2:16; 7:15; 4:13.
14. Mikhail M. Bakhtin, *Rabelais and His World*, trans. Helene Iswolsky (Bloomington: Indiana University Press, 1984), 39–40.

15 In order to explain 12:10, Longman is forced to ascribe to the frame narrator the subtlety and ironic wit that he elsewhere denies to Qoheleth. See Tremper Longman, *The Book of Ecclesiastes* (Grand Rapids: Eerdmans, 1998), 261, 278.
16 R. N. Whybray, "Qoheleth, Preacher of Joy," in *Wisdom: The Collected Articles of Norman Whybray*, ed. Katharine J. Dell and Margaret Baker (Aldershot: Ashgate, 2005), 141–52.
17 Longman, *The Book of Ecclesiastes*, 26–29.
18 The word translated as "breath" in Ecclesiastes is *ruach*, which is also commonly translated as "spirit," as in Genesis 1:2, "the Spirit of God was hovering over the waters."
19 Marion, *God Without Being*, 125.
20 Marion, *God Without Being*, 125.
21 Marion, *God Without Being*, 126.
22 Marion, *God Without Being*, 126.
23 Marion, *God Without Being*, 126.
24 Marion, *God Without Being*, 127.
25 Marion writes, "the *as if* plays from the nothing to being and from being to the nothing" (*God Without Being*, 89).
26 Marion, *God Without Being*, 128.
27 Giorgio Agamben, *The Time That Remains*, trans. Patricia Dailey (Stanford: Stanford University Press, 2005), 23.
28 Jürgen Moltmann, *Theology and Joy* (London: SCM Press, 1973), 37–38.
29 Moltmann, *Theology and Joy*, 40.
30 Karl Barth, *Ethics*, trans. Geoffrey Bromiley (London: T&T Clark, 1992), 504.
31 Barth, *Ethics*, 503.
32 All quotations of Byron are taken from Lord Byron, *The Major Works*, ed. Jerome McGann (Oxford: Oxford University Press, 2000).
33 Plato, *Laws*, trans. Benjamin Jowett (Oxford: Clarendon, 1871), II, 653.
34 Johan Huizinga, *Homo Ludens: A Study of the Play-Element in Culture* (Boston: Beacon Press, 1955), 32.
35 Hans-Georg Gadamer, "Play as the Clue to Ontological Explanation," in *Truth and Method*, , trans. Joel Weinsheimer and Donald Marshall (London: Continuum, 2004), 104.
36 W. H. Auden, *Collected Poems* (New York: Vintage, 1991), 567.
37 Schiller, *On the Aesthetic Education of Man*, 64.
38 Schiller, *On the Aesthetic Education of Man*, 67.
39 Schiller, *On the Aesthetic Education of Man*, 74.
40 Schiller, *On the Aesthetic Education of Man*, 80.

Notes to pp. 47–57 217

41 Max Beerbohm, *The Happy Hypocrite* (New York: John Lane, 1897), 17.
42 Beerbohm, *The Happy Hypocrite*, 19.
43 Beerbohm, *The Happy Hypocrite*, 33.
44 Gadamer, "Play as the Clue to Ontological Explanation," 109.
45 Gadamer, "Play as the Clue to Ontological Explanation," 111.
46 Gadamer, "Play as the Clue to Ontological Explanation," 105.
47 Beerbohm, *The Happy Hypocrite*, 52.
48 Beerbohm, *The Happy Hypocrite*, 62.
49 Gadamer, "Play as the Clue to Ontological Explanation," 112.
50 David Cohen, *The Development of Play* (London: Routledge, 2006), 20–32.
51 C. S. Lewis, *Mere Christianity* (London: Bles, 1952), 148.
52 Barth, *Ethics*, 503.
53 Moltmann, *Theology and Joy*, 36.
54 Barth, *Ethics*, 505.
55 Barth, *Ethics*, 510.

Chapter 4

1 Charles Neaves, *Songs and Verses, Social and Scientific* (Edinburgh: William Blackwood & Sons, 1868), 54.
2 Bakhtin, *Rabelais and His World*, 9.
3 Bakhtin, *Rabelais and His World*, 9.
4 Bakhtin, *Rabelais and His World*, 10.
5 Evagrius and Robert E. Sinkewicz, *Evagrius of Pontus: The Greek Ascetic Corpus* (Oxford: Oxford University Press, 2003), 99.
6 Roger Caillois, *Man and the Sacred*, trans. Meyer Barash (Chicago: University of Illinois Press, 2001), 103.
7 Bakhtin, *Rabelais and His World*, 34.
8 Bakhtin, *Rabelais and His World*, 10, 212.
9 Bakhtin often points in this direction in statements like "the basis of laughter which gives form to carnival rituals frees them completely from all religious and ecclesiastic dogmatism, from all mysticism and piety" (*Rabelais and His World*, 7).
10 Karl Barth, *Church Dogmatics*, ed. Thomas F. Torrance, trans. Geoffrey William Bromiley, 2nd ed., 14 vols. (London: T&T Clark, 2004), III/1, 225.
11 Jürgen Moltmann, *The Way of Jesus Christ* (London: SCM Press, 1990), 120.
12 Jürgen Moltmann, *The Trinity and the Kingdom of God*, trans. Margaret Kohl (London: SCM Press, 1981), 218.
13 Bakhtin, *Rabelais and His World*, 235.
14 Bakhtin, *Rabelais and His World*, 19.

15 R. Rawdon Wilson observes that in recent scholarship "carnival has been transformed into a synonym for undoing, for transgression, for destruction, and for *replacement*" (*In Palamedes' Shadow: Explorations in Play, Game, and Narrative Theory* [Boston: Northeastern University Press, 1990], 41).
16 Jan Kott, *The Bottom Translation*, trans. Daniela Miedzyrzecka and Lillian Vallee (Evanston, Ill.: Northwestern University Press, 1987), 49.
17 Mikhail M. Bakhtin, *The Dialogic Imagination*, trans. Michael Holquist and Caryl Emerson (Austin: University of Texas Press, 1981), 163.
18 *OED*, "preposterous, adj."
19 G. K. Chesterton, "A Midsummer Night's Dream," in *The Common Man* (London: Sheed & Ward, 1950), 14.
20 Chesterton, "A Midsummer Night's Dream," 14, 10.
21 Harvey Cox, *The Feast of Fools: A Theological Essay on Festivity and Fantasy* (Cambridge, Mass.: Harvard University Press, 1969), 140–41.
22 Barth, *Church Dogmatics*, III/1, 228.
23 Barth, *Church Dogmatics*, III/1, 228.
24 Barth, *Church Dogmatics*, III/4, 51.
25 Bakhtin, *Rabelais and His World*, 94.
26 Bakhtin, *Rabelais and His World*, 122–23.
27 Wilson, *Palamedes' Shadow*, 38.
28 Bakhtin, *Rabelais and His World*, 123.
29 Reinhold Niebuhr, "Humour and Faith," in *Discerning the Signs of the Times* (London: SCM Press, 1946), 107.
30 George R. Potter and Evelyn M. Simpson, eds., *The Sermons of John Donne*, 10 vols. (Berkeley: University of California Press, 1959), 4:82–83.
31 Barth, *Church Dogmatics*, III/4, 58.
32 Bakhtin, *Rabelais and His World*, 19.
33 Auden, *Forewords and Afterwords*, 471.
34 Chesterton, "A Midsummer Night's Dream," 17.
35 Bakhtin, *Rabelais and His World*, 78; Kott, *The Bottom Translation*, 44.
36 Kott, *The Bottom Translation*, 31.
37 Slavoj Žižek, *The Puppet and the Dwarf: The Perverse Core of Christianity* (Cambridge, Mass.: MIT Press, 2003).
38 Bakhtin, *Rabelais and His World*, 81.
39 Barth, *Church Dogmatics*, III/4, 56.
40 Agamben, *The Time That Remains*, 73, 72.
41 Moltmann, *Theology and Joy*, 53.
42 Manlove, "G. K. Chesterton and George MacDonald: Strangers and Brothers," 64.
43 George MacDonald, *David Elginbrod* (Whitehorn: Johannesen, 1995), 41.

44 George MacDonald, *Miracles of Our Lord* (Whitehorn: Johannesen, 2000), 249–50.
45 MacDonald, *Miracles of Our Lord*, 245–46.
46 MacDonald, *Miracles of Our Lord*, 249.
47 Chesterton, "George MacDonald and His Work."

Chapter 5

1   See, e.g., Bakhtin, *Rabelais and His World*. G. K. Chesterton, "A Drama of Dolls," in *Alarms and Discursions* (London: Methuen, 1910), 29–34.
2   Moltmann, *Theology and Joy*, 35.
3   Anonymous, *A Call to Seriousness in Religion* (London: Tho. Parkhurst, 1693), 1.
4   Neaves, *Songs and Verses, Social and Scientific*, 54.
5   Bakhtin uses this quotation before adding that "the Enlighteners had a lack of historical sense, an abstract and rationalist utopianism, a mechanistic conception of matter, a tendency to abstract generalizations and typification on one hand and to documentation on the other hand" (*Rabelais and His World*, 116).
6   This phrase is from Immanuel Kant's famous definition of Enlightenment as "mankind's exit from its self-incurred immaturity" ("An Answer to the Question: What is Enlightenment?" in *What is Enlightenment?* ed. James Schmidt [Berkeley: University of California Press, 1996], 58).
7   Kant argued that the performance of moral actions should arise "not from inclination, but from duty" (*The Moral Law: Groundwork of the Metaphysics of Morals*, trans. H. J. Paton [London: Routledge, 1997], 64).
8   Kant, "An Answer to the Question," 58.
9   John Henry Newman, *On Certain Difficulties Felt By Anglicans in Submitting to the Catholic Church*, 2nd ed. (London: Burns & Lambert, 1850), 239.
10 Donald Gray, "The Uses of Victorian Laughter," *Victorian Studies* 10 (1966): 145.
11 G. K. Chesterton, *The Victorian Age in Literature* (London: Williams & Norgate, 1923), 153, 155.
12 Gray, "The Uses of Victorian Laughter," 150.
13 Gray, "The Uses of Victorian Laughter," 165.
14 Gerald Massey, "Thomas Hood, Poet and Punster," *Hogg's Instructor* IV (1855): 323.
15 Massey, "Thomas Hood, Poet and Punster," 323.
16 Chesterton, *Victorian Age*, 25.
17 Quoted in Gray, "The Uses of Victorian Laughter," 160.
18 Gray, "The Uses of Victorian Laughter," 159.

19 Charles Dickens, *Hard Times* (London: Oxford University Press, 1968), 1.
20 John Stuart Mill, *Autobiography* (Oxford: Oxford University Press, 1971), 19.
21 Philip Davis observes how Utilitarians believed that "the Archimedean lever by which to lift society was the impersonally rational principle of utility, cutting a path through individualistic thickets of short-sighted sentiment and blind self-interest" (*The Victorians*, The Oxford English Literary History [Oxford: Oxford University Press, 2002], 43).
22 Dickens, *Hard Times*, 7.
23 Dickens, *Hard Times*, 49.
24 Walter E. Houghton claims that "except for 'God' the most popular word in the Victorian vocabulary must have been 'work'" (*The Victorian Frame of Mind, 1830–1870* [London: Yale University Press, 1957], 242).
25 Thomas Carlyle, *Past and Present: Chartism* (New York: Harper & Brothers, 1862), 197.
26 Davis, *The Victorians*, 14.
27 Colin Matthew, ed. *The Nineteenth Century*, Short Oxford History of the British Isles (Oxford: Oxford University Press, 2000), 71.
28 Carlyle, *Past and Present*, 210. Carlyle's epigraph to *Past and Present* is Schiller's line from the prologue to *Wallensteins Lager*, "Ernst ist das Leben."
29 Carlyle, *Past and Present*, 291.
30 Dickens, *Hard Times*, 22, 23.
31 Dickens, *Hard Times*, 23.
32 Matthew, ed. *The Nineteenth Century*, 203.
33 Matthew, ed. *The Nineteenth Century*, 207–9.
34 William Thackeray, *The Newcomes* (Leipzig: Bernhard Tauchnitz, 1854), 30.
35 Edwin Sidney, *The Life of the Reverend Rowland Hill* (London: Seeley, Burnside, & Seeley, 1844), 207.
36 Ian Bradley, *The Call to Seriousness: The Evangelical Impact on the Victorians* (London: Jonathan Cape, 1976), 32.
37 George MacDonald, *England's Antiphon* (Whitehorn, Calif.: Johannesen, 1996), 329.
38 For more on this, see Stephen Prickett, *Victorian Fantasy* (Waco, Tex.: Baylor University Press, 2005), 75–76.
39 Matthew Arnold, *Literature and Dogma* (London: Smith, Elder, 1873), 310–11.
40 George Eliot's translations of Straus' *The Life of Jesus Critically Examined* and Feuerbach's *The Essence of Christianity* reflect a similar sentiment.
41 Arnold, *Literature and Dogma*, 107.

42 Stephen Prickett summarizes Arnold's idea in this passage: "the age of fairy stories is past, and modern man, if he is to survive as a 'spiritual' being, must learn to demythologize his belief. He must separate the kernel of abstract truth from its poetic husk" (*Romanticism and Religion: The Tradition of Coleridge and Wordsworth in the Victorian Church* [Cambridge: Cambridge University Press, 1976], 214).
43 Chesterton, *Victorian Age*, 77.
44 Matthew Arnold, *Selected Prose* (London: Penguin, 1987), 207.
45 Arnold, *Selected Prose*, 355.
46 Arnold, *Selected Prose*, 404.
47 Thomas Carlyle and G. B. Tennyson, *A Carlyle Reader: Selections from the Writings of Thomas Carlyle* (Cambridge: Cambridge University Press, 1984), 204.
48 Matthew Arnold, "My Countrymen," *Cornhill Magazine*, vol. 13 (February 1866): 170.
49 Davis, *The Victorians*, 104.
50 T. R. Wright goes so far as to argue that "all the elements of the [Comtean] Religion of Humanity [. . .] can be found in some form in George Eliot's work" (*The Religion of Humanity: The Impact of Comtean Positivism on Victorian Britain* [Cambridge: Cambridge University Press, 1986], 180).
51 George Eliot, *Adam Bede* (New York: Modern Library, 2002), 177.
52 George Eliot, "The Natural History of German Life," in *The Essays of George Eliot*, ed. Thomas Pinney (London: Routledge & Kegan Paul, 1963), 271.
53 "Art is the nearest thing to life; it is a mode of amplifying experience and extending our contact with our fellowmen beyond the bounds of our personal lot. All the more sacred is the task of the artist when he undertakes to pain the life of the People. Falsification here is far more pernicious than in the more artificial aspects of life" (Eliot, "The Natural History of German Life," 271).
54 John Ruskin, *Modern Painters*, vol. 3 (New York: John Wiley, 1863), 105.
55 John Ruskin, *Modern Painters*, 110.
56 Alison Milbank, "Praeterita as Dantesque Journey to the Real," *Nineteenth-Century Prose* 35, no. 1 (2008): 50.
57 Stephen Prickett, *Words and The Word* (Cambridge: Cambridge University Press, 1986), 157.
58 Ruskin, *Modern Painters*, 110–11.
59 Newman, *On Certain Difficulties*, 238.
60 Maria Edgeworth, *Practical Education* (New York: Harper & Brothers, 1855), 250, 252–53.

61 Maria Edgeworth, *Moral Tales* (Leipzig: Bernhard Tauchnitz, 1866), 336.
62 "Before Henry and Charlotte began to read these Histories, they were taught to consider them, not as containing the real conversations of birds (for that is impossible we should ever understand) but as a series of Fables, intended to convey moral instruction applicable to themselves" (Sarah Trimmer, *Fabulous Histories* [London: J. G. & F. Rivington, 1838], 1).
63 Charles Dickens, *Miscellaneous Papers* (London: Chapman & Hall, 1908), 407.
64 Lewis Carroll, *The Complete Works of Lewis Carroll* (New York: Barnes & Noble, 1994), 88.
65 Carroll, *The Complete Works of Lewis Carroll*, 88.
66 Carroll, *The Complete Works of Lewis Carroll*, 61.
67 Carroll, *The Complete Works of Lewis Carroll*, 88.
68 Morton N. Cohen, ed., *The Letters of Lewis Carroll*, 2 vols. (London: Macmillan, 1979), 1:96.
69 Oscar Wilde, *The Picture of Dorian Gray* (Leipzig: Bernhard Tauchnitz, 1908), 5.
70 Oscar Wilde, *The Happy Prince and Other Stories* (London: Penguin, 1994), 55.
71 Wilde, *The Happy Prince and Other Stories*, 55.
72 Wilde, *The Happy Prince and Other Stories*, 41.
73 Wilde is more odd and complex than this, of course, and one could construct arguments either for a stronger version of his morality (as seen, e.g., in *De profundis*) or conversely for a stronger version of his immorality (as demonstrated by his trial). Yet this ambiguity only highlights Wilde's desire for the multiplicity and mobility of meaning. On this subject G. K. Chesterton comments: "Like a many-coloured humming top, [Wilde] was at once a bewilderment and a balance. He was so fond of being many-sided that among his sides he even admitted the right side. He loved so much to multiply his souls that he had among them one soul at least that was saved" ("Oscar Wilde," in *Oscar Wilde: The Critical Heritage*, ed. Karl Beckson [London: Routledge & Kegan Paul, 1997], 314).
74 Ruskin, *Modern Painters*, 96.
75 Ruskin, *Modern Painters*, 97.
76 W. H. Auden, "Afterword," in *The Golden Key*, by George MacDonald (New York: Farrar, Straus & Giroux, 1967), 86.
77 Chesterton, "George MacDonald and His Work."
78 Most scholars seem to agree with John Pennington that MacDonald's fairytales are less interesting from a literary perspective than *Phantastes*, *Lilith*, or *At the Back of the North Wind* because in the fairytales

MacDonald "is conservative" and the tales only play "a variation on theme" from traditional fairytales. John Pennington, "Alice at the Back of the North Wind," in *Behind the Back of the North Wind*, ed. John Pennington and Roderick McGillis (Hamden: Winged Lion Press, 2011), 54. Jack Zipes' commentary on MacDonald's fairytales in *Fairy Tales and the Art of Subversion* is probably the best structural analysis to date; however, Zipes is not sensitive to MacDonald's theological outlook, nor does he consider how lightness functions within the stories. See Jack Zipes, *Fairy Tales and the Art of Subversion* (New York: Wildman, 1983).

79 This event also gave Freudian scholars like Robert Lee Wolf and U. C. Knoepflmacher the hermeneutical key to interpreting his fantasies. U. C. Knoepflmacher, *Ventures into Childland* (London: University of Chicago Press, 1998), 122–24.
80 Greville MacDonald, *George MacDonald and His Wife* (London: G. Allen & Unwin, 1924), 62. Henceforth in the notes, "MacDonald" by itself refers to George MacDonald.
81 Greville MacDonald, *George MacDonald and His Wife*, 64.
82 Greville MacDonald, *George MacDonald and His Wife*, 62.
83 William Raeper, *George MacDonald: Novelist and Victorian Visionary* (Tring: Lion, 1987), 38.
84 Greville MacDonald, *George MacDonald and His Wife*, 51.
85 Greville MacDonald, *George MacDonald and His Wife*, 51–66.
86 Glenn Edward Sadler, ed. *An Expression of Character: The Letters of George MacDonald* (Grand Rapids: Eerdmans, 1994), 17.
87 Sadler, *An Expression of Character*, 18.
88 George MacDonald, *A Dish of Orts* (1893). For a modern printing of this work, see *A Dish of Orts* (Whitehorn: Johannesen, 1996), 195.
89 MacDonald, *A Dish of Orts*, 195.
90 MacDonald, *A Dish of Orts*, 197–98.
91 MacDonald, *A Dish of Orts*, 200.
92 MacDonald, *A Dish of Orts*, 217.
93 Friedrich Nietzsche, *The Gay Science*, trans. Thomas Common (Mineola: Dover, 2006), 196.
94 Raeper, *George MacDonald*, 314.
95 MacDonald, *A Dish of Orts*, 318.
96 MacDonald, *A Dish of Orts*, 321.
97 MacDonald, *A Dish of Orts*, 320.
98 MacDonald, *A Dish of Orts*, 319.
99 Chesterton, *Orthodoxy*, 221.
100 The philosopher of history R. G. Collingwood succinctly describes the

first three of these methods in his only recently published book *The Philosophy of Enchantment*. The "philological" school began with the Grimm brothers in 1812 and culminated with Max Müller at the end of the nineteenth century. It essentially argued that myths were a "disease of language" in that early people personified abstract forces like fertility and death because language allowed them to name them. The "functional" school is best represented by Sir James Frazer's *The Golden Bough*, and it argued that folk stories are leftovers of customs and rituals—each had some original "function" in society. The psychological school was initiated by Freud and extended by Jung. In their different ways, Freud and Jung each argue that stories represent psychic states within individuals (fears, hopes, desires). Structuralism is best exemplified by Vladimir Propp and his book *The Morphology of the Folktale*, in which he attempts to show how all stories share the same component parts and can therefore be analysed in a scientific manner. Poststructuralism, meanwhile, is widely fragmented and thus not really a "school"; nevertheless, whether it is Marxist, feminist, or a reconceived psychoanalytical approach, poststructuralists tend to be concerned with power relations and the formation of personal identity. They recognize the latent power of fairytales and want to expose it either to liberate people or to harness it.

101 MacDonald, *A Dish of Orts*, 316.
102 MacDonald, *A Dish of Orts*, 317.
103 Thomas Gerold has observed in his recent monograph *Die Gotteskindschaft des Menschen*, "the fatherhood of God and the human as his child stands at the centre of MacDonald's theology" (*Die Gotteskindschaft des Menschen: Die Theologische Anthropologie bei George MacDonald* [Berlin: LIT, 2007], 2; my translation).
104 Originally titled *Good Words for the Young*, then changed in 1872 to the longer title. The periodical was a children's offshoot of Norman MacLeod's more popular *Good Words*, which ran from 1860–1905.
105 In this brief essay, MacDonald quotes the entirety of "My Heart Leaps Up When I Behold," which concludes with the three lines that MacDonald reworks in the above quotation: "The Child is father of the Man; / And I could wish my days to be / bound each to each by natural piety" ("The Child and the Man," in *Good Things for the Young of All Ages* [1873], 2).
106 Wordsworth prefaced "Intimations of Immortality" with the key final lines of "My Heart Leaps Up When I Behold," which he apparently composed the day before starting "Intimations." MacDonald called this poem "the outcome and essence of all Wordsworth's theories" (*England's Antiphon*, 255).

107 MacDonald, *England's Antiphon*, 255, 256.
108 John Pridmore, "George MacDonald's Estimate of Childhood," *International Journal of Children's Spirituality* 12, no. 1 (2007): 72.
109 U. C. Knoepflmacher, "The Balancing of Child and Adult: An Approach to Victorian Fantasies for Children," *Nineteenth-Century Fiction* 37, no. 4 (1983): 497.
110 Morton N. Cohen, *Lewis Carroll: A Biography* (New York: Papermac, 1995), 294. Toward the end of his life, Lewis Carroll did attempt to harmonize these two worlds more intentionally in his *Sylvie and Bruno* books, especially in the prefaces, where he speaks of combining "innocent merriment" with "the graver cadences of Life" (Carroll, *The Complete Works of Lewis Carroll*, 257).
111 Some critics argue that this hovering between two worlds is applicable to George MacDonald. Amy Billone, for example, claims that in "The Light Princess" "MacDonald forces readers to hover not only between innocence and experience but also between alternative methods of expression." While the levitating imagery is in one sense correct, Billone misses the crucial element of a directed hope when she says that there is a "vertiginous impossibility of progression" (Billone, "Hovering Between Irony and Innocence: George MacDonald's 'The Light Princess' and the Gravity of Childhood," *Mosaic* [2004]: 145).
112 MacDonald, *David Elginbrod*, 33.
113 In *The Princess and Curdie*, Curdie is given the ability to feel people's "true" hands, whether beast or human, and thereby know if they are regressing toward their animal nature or progressing toward their ultimate human one.
114 MacDonald, *A Dish of Orts*, 75.
115 George MacDonald, *The Hope of the Gospel* (Whitehorn: Johannesen, 2000), 202.
116 MacDonald, *The Hope of the Gospel*, 152.
117 MacDonald, *The Hope of the Gospel*, 49.
118 MacDonald, *The Hope of the Gospel*, 51–52.
119 MacDonald, *Miracles of Our Lord*, 372.
120 MacDonald, *The Hope of the Gospel*, 53.
121 MacDonald, *The Hope of the Gospel*, 55.
122 MacDonald, *The Hope of the Gospel*, 59.
123 George MacDonald, *Unspoken Sermons* (Whitehorn: Johannesen, 2004), 444. William Wordsworth, "Essay Supplementary to the Preface," in *The Poetical Works* (New Haven: Peck & Newton, 1836), xvi.
124 MacDonald, *The Hope of the Gospel*, 153.

125 Rolland Hein, *The Harmony Within* (Chicago: Cornerstone Press, 1999), 178.
126 Alison Milbank sets a precedent for this sort of approach with related authors in her recent book on Chesterton and Tolkien. She says, "I am not so much seeking to find Christian doctrines in the *content* of their fiction as in the *manner* in which they write" (*Chesterton and Tolkien as Theologians: The Fantasy of the Real* [London: T&T Clark, 2007], xv).

Chapter 6

1 Tolkien, *A Tolkien Miscellany*, 103.
2 George MacDonald, *Robert Falconer* (Whitehorn: Johannesen, 1999), 116. Earlier in the same book he also says, "boys are not unfrequently more given to metaphysics than older people are capable or, perhaps, willing to believe" (12).
3 In attempting to salvage fairytales from the nursery, Tolkien oddly overlooks this connection of children and fairytales. Tolkien, *A Tolkien Miscellany*, 115–22.
4 Tolkien, *A Tolkien Miscellany*, 114.
5 Tolkien, *A Tolkien Miscellany*, 145.
6 In this transition beyond the quotidian, the fairytale displays characteristics of play. To use Huizinga's description, one of the elements of play is that "[it] is distinct from 'ordinary life' both as to locality and duration. [. . .] It is 'played out' within certain limits of time and place" (*Homo Ludens*, 9).
7 Both sporting events and religious festivals create their own experiences of time, which are separate from mundane temporality. Hans-Georg Gadamer highlights how festivals have a "highly puzzling temporal structure" which excludes "the familiar distinction in time experience between present, memory, and expectation." Instead, he says, "the time experience of the festival is rather its *celebration*" (*Truth and Method*, 121).
8 MacDonald's first fairytale published in a periodical was "Cross Purposes," which appeared in the 1862 edition of *Beeton's Christmas Annual*. He also published "The Giant's Heart" immediately prior to *Adela Cathcart* (April 1864) in the Christmas edition of the *Illustrated London News* in 1863 under the title "Tell Us a Story." The important point, however, is that both appeared in a Christmas context.
9 The epithet to the novel is from "The Man of Lawes Tale" (lines 571–72): "Me list not of the chaf ne of the stre / Maken so long a tale as of the corn."
10 Up to 1864, MacDonald had yet to repeat any major literary genre, having also attempted lyric poetry (*Poems*, 1857), a drama (*If I Had a Father*,

never published), translations (*Twelve of the Spiritual Songs of Novalis*, 1851), literary essays ("Browning's 'Christmas Eve,'" 1853), and gothic short stories ("The Broken Swords," 1854). After 1864, however, his experimentation with form became more and more limited to that towering Victorian genre—the novel.

11 Raeper, *George MacDonald*, 173.
12 Sadler, *An Expression of Character*, 143.
13 The *Athenaeum* accused MacDonald of cobbling together "old bits of writing he had in his possession" (R. B. Shaberman, *George MacDonald: A Bibliographical Study* [Winchester: St. Paul's Bibliographies, 1990], 21).
14 Most recent critics note the parallels between Adela's listlessness and the Light Princess' lack of gravity, but otherwise discussion of the novel is rare. A prominent exception is Knoepflmacher, *Ventures into Childland*, 142–45.
15 George MacDonald, *Adela Cathcart* (Whitehorn: Johannesen, 1994), 1.
16 MacDonald, *Adela Cathcart*, 4.
17 MacDonald, *Adela Cathcart*, 4.
18 MacDonald, *Adela Cathcart*, 14.
19 MacDonald, *Adela Cathcart*, 4.
20 MacDonald, *Adela Cathcart*, 6.
21 Strangely, with the exception of his poetry, these and other comments in *Adela Cathcart* seem to be some of MacDonald's only extended reflections on Christmas. It was something of a ritual for MacDonald to write a Christmas poem every year that he would send to his friends and family. See Daniel Gabelman, "'The Day of All the Year': MacDonald's Christmas Aesthetic," *North Wind* 29 (2010).
22 MacDonald, *Adela Cathcart*, 19.
23 MacDonald, *Adela Cathcart*, 20.
24 Gadamer notes the "highly puzzling temporal structure" of festivals and claims that "a festival exists only in being celebrated" (*Truth and Method*, 121).
25 George MacDonald, *Sir Gibbie* (Whitehorn: Johannesen, 2000), 7.
26 MacDonald, *Adela Cathcart*, 52.
27 MacDonald, *Adela Cathcart*, 55.
28 MacDonald, *Adela Cathcart*, 55.
29 MacDonald, *Adela Cathcart*, 56.
30 MacDonald, *Adela Cathcart*, 56.
31 George MacDonald, *At the Back of the North Wind* (Whitehorn: Johannesen, 2002), 257.
32 MacDonald, *Adela Cathcart*, 57.

33 Max Lüthi states that the "formula immediately sets the beginning narrative off from the present, from the everyday world of teller and listener (or reader)" (*The Fairytale as Art Form and Portrait of Man*, trans. Jon Erickson [Bloomington: Indiana University Press, 1987], 49).

34 MacDonald interestingly puts some of John Ruskin's comments about the propriety of fairytales into the mouth of Mrs. Cathcart. Ruskin complained in a letter to MacDonald, "You *did* make me into Mrs Cathcart." Ruskin's primary criticism of "The Light Princess" was that sexuality should not be approached in a lighthearted way; rather, it needed "a graver and grander manner." In this most intimate of places, Ruskin struggled to take things lightly. Quoted in Knoepflmacher, *Ventures into Childland*, 140, 142.

35 MacDonald, *Adela Cathcart*, 60.

36 Little Daylight also has a christening scene with an evil witch, which MacDonald justifies by saying, "I never knew of any interference on the part of a wicked fairy that did not turn out a good thing in the end" (*At the Back of the North Wind*, 260).

37 MacDonald, *Adela Cathcart*, 99.

38 MacDonald, *Adela Cathcart*, 310. "My Uncle Peter" had been published previously in a Christmas edition of *The Queen* in 1861, which also included two poems: "Born on Christmas Eve" and "Died on Christmas Eve." Clearly, Christmas was prominently on MacDonald's mind in the early 1860s.

39 The other exception is "Little Daylight."

40 MacDonald, *Adela Cathcart*, 186–87.

41 Greville MacDonald, *George MacDonald and His Wife*, 285; MacDonald, *Adela Cathcart*, 186–87. Greville notes that "the germinal idea of *The Shadows*" appears in a collection of pieces gathered together for Louisa's father's seventy-fifth birthday.

42 MacDonald, *Adela Cathcart*, 197.

43 MacDonald, *Adela Cathcart*, 133.

44 MacDonald, *A Dish of Orts*, 200.

45 This phrase refers specifically to the red stones in the crown that the Shadows place on Ralph's head, but of course the crown is itself symbolic of their legitimacy and source of vitality. MacDonald is also recalling Smith's earlier comments about "the red of joy" from "the happy fires" on Christmas Eve. MacDonald, *Adela Cathcart*, 192, 6.

46 MacDonald, *Adela Cathcart*, 204.

47 The only complete exception is "Little Daylight," which was interpolated in *At the Back of the North Wind* and appeared in June 1870. "The

Carasoyn" meanwhile appeared in two parts, the first of which was not in a Christmas edition ("The Fairy Fleet," *The Argosy*, April 1866) but the second of which was ("The Fairy Cobbler," *Good Cheer*, December 1867). "The Golden Key," though not published serially, first appeared in *Dealings with Fairies* in time for the Christmas season of 1866. "The Wise Woman" began its serialization in *Good Things* during Christmas 1874, though it continued to run through July.

48 Greville MacDonald, *George MacDonald and His Wife*, 286–87.
49 Mieke Bal, *Narratology: Introduction to the Theory of Narrative*, 3rd ed. (Toronto: University of Toronto Press, 2009), 78.
50 MacDonald, *Adela Cathcart*, 6.
51 Bede, *The Reckoning of Time*, trans. Faith Wallis (Liverpool: Liverpool University Press, 1999), 13.
52 John Milbank, Graham Ward, and Catherine Pickstock, *Radical Orthodoxy: A New Theology* (London: Routledge, 1999), 247.
53 As we saw in a previous chapter, Karl Barth argues that Sabbath is a "continually recurring interruption" or "temporal pause" which is "the true time from which alone [humanity] can have other time" (*Church Dogmatics*, III.iv, 68, 69).
54 Gerhard von Rad, *Old Testament Theology*, trans. D. M. G. Stalker, vol. 2 (London: SCM Press, 1965), 102–3.
55 Karl Barth argues, "The time of man begins with a day of rest and not a day of work; with freedom and not with obligation; with a holiday and not with a task" (*Church Dogmatics*, III.ii, 458).
56 Catherine Pickstock, *After Writing: On the Liturgical Consummation of Philosophy* (Oxford: Blackwell, 1998), 222, 223.
57 In Judaism, Havdalah, Hebrew for "separation," is the ceremony that ends the Sabbath and ushers in the new week. It takes place at twilight when three stars appear in the night sky and begins with the prayer, "Blessed are you Lord, King of the universe who separates the holy from the mundane."
58 Pickstock, *After Writing*, 222.
59 George MacDonald, *The Complete Fairy Tales* (New York: Penguin, 1999), 120.
60 MacDonald, *The Complete Fairy Tales*, 133.
61 MacDonald, *The Complete Fairy Tales*, 104.
62 Robert Kirk, *The Secret Commonwealth of Elves, Fauns and Fairies* (New York: New York Review of Books, 2007), 5–6.
63 MacDonald, *The Complete Fairy Tales*, 106; George MacDonald, *Phantastes: A Faerie Romance for Men and Women* (Whitehorn: Johannesen, 2000), 22.

64 Knoepflmacher in his notes on "Cross Purposes" ambiguously refers to Alice's "namesake," seeming to suggest that MacDonald wrote the story in response to Carroll. This, however, is anachronistic, since "Cross Purposes" was published in December of 1862 (therefore finished by November at the latest), and Carroll did not begin composing *Alice* until November 13, 1862. The similarity of date, structure, and theme is highly suggestive, so much so that despite any explicit evidence, John Docherty claims that both authors agreed to create stories with similar plots as a sort of literary game. John Docherty, *The Literary Products of the Lewis Carroll-George MacDonald Friendship* (Lewiston, N.Y.: Mellen, 1995), 105–8.

65 Donald Rackin says that at the Mad Hatter's tea party, "time is frozen, and one of the most important concepts of common human experience is laughed out of existence" (Robert Phillips, ed. *Aspects of Alice* [Bungay: Penguin, 1971], 469).

66 In his preface to *Sylvie and Bruno Concluded* (1893), Carroll spends a long time complaining about "the waning spirit of reverence" toward religion. Speaking of innocent jests about faith, Carroll says, "surely such jests, if uttered with no consciousness of harm, must necessarily be also uttered with no consciousness, at the moment, of the *reality* of God, as a *living being*" (*The Complete Works of Lewis Carroll*, 257, 471).

67 Carroll, *The Complete Works of Lewis Carroll*, 120.

68 For MacDonald, memory points both backward and forward. There is no past in God; therefore, all past experiences are still alive in the eternal realm.

69 MacDonald, *The Complete Fairy Tales*, 119.

70 MacDonald, *Adela Cathcart*, 226–27.

71 MacDonald, *Adela Cathcart*, 74.

72 The subject of readerly transformation is explored more fully in chap. 8.

73 MacDonald, *Phantastes*, 47.

74 Bakhtin, *Rabelais and His World*, 10.

75 MacDonald, *Miracles of Our Lord*, 256.

76 Greville MacDonald, *George MacDonald and His Wife*, 285.

77 Exceptions include Patrick Maiwald, *The Journey in George MacDonald's Fantastic Fiction* (Trier: Wissenschaftlicher Verlag Trier, 2008), 64–68; John Pennington, "Thematic and Structual Subversion in the Fairy Tales and Fantasies of George MacDonald" (Ph.D. diss., Purdue University, 1987), 132–35.

78 MacDonald, *Adela Cathcart*, 186.

79 Even electing a sovereign is a grotesque combination of democracy and

monarchy, somewhat prescient of Chesterton's first fantasy, *The Napoleon of Nottinghill*.
80 MacDonald, *Adela Cathcart*, 187.
81 MacDonald, *Adela Cathcart*, 195, 217.
82 MacDonald, *Adela Cathcart*, 189.
83 MacDonald, *Adela Cathcart*, 196.
84 John Ruskin, *The Stones of Venice*, vol. 3 (London: J. M. Dent, 1905), 115. MacDonald and Ruskin met in 1863. In 1864 Ruskin also gave MacDonald a complete original set of *Modern Painters*. Greville MacDonald, *George MacDonald and His Wife*, 329.
85 MacDonald, *Adela Cathcart*, 195.
86 Ruskin, *Modern Painters*, III, 97.
87 MacDonald, *Adela Cathcart*, 194.
88 Bakhtin, *Rabelais and His World*, 39.
89 MacDonald, *Adela Cathcart*, 198.
90 According to Bakhtin, "[the grotesque] frees human consciousness, thought, and imagination for new potentialities" (*Rabelais and His World*, 49).
91 MacDonald, *Adela Cathcart*, 204.
92 MacDonald, *Adela Cathcart*, 213.
93 *Within and Without*, set in Catholic Italy, opens with a mention of carnival, while in *Phantastes* the fairy garden is described as a carnival. The other instances occur a decade and more later, once each in *St George and St Michael* (1876), *Castle Warlock* (1882), and *Donal Grant* (1883).
94 George MacDonald, *Rampolli* (Whitehorn: Johannesen, 1995), 69–71.
95 Bakhtin, *Rabelais and His World*, 245.
96 MacDonald, *Adela Cathcart*, 75.
97 MacDonald, *Adela Cathcart*, 75.
98 John Milbank, "Fictioning Things: Gift and Narrative," *Religion & Literature* 37, no. 3 (2005): 6.
99 Tolkien, *A Tolkien Miscellany*, 135.
100 MacDonald, *Unspoken Sermons*, 302.
101 MacDonald, *The Complete Fairy Tales*, 141.
102 MacDonald, *Unspoken Sermons*, 296.
103 MacDonald, *The Complete Fairy Tales*, 142.
104 Bakhtin, *Rabelais and His World*, 9.
105 Bakhtin, *Rabelais and His World*, 53.
106 MacDonald, *The Complete Fairy Tales*, 290.
107 MacDonald, *The Complete Fairy Tales*, 292.
108 MacDonald, *The Complete Fairy Tales*, 292.

109 MacDonald, *The Complete Fairy Tales*, 293.
110 MacDonald, *The Complete Fairy Tales*, 293.
111 MacDonald, *The Complete Fairy Tales*, 293.
112 In his fantasies, wise women appear in "The Golden Key," "The Wise Woman," "The Carasoyn," "Little Daylight," *The Princess and the Goblin*, *The Princess and Curdie*, *At the Back of the North Wind*, *Phantastes*, and *Lilith*. For a recent Jungian discussion of this archetype, see Katharine Bubel, "Knowing God Other-wise," *North Wind* 25 (2006): 1–17.
113 MacDonald, *The Complete Fairy Tales*, 125.
114 MacDonald, *Unspoken Sermons*, 308.
115 MacDonald, *Unspoken Sermons*, 308–9.
116 Erin Sheley argues that MacDonald "intended a direct allusion to pre-lapsarian figures" when he utilized the two "time patterns in Genesis"—the chronology of the patriarchs and the time compression of creation. Sheley, "From Eden to Eternity: The Timescales of Genesis in George MacDonald's 'The Golden Key' and *Lilith*," *Children's Literature Association Quarterly* 29, no. 4 (2004): 334.
117 Sheley, "From Eden to Eternity," 335. Sheley misreads death into the story when she says, "the Old Men also live for centuries in states of relative youth." The resonances with Genesis are intriguing and suggestive, but Sheley goes too far in claiming a direct allusion. Other scholars have made much more convincing cases for the connections with Greek mythology: see Fernando Soto, "Unearthing Ancient Sources in MacDonald's 'The Golden Key,'" *North Wind* 26 (2007).
118 MacDonald, *The Complete Fairy Tales*, 136.
119 MacDonald, *The Complete Fairy Tales*, 137.
120 MacDonald, *The Complete Fairy Tales*, 137.
121 MacDonald, *The Complete Fairy Tales*, 139.
122 Chesterton, *Orthodoxy*, 106.
123 Chesterton, *Orthodoxy*, 107.
124 MacDonald, *The Complete Fairy Tales*, 140.
125 MacDonald, *The Complete Fairy Tales*, 143.
126 MacDonald, *The Complete Fairy Tales*, 197.
127 MacDonald, *The Complete Fairy Tales*, 216.
128 MacDonald, *The Complete Fairy Tales*, 204.
129 MacDonald, *The Complete Fairy Tales*, 189.
130 MacDonald, *The Complete Fairy Tales*, 53.
131 Oscar Wilde, *Complete Shorter Fiction* (Oxford: Oxford University Press, 1979), 184.
132 Critics frequently miss this point. Whether it is pre-lapsarian Eden or a

purgatorial afterlife, most critics disassociate fairyland from all human historical temporality. Sheley argues that fairyland represents Eden and concludes, "[MacDonald's] desire to preserve [children's] pre-lapsarian spiritual purity as Adam and Eve in miniature, by rushing them quickly into the 'death' of salvation, is a more pleasant idea for adults than children themselves" ("From Eden to Eternity," 341). Marilyn Pemberton and Rolland Hein, on the other hand, argue the opposite, saying that fairyland is "ahistoric," a kind of purgatorial "afterlife," and "a type of intermediate world between the one we know and that of humanity's ultimate destination" (Pemberton, "The Ultimate Rite of Passage: Death and Beyond in 'The Golden Key' and *At the Back of the North Wind*," *North Wind* 27 [2008]: 38, 44; Hein, *The Harmony Within*, 188).

133 George MacDonald, *Poetical Works of George MacDonald*, vol. 1 (Whitehorn: Johannesen, 1996), 302–3.
134 MacDonald, *England's Antiphon*, 332.
135 MacDonald, *Poetical Works*, 1:304.
136 Barth, *Church Dogmatics*, III.2, 469.
137 MacDonald, *The Complete Fairy Tales*, 150.
138 MacDonald, *The Complete Fairy Tales*, 161.
139 MacDonald, *The Complete Fairy Tales*, 16.
140 George MacDonald, *The Princess and the Goblin* (Whitehorn: Johannesen, 2002), 13.
141 First appearing in the Christmas edition of *The Graphic* in 1879, "The History of Photogen and Nycteris: A Day and Night Märchen" was MacDonald's last fairytale, at the age of 53. *The Princess and Curdie*, though not published in book form until 1882, appeared in *Good Things* in 1877.
142 MacDonald, *The Complete Fairy Tales*, 304.
143 Lüthi, *The Fairytale as Art Form and Portrait of Man*, 133.
144 MacDonald, *The Complete Fairy Tales*, 340.
145 This passage comes in the middle of a Christmas sermon that concludes, "In the name of the holy child Jesus, I call upon you, this Christmas day, to cast care to the winds, and trust in God" (George MacDonald, *Annals of a Quiet Neighbourhood* [Whitehorn: Johannesen, 2004], 204, 208).
146 MacDonald, *The Complete Fairy Tales*, 119.
147 MacDonald, *The Complete Fairy Tales*, 209.
148 MacDonald, *The Complete Fairy Tales*, 223.
149 Jürgen Moltmann argues, "we therefore have to understand the liberating activity of God as the *immanence* of the eschatological kingdom of God, and the coming kingdom as the *transcendence* of the present lordship of God" (*The Way of Jesus Christ*, 98).

150 MacDonald, *The Complete Fairy Tales*, 196.
151 MacDonald, *The Complete Fairy Tales*, 44.
152 Jürgen Moltmann, *Theology of Hope* (London: SCM Press, 1967), 16.
153 MacDonald, *The Complete Fairy Tales*, 120. Speculating on the symbolic meaning of the golden key is a favorite scholarly game and one that shows the multivalence of MacDonald's image, so it seems strange that no critic has suggested hope as a primary meaning. Suggestions include a phallus or male-power, kindness, love, the imagination, Christ, and the "keys of the kingdom," to name a few. It could be argued that some of these have hope already embodied in them (the imagination, Christ, etc.)—oddly, though, no one explicitly makes the connection. Robert Lee Wolff, *The Golden Key: A Study of the Fiction of George MacDonald* (New Haven: Yale University Press, 1961), 137–38; Hein, *The Harmony Within*, 191; Pemberton, "The Ultimate Rite of Passage: Death and Beyond in 'The Golden Key' and *At the Back of the North Wind*," 39; Bonnie Gaarden, "'The Golden Key': A Double Reading," *Mythlore* 93 (2006): 38–39.
154 Dante, *The Portable Dante*, 584.
155 George MacDonald, *Poems* (London: Longman, Brown, Green, 1857), 143. MacDonald strangely seems to have edited this beautiful image out of the poem in later versions.
156 George MacDonald, *Poetical Works of George MacDonald*, vol. 2 (Whitehorn: Johannesen, 1996), 139.
157 Sadler, *An Expression of Character*, 354.
158 MacDonald, *The Complete Fairy Tales*, 144.
159 Dante, *The Portable Dante*, 585.
160 MacDonald, *The Complete Fairy Tales*, 164, 341.
161 *The Last Battle* concludes, "All their adventures in Narnia had only been the cover and the title page: now at last they were beginning Chapter One of the Great Story which no one on earth has read: which goes on for ever: in which every chapter is better than the one before" (C. S. Lewis, *The Chronicles of Narnia* [London: HarperCollins, 2004], 767).
162 "The Endless Ending" is the title of the final chapter of *Lilith*.
163 George MacDonald, *The Princess and Curdie* (Whitehorn: Johannesen, 2005), 319–20.
164 Moltmann, *Theology of Hope*, 338.

Chapter 7

1 Tolkien, *A Tolkien Miscellany*, 101.
2 MacDonald begins "The Fantastic Imagination" with a similar refusal to define the fairytale directly. MacDonald, *A Dish of Orts*, 313.

3   As Alison Milbank has shown, Tolkien's statement goes slightly against his bold poetic practice of using "Faerie" as a site of mediating the divine and "a way of rendering [the divine] visible" (*Chesterton and Tolkien as Theologians: The Fantasy of the Real*, 168).
4   G. K. Chesterton, *Selected Essays* (London: Collins Clear-Type Press, 1939), 205.
5   MacDonald, *The Complete Fairy Tales*, 209.
6   MacDonald, *The Complete Fairy Tales*, 209.
7   MacDonald, *A Dish of Orts*, 211–12.
8   MacDonald, *At the Back of the North Wind*, 83.
9   Lüthi, *Once Upon a Time*, 140.
10 MacDonald, *The Complete Fairy Tales*, 32.
11 MacDonald, *The Complete Fairy Tales*, 154.
12 MacDonald, *The Complete Fairy Tales*, 105.
13 MacDonald, *The Complete Fairy Tales*, 106.
14 MacDonald, *The Complete Fairy Tales*, 108.
15 MacDonald, *The Complete Fairy Tales*, 113.
16 MacDonald, *The Complete Fairy Tales*, 81.
17 Reis, *George MacDonald*, 81; Wolff, *The Golden Key*, 126; Humphrey Carpenter, *Secret Gardens: The Golden Age of Children's Literature* (Boston: Houghton Mifflin, 1985), 81.
18 Despite his otherwise careful reading of the story, Roderick McGillis oddly assumes that "Giantland and Fairyland are the same" (*For the Childlike*, ed. Roderick McGillis [Metuchen: Scarecrow, 1992], 8).
19 It is probably unwise to press the point too far, but it should also be noted that unlike fairyland, which in "Cross Purposes" borders on "a nice country village" with "nice country people," Giantland borders on "the country of common people." The word "common" typically connotes for MacDonald the unchildlike, especially in the construct "commonplace." In addition, Tricksey-Wee and Buffy-Bob are MacDonald's only blatantly "unchildlike" child protagonists. It would have been odd for MacDonald to have overlooked a point so crucial to his life philosophy.
20 McGillis, *For the Childlike*, 12–14.
21 MacDonald, *Adela Cathcart*, 338.
22 Lüthi, *Once Upon a Time*, 143.
23 Max Lüthi, *The European Folktale: Form and Nature* (Bloomington: Indiana University Press, 1986), 37–65.
24 See, e.g., his letters to Mrs. William Cowper-Temple in Sadler, *An Expression of Character*, 275–76.

25 George MacDonald, "The Family of Jesus," in *Proving the Unseen*, ed. William J. Peterson (New York: Ballantine, 1989).
26 MacDonald, *Miracles of Our Lord*, 304.
27 MacDonald, *The Complete Fairy Tales*, 121, 122.
28 MacDonald, *The Complete Fairy Tales*, 151.
29 MacDonald, *The Complete Fairy Tales*, 152.
30 MacDonald, *The Complete Fairy Tales*, 155.
31 MacDonald, *The Complete Fairy Tales*, 155.
32 MacDonald, *The Complete Fairy Tales*, 155.
33 MacDonald, *The Complete Fairy Tales*, 156.
34 Marion, *God Without Being*, 138.
35 MacDonald, *The Complete Fairy Tales*, 163.
36 MacDonald, *The Complete Fairy Tales*, 32.
37 MacDonald, *The Complete Fairy Tales*, 33.
38 Augustine, *Summa* II-II, 175.
39 MacDonald, *Unspoken Sermons*, 365. The carnival revelation of the salutatory effect of water discussed in the previous chapter also results from a kind of rapture as the king violently—though unintentionally—throws the princess into a new realm.
40 MacDonald, *The Complete Fairy Tales*, 33.
41 MacDonald, *The Complete Fairy Tales*, 38.
42 MacDonald, *The Complete Fairy Tales*, 38.
43 MacDonald, *The Complete Fairy Tales*, 38-39.
44 MacDonald, *The Complete Fairy Tales*, 43.
45 Jesus, interestingly, is the archetypal fairytale hero as seen by Lüthi's categories of complete "isolation" (freedom) and capacity for "universal interconnection" (love).
46 MacDonald, *The Complete Fairy Tales*, 50.
47 MacDonald, *The Complete Fairy Tales*, 50.
48 Milbank, "Fictioning Things," 6.
49 MacDonald, *The Complete Fairy Tales*, 59.
50 MacDonald, *What's Mine's Mine* (Whitehorn: Johannesen, 2000), 126.
51 MacDonald, *The Complete Fairy Tales*, 60.
52 MacDonald, *The Complete Fairy Tales*, 64.
53 Frank Riga, "The Platonic Imagery of George MacDonald and C. S. Lewis," in *For the Childlike*, ed. McGillis, 114.
54 MacDonald, *The Complete Fairy Tales*, 64.
55 MacDonald, *A Dish of Orts*, 30.
56 MacDonald borrows this phrase from Coleridge's "Hymn before Sunrise, in the Vale of Chamouni."

57 MacDonald, *The Complete Fairy Tales*, 307, 309.
58 MacDonald, *The Complete Fairy Tales*, 309.
59 MacDonald, *The Complete Fairy Tales*, 311.
60 MacDonald, *The Complete Fairy Tales*, 312.
61 MacDonald, *The Complete Fairy Tales*, 312.
62 Greville MacDonald, *George MacDonald and His Wife*, 481.
63 Greville MacDonald, *George MacDonald and His Wife*, 349.
64 MacDonald, *The Complete Fairy Tales*, 312–313.
65 MacDonald, *The Complete Fairy Tales*, 313.
66 MacDonald, *The Complete Fairy Tales*, 323.
67 MacDonald, *The Complete Fairy Tales*, 314.
68 MacDonald, *A Dish of Orts*, 314–15.
69 Colin N. Manlove calls this one of the major "inconsistencies" in MacDonald's work, saying that "the chaotic element" so frightened MacDonald that he was "driven to impose meaning on it." Manlove dichotomizes MacDonald into a conscious and unconscious artist who privileges the unconscious (the mystical and symbolic) but who nevertheless cannot fully suppress the conscious (the scientific and rational). Manlove, *Modern Fantasy* (Cambridge: Cambridge University Press, 1978), 77.
70 MacDonald, *Phantastes*, 12. The Johannesen edition retains the two original textual errors noted by Robert Lee Wolff (*Golden Key*, 42–44). The German text I have translated, therefore, is as follows: "Ein Mährchen ist wie ein Traumbild ohne Zuzammenhang. Ein Ensemble wunderbarer Dinge und Begebenheiten [. . .] In einem echten Mährchen muss alles wunderbar, geheimnissvoll und zusammenhängend sein; alles belebt, jedes auf eine andere Art. Die ganze Nautr muss wunderlich mit der ganzen Geisterwelt gemischt sein; hier tritt die Zeit der Anarchie, der Gestzlosigkeit, Freiheit, der Naturstand der Natur, die Zeit vor der Welt."
71 Where Luther's Bible uses the word *wunder*, the Authorized Version uses both "wonder" and "miracle" (cf. Exod 7:3, 9). In English, "miracle" has retained more of its association with the supernatural, whereas "wonder" is often just a mundane mode of questioning ("I wonder," "I was wondering").
72 Recent scholarship has noted some connections between miracles and MacDonald's artistic practice. John Pridmore argues that MacDonald's work is "transfiguring fantasy" in that he calls into question "the distinctions we customarily make between the worlds we move in" and between fiction and reality, and Roderick McGillis believes that MacDonald presents "fantasy as miracle" because "[fantasy] delivers impossible things, including impossible communities we sometimes refer to as utopias."

Both articles are highly suggestive, but neither listens closely enough to what MacDonald actually says. Despite being full of keen insights into the transfiguration and MacDonald, the most striking thing about Pridmore's article is that he never mentions MacDonald's view of the transfiguration, while McGillis seems more interested in expounding Lacanian theory than exploring MacDonald's understanding of miracles. Yet their general intuition of relating miracles to MacDonald's aesthetic practice is vital to the cosmology of fairyland. John Pridmore, "George MacDonald's Transfiguring Fantasy," *Seven* 20 (2000): 62. Roderick McGillis, "Fantasy as Miracle: George MacDonald's The Miracles of Our Lord," in *George MacDonald: Literary Heritage and Heirs*, ed. Roderick McGillis (Wayne: Zossima, 2008), 214.

73 MacDonald, *Miracles of Our Lord*, 434.
74 MacDonald, *Miracles of Our Lord*, 436.
75 MacDonald, *Miracles of Our Lord*, 437.
76 MacDonald, *Miracles of Our Lord*, 439.
77 MacDonald, *The Complete Fairy Tales*, 115.
78 This is a typical allegorical reading. See, e.g., Hein, *The Harmony Within*, 186.
79 MacDonald, *Miracles of Our Lord*, 438.
80 MacDonald, *Miracles of Our Lord*, 405.
81 MacDonald, *Miracles of Our Lord*, 233.
82 MacDonald, *The Complete Fairy Tales*, 218–19.
83 For an interesting exploration of this connection, see Jason Fisher, "Reluctantly Inspired: George MacDonald and J. R. R. Tolkien," *North Wind* 25 (2006): 113–20.
84 MacDonald, *The Complete Fairy Tales*, 236.
85 MacDonald, *The Complete Fairy Tales*, 237.
86 MacDonald, *Miracles of Our Lord*, 411.
87 MacDonald, *Miracles of Our Lord*, 403.
88 MacDonald, *Miracles of Our Lord*, 400.
89 Katharine Briggs, *The Fairies in Tradition and Literature* (London: Routledge, 1967), 232; Bubel, "Knowing God Other-wise," 15; Rolland Hein, *George MacDonald: Victorian Mythmaker* (Nashville: StarSong, 1993), 187.
90 MacDonald, *The Complete Fairy Tales*, 142. This reading would also eliminate some of the wild speculation about the separation of Mossy and Tangle and their different paths. Roderick McGillis, for instance, says that Mossy's leaving Tangle "may signal his mid-life crisis" ("A Fairytale Is Just a Fairytale: George MacDonald and the Queering of Fairy," *Marvels & Tales* 17, no. 1 [2003]: 96).

91 The best case for a Christ figure is the Old Man of the Fire, who is "the oldest man of all" and simultaneously the most childlike and is also the only person who has been to the country whence the shadows fall.
92 MacDonald, *Hope of the Gospel*, 128.
93 George MacDonald, *The Portent and Other Stories* (Whitehorn: Johannesen, 1999), 45.
94 This is the belief of Diamond in MacDonald's *At the Back of the North Wind*: "Little Diamond possessed the secret of life, and was himself what he was so ready to think the lowest living thing—an angel of God with something special to say or do" (345).
95 MacDonald, *The Complete Fairy Tales*, 30.
96 MacDonald, *The Complete Fairy Tales*, 51.
97 Ironically, despite his dislike for people calling his stories allegories, Tolkien indulged in the same criticism of MacDonald's stories.
98 MacDonald, *A Dish of Orts*, 317.
99 MacDonald, *A Dish of Orts*, 320.
100 MacDonald comments on this passage in his chapter on nature in *Miracles of Our Lord*, 410.
101 MacDonald, *Unspoken Sermons*, 428.
102 MacDonald's stance on the Trinity is somewhat ambiguous since he almost never uses the word except when translating others. He does, however, speak of all three persons of the Trinity throughout his works. It is probable that MacDonald avoided discussing the doctrine because of his connections with Unitarians and because he believed that Christian unity was more important than any single teaching. In a sermon preached at Unitarian chapel, for example, MacDonald says, "we are not here to convince men, but to let our light shine." Intriguingly though, MacDonald then concludes his sermon with a Trinitarian prayer: "May the God of peace give you his peace; may the love of Christ constrain you; may the gift of the Holy Spirit be yours" (*A Dish of Orts*, 297).
103 Sadler, *An Expression of Character*, 287.

Chapter 8

1 Tolkien, *A Tolkien Miscellany*, 115–16; C. S. Lewis, "On Three Ways of Writing for Children," in *C. S. Lewis: Essay Collection & Other Short Pieces*, ed. Lesley Walmsley (London: HarperCollins, 2000), 508.
2 Pierre Mabille, *Mirror of the Marvelous* (Rochester: Inner Traditions, 1998), 7.
3 Lüthi, *European Folktale*, 89.
4 Tolkien calls this "Secondary Belief," but he questions whether or not

children are specially gifted at achieving this condition. He does, however, grudgingly admit that having the heart of a little child "is necessary to all high adventure, into kingdoms both less and far greater than Faerie" (*A Tolkien Miscellany*, 119, 121).

5. The two exceptions are "The History of Photogen and Nycteris" and "The Wise Woman."
6. MacDonald, *The Complete Fairy Tales*, 56.
7. Marion, *God Without Being*, 126.
8. Marion, *God Without Being*, 11, 18.
9. Augustine, *City of God*, 477. XII, 6.
10. Augustine, *City of God*, 572. XIV, 13.
11. Jenson, *The Gravity of Sin*, 24.
12. MacDonald hints at and sketches an entire shadow-cosmology in this story, including, in addition to the mirror-creatures, ghosts (with whom "Fairyland will not willingly have much to do"), angels ("white shadows cast in heaven from the Light of Light"), and "shadows of the mind" (strange shadows with human eyes and faces which Adela calls the "mysteries in the midst of mystery"). MacDonald here speculates that there might be other beings with a unique ontological status. The Shadows have an entire political and religious structure (their public forum is their church), and MacDonald suggests that so might these other creatures.
13. MacDonald, *The Complete Fairy Tales*.
14. MacDonald believed that mirrors and reflections had polarized potentialities in that they could either fix the gaze of the self upon itself or reveal strangeness and draw the viewer out of the self.
15. Marion, *God Without Being*, 128.
16. MacDonald, *The Complete Fairy Tales*, 61.
17. MacDonald, *Adela Cathcart*, 217.
18. MacDonald, *The Complete Fairy Tales*, 80.
19. MacDonald, *Miracles of Our Lord*, 205–6.
20. MacDonald, *The Complete Fairy Tales*, 69.
21. Potter and Simpson, eds., *The Sermons of John Donne*, 83.
22. MacDonald, *The Complete Fairy Tales*, 60.
23. "The Wise Woman" has two girls, and "The Carasoyn" only really focuses on Colin, though Fairy does play an important role. With just one old man, "The Shadows" is the most anomalous.
24. At one point in the telling of "The Shadows" in *Adela Cathcart*, there is a poem within a shadow's story within Rinkelmann's story within John Smith's story within MacDonald's novel.

25 MacDonald, *The Complete Fairy Tales*, 106.
26 See McGillis, "A Fairytale Is Just a Fairytale: George MacDonald and the Queering of Fairy."
27 Since Jack Zipes' book *Fairy Tales and the Art of Subversion*, many scholars have argued that MacDonald's fairytales contain acute criticisms of Victorian culture.
28 Roger Lancelyn Green, *Tellers of Tales* (Leicester: Edmund Ward, 1946), 63.
29 MacDonald, *The Complete Fairy Tales*, 255.
30 MacDonald, *The Complete Fairy Tales*, 248.
31 MacDonald, *The Portent*, i.
32 MacDonald, *Poetical Works*, 2:13.
33 George MacDonald, *Castle Warlock* (Whitehorn: Johannesen, 1998), 47–48.
34 Hein, *The Harmony Within*, 178.
35 Prickett, *Romanticism and Religion*, 239.
36 MacDonald, *Phantastes*, 119.
37 MacDonald, *Phantastes*, 130.
38 MacDonald, *Phantastes*, 132.
39 MacDonald, *Phantastes*, 135–37.
40 MacDonald, *Phantastes*, 124.
41 MacDonald, *Phantastes*, 123.
42 MacDonald, *Poetical Works*, 2:14.
43 MacDonald, *Phantastes*, 162.
44 MacDonald, *Phantastes*, 162.
45 Samuel Taylor Coleridge, *The Major Works*, ed. H. J. Jackson (Oxford: Oxford University Press, 2000), 314. See also Shelley's "Mont Blanc" for a similar view of the power of the imagination.
46 Oscar Wilde, *De Profundis and Other Writings* (London: Penguin, 1986), 79.
47 MacDonald, *Phantastes*, 137.
48 MacDonald, *Phantastes*, 134.
49 Sadler, *An Expression of Character*, 354.
50 MacDonald, *Robert Falconer*, 452.
51 Fernando Soto, "Mirrors in MacDonald's *Phantastes*: A Reflective Structure," *North Wind* 23 (2004): 28. See also John Docherty, "A Note on the Structure and Conclusion of *Phantastes*," *North Wind* 7 (1988); Roderick McGillis, "The Community of the Centre: Structure and Theme in *Phantastes*," in *For the Childlike*, ed. Roderick McGillis (Metuchen: Scarecrow, 1992).

52 Wolff says that on account of its earthly setting, the story of Cosmo is "out of place in the library of the fairy palace," but this surely misses MacDonald's point that "Faerie invades the world of men" (*The Golden Key*, 78; MacDonald, *Phantastes*, 154).
53 MacDonald, *Phantastes*, 139.
54 MacDonald, *Phantastes*, 140.
55 MacDonald, *Phantastes*, 187.
56 There is a Dantesque ascent via descent. While Anodos still fails in the second half—most notably in allowing himself to be imprisoned by his shadow—these failures spur him on to greater acts of humility and letting go of himself.
57 MacDonald here quotes from the revised version. After its release in 1881, MacDonald strongly supported the revised version as the most accurate of all English translations.
58 MacDonald, *Unspoken Sermons*, 452. MacDonald interestingly defines mysticism in this sermon as "the exercise of a power of seeing, as by spiritual refraction, truths that had not, perhaps have not yet, risen above the human horizon; at another, the result of a wide-eyed habit of noting the analogies and correspondences between the concentric regions of creation."
59 MacDonald, *Unspoken Sermons*, 454.
60 MacDonald, *Unspoken Sermons*, 457.
61 MacDonald, *Phantastes*, 153–54.
62 Wordsworth in *The Prelude* says that when musing on his childhood "often do I seem / Two consciousnesses, conscience of myself / and of some other Being" (2.31–33). MacDonald takes this concept of personal memory and applies it to the reading of stories, suggesting that the stories have a power as emotive and powerful as that of personal memory.
63 MacDonald, *A Dish of Orts*, 320.
64 MacDonald, *A Dish of Orts*, 321.
65 MacDonald, *A Dish of Orts*, 321.
66 MacDonald, *A Dish of Orts*, 322.
67 Barth, *Ethics*, 505.
68 MacDonald, *Miracles of Our Lord*, 379.
69 MacDonald, *Miracles of Our Lord*, 267.
70 MacDonald, *Miracles of Our Lord*, 281.
71 This is Sir Walter Raleigh's phrase from the first chapter of *The History of the World*. MacDonald quotes it while discussing the transfiguration in *Miracles of Our Lord*, 434.
72 Wilhelm Worringer, *Abstraction and Empathy: A Contribution to the*

Psychology of Style, trans. Michael Bullock (New York: International Universities Press, 1980), 13.

73 G. K. Chesterton, *Robert Browning* (London: Macmillan, 1903), 185. This argument also harmonizes with how MacDonald describes fairytales as like "a sonata" which rouses "related, if not identical, feelings, but probably not one common thought" (*A Dish of Orts*, 318).
74 MacDonald, *Miracles of Our Lord*, 234.
75 MacDonald, *Miracles of Our Lord*, 235, 233.
76 MacDonald, *Miracles of Our Lord*, 247.
77 MacDonald, *Miracles of Our Lord*, 247.
78 MacDonald, *The Complete Fairy Tales*, 142.
79 MacDonald, *The Complete Fairy Tales*, 163–64.
80 Lüthi, *European Folktale*, 97; MacDonald, *A Dish of Orts*, 130.
81 Lüthi, *European Folktale*, 36.
82 MacDonald, *A Dish of Orts*, 320.
83 Roderick McGillis observes how "MacDonald has a tendency to observe a miracle from the perspective of a particular person" ("Fantasy as Miracle: George MacDonald's *The Miracles of Our Lord*," 213).
84 MacDonald, *Miracles of Our Lord*, 439.
85 MacDonald, *Miracles of Our Lord*, 351.
86 MacDonald, *Miracles of Our Lord*, 412.
87 Moltmann, *Theology and Joy*, 28.
88 MacDonald, *Poetical Works*, 1:177.
89 MacDonald, *A Dish of Orts*, 42.

Conclusion

1 David Darling, *Gravity's Arc: The Story of Gravity, from Aristotle to Einstein and Beyond* (Hoboken, N.J.: Wiley, 2006), 196.
2 Wilczek, *The Lightness of Being*, 177–204.
3 G. K. Chesterton, "Introduction," in *George MacDonald and His Wife* (London: George Allen & Unwin, 1924), 9.
4 Chesterton, "Introduction," 10–11.
5 The fact that white horses were also associated in Chesterton's mind with Alfred the Great and the prehistoric art of England does not invalidate the impact of MacDonald's image. It rather serves to substantiate MacDonald's claim that no writer can "help his words and figures falling into such combinations in the mind of another as he had himself not foreseen" and that by lightly stimulating his reader through symbols and images he can "gladly wake" the "music in [his] reader" (*A Dish of Orts*, 320, 321).
6 "It is not that [MacDonald] dresses up men and movements as knights

and dragons, but that he thinks that knights and dragons, really existing in the eternal world, are dressed up here as men and movements." Chesterton, "George MacDonald and His Work."
7. Chesterton, "Introduction," 11.
8. C. S. Lewis, *Surprised by Joy* (London: Bles, 1955), 169–71.
9. Prickett has an extended discussion of this passage in which he concludes "What *Phantastes* seems to have given to Lewis above all was a glimpse of the possibility of a developing synthesis in which language, literature, and thus the entire record of human imaginative experience could be brought into a unified whole" (*Victorian Fantasy*, 179).
10. This description, of course, is analogous to MacDonald's discussion of how a true vision of fairyland does not make the everyday world seem less real but more: "it had made common things disclose the wonderful that was in them" (*The Complete Fairy Tales*, 64).
11. Lewis, *Surprised by Joy*, 171.
12. Chesterton, "George MacDonald and His Work."
13. MacDonald, *The Complete Fairy Tales*, 341.

Bibliography

Agamben, Giorgio. *The Time That Remains*. Translated by Patricia Dailey. Stanford: Stanford University Press, 2005.
Anonymous. *A Call to Seriousness in Religion*. London: Tho. Parkhurst, 1693.
Aquinas, Thomas, St. *Summa Theologiae*. Translated by Fathers of the English Dominican Province. London: Burns, Oates & Washbourne, 1922.
Aristotle. *Physica: Translatio Vaticana*. Leiden: Brill, 1990.
Aristotle. *Physics*. Translated by Robin Waterfield. Oxford: Oxford University Press, 1999.
Arnold, Matthew. *Literature and Dogma*. London: Smith, Elder, 1873.
———. "My Countrymen," *Cornhill Magazine*, vol. 13, February 1866.
———. *Selected Prose*. London: Penguin, 1987.
Auden, W. H. "Afterword." In *The Golden Key*, by George MacDonald. New York: Farrar, Straus & Giroux, 1967.
———. *Collected Poems*. New York: Vintage International, 1991.
———. *Forewords and Afterwords*. London: Faber & Faber, 1973.
Augustine. *City of God*. Translated by Henry Bettenson. London: Penguin, 2003.
———. *The Confessions of St. Augustine*. Translated by E. B. Pusey. London: Dent, 1907.
Bakhtin, Mikhail M. *The Dialogic Imagination*. Translated by Michael Holquist and Caryl Emerson. Austin: University of Texas Press, 1981.

———. *Rabelais and His World*. Translated by Helene Iswolsky. Bloomington: Indiana University Press, 1984.

Bal, Mieke. *Narratology: Introduction to the Theory of Narrative*. 3rd ed. Toronto: University of Toronto Press, 2009.

Balthasar, Hans Urs von. *The Glory of the Lord: A Theological Aesthetics*. Vol. 1, *Seeing the Form*. Translated by Erasmo Leiva-Merikakis. Edited by Joseph Fessio and John Kenneth Riches. 7 vols. New York: Ignatius Press, 1983.

Barth, Karl. *Church Dogmatics*. Edited by Thomas F. Torrance. Translated by Geoffrey William Bromiley. 2nd ed. 14 vols. London: T&T Clark, 2004.

———. *Ethics*. Translated by Geoffrey Bromiley. London: T&T Clark, 1992.

Bede. *The Reckoning of Time*. Translated by Faith Wallis. Liverpool: Liverpool University Press, 1999.

Beerbohm, Max. *The Happy Hypocrite*. New York: John Lane, 1897.

Berger, Peter L. *Redeeming Laughter: The Comic Dimension of Human Experience*. Berlin: de Gruyter, 1997.

Billone, Amy. "Hovering between Irony and Innocence: George MacDonald's 'The Light Princess' and the Gravity of Childhood." *Mosaic* (2004): 135–48.

Bradley, Ian. *The Call to Seriousness: The Evangelical Impact on the Victorians*. London: Jonathan Cape, 1976.

Briggs, Katharine. *The Fairies in Tradition and Literature*. London: Routledge, 1967.

Bubel, Katharine. "Knowing God Other-Wise." *North Wind* 25 (2006): 1–17.

Butler, Alban. *Butler's Lives of the Saints*, vol. 3. Edited by Herbert Thurston and Donald Attwater. New York: P. J. Kennedy & Sons, 1956.

Byron, Lord. *The Major Works*. Edited by Jerome McGann. Oxford: Oxford University Press, 2000.

Caillois, Roger. *Man and the Sacred*. Translated by Meyer Barash. Chicago: University of Illinois Press, 2001.

Carlyle, Thomas. *Past and Present; Chartism*. New York: Harper & Brothers, 1862.

Carlyle, Thomas, and G. B. Tennyson. *A Carlyle Reader: Selections from the Writings of Thomas Carlyle*. Cambridge: Cambridge University Press, 1984.

Carpenter, Humphrey. *Secret Gardens: The Golden Age of Children's Literature*. Boston: Houghton Mifflin, 1985.
Carroll, Lewis. *The Complete Works of Lewis Carroll*. New York: Barnes & Noble, 1994.
Chesterton, G. K. *Autobiography*. London: Hutchinson, 1950.
———. "A Drama of Dolls." In *Alarms and Discursions*, 29–34. London: Methuen, 1910.
———. *The Everlasting Man*. San Francisco: Ignatius, 1993.
———. "George Macdonald." *The Daily News*, September 23, 1905.
———. "George Macdonald and His Work." *The Daily News*, June 11, 1901.
———. "Introduction." In *George MacDonald and His Wife*. London: George Allen & Unwin, 1924.
———. "A Midsummer Night's Dream." In *The Common Man*, 10–21. London: Sheed & Ward, 1950.
———. *Orthodoxy*. London: John Lane, 1927.
———. "Oscar Wilde." In *Oscar Wilde: The Critical Heritage*. Edited by Karl Beckson, 311–13. London: Routledge & Kegan Paul, 1997.
———. *Robert Browning*. London: Macmillan, 1903.
———. *Selected Essays*. London: Collins Clear-Type Press, 1939.
———. *The Victorian Age in Literature*. London: Williams & Norgate, 1923.
Clemens, David M. "The Law of Sin and Death: Ecclesiastes and Genesis 1–3." *Themelios* 19, no. 3 (1994): 5–8.
Cohen, David. *The Development of Play*. London: Routledge, 2006.
Cohen, Morton N., ed. *The Letters of Lewis Carroll*. 2 vols. London: Macmillan, 1979.
———. *Lewis Carroll: A Biography*. New York: Papermac, 1995.
Coleridge, Samuel Taylor. *The Major Works*. Edited by H. J. Jackson. Oxford: Oxford University Press, 2000.
Cox, Harvey. *The Feast of Fools: A Theological Essay on Festivity and Fantasy*. Cambridge, Mass.: Harvard University Press, 1969.
Crossan, John Dominic. *Cliffs of Fall: Paradox and Polyvalence in the Parables of Jesus*. New York: Seabury Press, 1980.
———. *The Dark Interval: Towards a Theology of Story*. Niles: Argus Communications, 1975.
Dante. *The Portable Dante*. Translated by Mark Musa. London: Penguin, 2003.

Darling, David. *Gravity's Arc: The Story of Gravity, from Aristotle to Einstein and Beyond*. Hoboken, N.J.: Wiley, 2006.

Davis, Philip. *The Victorians*, The Oxford English Literary History. Oxford: Oxford University Press, 2002.

Derrida, Jacques. "Structure, Sign and Play in the Discourse of the Human Sciences." In *Writing & Difference*, translated by Alan Bass, 278–93. London: Routledge, 1978.

Dickens, Charles. *Hard Times*. London: Oxford University Press, 1968.

———. *Miscellaneous Papers*. London: Chapman & Hall, 1908.

Dickson, Gwen Griffith, and Johann Georg Hamann. *Johann Georg Hamann's Relational Metacriticism*. Berlin: de Gruyter, 1995.

Docherty, John. *The Literary Products of the Lewis Carroll-George MacDonald Friendship*. Lewiston, N.Y.: Mellen, 1995.

———. "A Note on the Structure and Conclusion of *Phantastes*." *North Wind* 7 (1988): 25–30.

Edgeworth, Maria. *Moral Tales*. Leipzig: Bernhard Tauchnitz, 1866.

———. *Practical Education*. New York: Harper & Brothers, 1855.

Eliot, George. *Adam Bede*. New York: The Modern Library, 2002.

———. "The Natural History of German Life." In *The Essays of George Eliot*, edited by Thomas Pinney, 266–99. London: Routledge & Kegan Paul, 1963.

Erasmus, Desiderius. *The Praise of Folly and Other Writings*. Translated by Robert M. Adams. New York: W.W. Norton, 1989.

Evagrius Ponticus and Robert E. Sinkewicz. *Evagrius of Pontus: The Greek Ascetic Corpus*. Oxford: Oxford University Press, 2003.

Fisher, Jason. "Reluctantly Inspired: George MacDonald and J. R. R. Tolkien." *North Wind* 25 (2006): 113–20.

France, R. T. *The Gospel of Mark: A Commentary on the Greek Text*. Carlisle: Paternoster, 2002.

Furnish, Victor Paul. *II Corinthians*, The Anchor Bible. London: Yale University Press, 2005.

Gaarden, Bonnie. "'The Golden Key': A Double Reading." *Mythlore* 93 (2006): 35–52.

Gabelman, Daniel. "'The Day of All the Year': MacDonald's Christmas Aesthetic," *North Wind* 29 (2010): 11–23.

Gadamer, Hans-Georg. *Truth and Method*. Translated by Joel Weinsheimer and Donald Marshall. New York: Continuum, 2004.

Gerold, Thomas. *Die Gotteskindschaft des Menschen: Die Theologische Anthropologie bei George MacDonald*. Berlin: LIT, 2007.
Gray, Donald. "The Uses of Victorian Laughter." *Victorian Studies* 10 (1966): 145–76.
Green, Roger Lancelyn. *Tellers of Tales*. Leicester: Edmund Ward, 1946.
Hart, David Bentley. *The Beauty of the Infinite*. Grand Rapids: Eerdmans, 2003.
Hein, Rolland. *George MacDonald: Victorian Mythmaker*. Nashville: StarSong, 1993.
———. *The Harmony Within*. Chicago: Cornerstone Press, 1999.
The Holy Bible, English Standard Version. Wheaton, Ill.: Good News Publishers, 2001.
Houghton, Walter E. *The Victorian Frame of Mind, 1830–1870*. London: Yale University Press, 1957.
Huizinga, Johan. *Homo Ludens: A Study of the Play-Element in Culture*. Boston: Beacon Press, 1955.
Jacobs, Alan. *A Theology of Reading: The Hermeneutics of Love*. Oxford: Westview, 2001.
Jenson, Matt. *The Gravity of Sin*. London: T&T Clark, 2006.
Kant, Immanuel. "An Answer to the Question: What is Enlightenment?" In *What is Enlightenment?*, edited by James Schmidt, 58–64. Berkeley: University of California Press, 1996.
———. *The Moral Law: Groundwork of the Metaphysics of Morals*. Translated by H. J. Paton. London: Routledge, 1997.
Ker, Ian. *G. K. Chesterton: A Biography*. Oxford: Oxford University Press, 2011.
Kirk, Robert. *The Secret Commonwealth of Elves, Fauns and Fairies*. New York: New York Review of Books, 2007.
Knoepflmacher, U. C. "The Balancing of Child and Adult: An Approach to Victorian Fantasies for Children." *Nineteenth-Century Fiction* 37, no. 4 (1983): 497–530.
———. "Introduction." In *The Complete Fairy Tales of George MacDonald*, edited by U. C. Knoepflmacher, vii–xx. Penguin: New York, 1999.
———. *Ventures into Childland*. London: University of Chicago Press, 1998.
Kott, Jan. *The Bottom Translation*. Translated by Daniela Miedzyrzecka

and Lillian Vallee. Evanston, Ill.: Northwestern University Press, 1987.

Kundera, Milan. *The Unbearable Lightness of Being*. Translated by Michael Henry Heim. New York: HarperPerennial, 1999.

Laski, Marghanita. *Ecstasy: A Study of Some Secular & Religious Experiences*. London: The Cresset Press, 1961.

Lewis, C. S. *The Chronicles of Narnia*. London: HarperCollins, 2004.

———. *Experiment in Criticism*. Cambridge: Cambridge University Press, 1961.

———. *George MacDonald: An Anthology*. London: Bles, 1946.

———. *The Great Divorce*. London: Bles, 1946.

———. *Mere Christianity*. London: Bles, 1952.

———. *Surprised by Joy*. London: Bles, 1955.

———. "On Three Ways of Writing for Children." In *C. S. Lewis: Essay Collection & Other Short Pieces*, edited by Lesley Walmsley, 505–14. London: HarperCollins, 2000.

Lewis, Charlton, and Charles Short. *A Latin Dictionary*. Glasgow: Oxford University Press, 1951.

Longman, Tremper. *The Book of Ecclesiastes*. Grand Rapids: Eerdmans, 1998.

Lüthi, Max. *The European Folktale: Form and Nature*. Bloomington: Indiana University Press, 1986.

———. *The Fairytale as Art Form and Portrait of Man*. Translated by Jon Erickson. Bloomington: Indiana University Press, 1987.

———. *Once Upon a Time: On the Nature of Fairy Tales*. Translated by Lee Chadeayne and Paul Gottwald. Bloomington: Indiana University Press, 1976.

Lux, Rüdiger. "'Ich, Kohelet, Big König . . .' Die Fiktion Als Schlüssel Zur Wirklichkeit in Kohelet 1.12–2.26." *EvT* 50 (1990): 331–42.

Mabille, Pierre. *Mirror of the Marvelous*. Rochester: Inner Traditions, 1998.

MacDonald, George. *Adela Cathcart*. Whitehorn: Johannesen, 1994.

———. *Annals of a Quiet Neighbourhood*. Whitehorn: Johannesen, 2004.

———. *At the Back of the North Wind*. Whitehorn: Johannesen, 2002.

———. *Castle Warlock*. Whitehorn: Johannesen, 1998.

———. "The Child and the Man." In *Good Things for the Young of All Ages*. London: Henry S. King, 1872.

———. *The Complete Fairy Tales*. New York: Penguin, 1999.
———. *David Elginbrod*. Whitehorn: Johannesen, 1995.
———. *A Dish of Orts*. Whitehorn: Johannesen, 1996.
———. *England's Antiphon*. Whitehorn, Calif.: Johannesen, 1996.
———. "The Family of Jesus." In *Proving the Unseen*, edited by William J. Peterson, 10–20. New York: Ballantine, 1989.
———. *The Hope of the Gospel*. Whitehorn: Johannesen, 2000.
———. *Miracles of Our Lord*. Whitehorn: Johannesen, 2000.
———. *Phantastes: A Faerie Romance for Men and Women*. Whitehorn: Johannesen, 2000.
———. *Poems*. London: Longman, Brown, Green, 1857.
———. *Poetical Works of George MacDonald*, vols. 1 & 2. Whitehorn: Johannesen, 1996.
———. *The Portent and Other Stories*. Whitehorn: Johannesen, 1999.
———. *The Princess and Curdie*. Whitehorn: Johannesen, 2005.
———. *The Princess and the Goblin*. Whitehorn: Johannesen, 2002.
———. *Rampolli*. Whitehorn: Johannesen, 1995.
———. *Robert Falconer*. Whitehorn: Johannesen, 1999.
———. *Sir Gibbie*. Whitehorn: Johannesen, 2000.
———. *Unspoken Sermons*. Whitehorn: Johannesen, 2004.
———. *What's Mine's Mine*. Whitehorn: Johannesen, 2000.
MacDonald, Greville. *George MacDonald and His Wife*. London: G. Allen & Unwin, 1924.
Maiwald, Patrick. *The Journey in George MacDonald's Fantastic Fiction*. Trier: Wissenschaftlicher Verlag Trier, 2008.
Manlove, Colin N. *Modern Fantasy*. Cambridge: Cambridge University Press, 1978.
———. "G. K. Chesterton and George MacDonald: Strangers and Brothers." *The Chesterton Review* 27, nos. 1–2 (2001): 55–64.
Marion, Jean-Luc. *God Without Being*. Translated by Thomas A. Carlson. Chicago: University of Chicago Press, 1991.
Martin, Ralph P. *2 Corinthians*. Word Biblical Commentary. Milton Keynes: Word Publishing, 1986.
Massey, Gerald. "Thomas Hood, Poet and Punster." *Hogg's Instructor* IV (1855).
Matthew, Colin, ed. *The Nineteenth Century*. Short Oxford History of the British Isles. Oxford: Oxford University Press, 2000.

McGillis, Roderick. "The Community of the Centre: Structure and Theme in *Phantastes*." In *For the Childlike*, edited by Roderick McGillis, 51–65. Metuchen: Scarecrow, 1992.

———. "A Fairytale Is Just a Fairytale: George MacDonald and the Queering of Fairy." *Marvels & Tales* 17, no. 1 (2003): 85–99.

———. *For the Childlike*. London: Scarecrow Press, 1992.

———, ed. *George MacDonald: Literary Heritage and Heirs*. Wayne, Penn.: Zossima, 2008.

McIntosh, Mark Allen. *Mystical Theology: The Integrity of Spirituality and Theology*. Oxford: Blackwell, 1997.

Milbank, Alison. *Chesterton and Tolkien as Theologians: The Fantasy of the Real*. London: T&T Clark, 2007.

———. "Praeterita as Dantesque Journey to the Real." *Nineteenth-Century Prose* 35, no. 1 (2008): 46–70.

Milbank, John. "Fictioning Things: Gift and Narrative." *Religion & Literature* 37, no. 3 (2005): 1–35.

Milbank, John, Graham Ward, and Catherine Pickstock. *Radical Orthodoxy: A New Theology*. London: Routledge, 1999.

Mill, John Stuart. *Autobiography*. Oxford: Oxford University Press, 1971.

Moltmann, Jürgen. *Theology of Hope*. London: SCM Press, 1967.

———. *Theology and Joy*. London: SCM Press, 1973.

———. *The Trinity and the Kingdom of God*. Translated by Margaret Kohl. London: SCM Press, 1981.

———. *The Way of Jesus Christ*. London: SCM Press, 1990.

Neaves, Charles. *Songs and Verses, Social and Scientific*. Edinburgh: William Blackwood & Sons, 1868.

Newman, John Henry. *On Certain Difficulties Felt by Anglicans in Submitting to the Catholic Church*. 2nd ed. London: Burns & Lambert, 1850.

Newton, Isaac. *Principia*. Translated by Andrew Motte and Florian Cajori. Berkeley: University of California Press, 1934.

Niebuhr, Reinhold. "Humour and Faith." In *Discerning the Signs of the Times*, 99–115. London: SCM Press, 1946.

Nietzsche, Friedrich. *The Gay Science*. Translated by Thomas Common. Mineola: Dover, 2006.

Oddie, William. *Chesterton and the Romance of Orthodoxy*. Oxford: Oxford University Press, 2008.

Oxford English Dictionary. 2nd ed. Oxford: Clarendon, 1989.

Pemberton, Marilyn. "The Ultimate Rite of Passage: Death and Beyond in 'The Golden Key' and *At the Back of the North Wind*." *North Wind* 27 (2008): 35–50.
Pennington, John. "Alice at the Back of the North Wind." In *Behind the Back of the North Wind*, edited by John Pennington and Roderick McGillis, 52–62. Hamden: Winged Lion Press, 2011.
———. "Thematic and Structural Subversion in the Fairy Tales and Fantasies of George MacDonald." Ph.D. diss., Purdue University, 1987.
———. "A 'Wolff' in Sheep's Clothing: The George MacDonald Industry and the Difficult Rehabilitation of a Reputation." In McGillis, *George MacDonald*, 239–59.
Petersson, Robert Torsten. *The Art of Ecstasy: Teresa, Bernini, and Crashaw*. London: Routledge & Kegan Paul, 1970.
Phillips, Robert, ed. *Aspects of Alice*. Bungay: Penguin, 1971.
Pick, B. "Ecclesiastes or the Sphinx of Hebrew Literature." *Open Court* 17 (1903): 361–71.
Pickstock, Catherine. *After Writing: On the Liturgical Consummation of Philosophy*. Oxford: Blackwell, 1998.
Plato. *Laws*. Translated by Benjamin Jowett. Oxford: Clarendon, 1871.
———. *The Phaedrus, Lysis, and Protagoras*. Translated by J. Wright. London: Macmillan, 1925.
Plotinus. *The Enneads*. Translated by Stephen MacKenna. London: Penguin, 1991.
Potter, George R., and Evelyn M. Simpson, eds. *The Sermons of John Donne*. 10 vols. Berkeley: University of California Press, 1959.
Prickett, Stephen. *Romanticism and Religion: The Tradition of Coleridge and Wordsworth in the Victorian Church*. Cambridge: Cambridge University Press, 1976.
———. *Victorian Fantasy*. Waco, Tex.: Baylor University Press, 2005.
———. *Words and the Word*. Cambridge: Cambridge University Press, 1986.
Pridmore, John. "George MacDonald's Estimate of Childhood." *International Journal of Children's Spirituality* 12, no. 1 (2007): 61–74.
———. "George MacDonald's Transfiguring Fantasy." *Seven* 20 (2000): 49–65.
Pseudo-Dionysius. *Pseudo-Dionysius: The Complete Works*. Translated by Colm Luibhéid and Paul Rorem. New York: Paulist Press, 1987.

Rad, Gerhard von. *Old Testament Theology*. Translated by D. M. G. Stalker. Vol. 2. London: SCM Press, 1965.
Raeper, William. *George MacDonald: Novelist and Victorian Visionary*. Tring: Lion, 1987.
Raymond, Joad. *Milton's Angels*. Oxford: Oxford University Press, 2010.
Reis, Richard. *George MacDonald*. New York: Twayne, 1972.
Riga, Frank. "The Platonic Imagery of George MacDonald and C. S. Lewis." In McGillis, *For the Childlike*, 111–32.
Ruskin, John. *Modern Painters*, vol. 3. New York: John Wiley, 1863.
———. *The Stones of Venice*, vol. 3. London: J. M. Dent, 1905.
Ryden, Lennart, ed. *The Life of St Andrew the Fool*. Vol. 2: *Text, Translation and Notes*. Uppsala, Sweden: Uppsala University Press, 1995.
Sadler, Glenn Edward, ed. *An Expression of Character: The Letters of George MacDonald*. Grand Rapids: Eerdmans, 1994.
Salyer, Gary D. *Vain Rhetoric: Private Insight and Public Debate in Ecclesiastes*, JSOTS. Sheffield: Sheffield Academic Press, 2001.
Saward, John. *Perfect Fools: Folly for Christ's Sake in Catholic and Orthodox Spirituality*. Oxford: Oxford University Press, 1980.
Schiller, Friedrich. *On the Aesthetic Education of Man*. Translated by Reginald Snell. New York: Dover, 2004.
Screech, M. A. *Ecstasy and the Praise of Folly*. London: Duckworth, 1980.
———. *Laughter at the Foot of the Cross*. London: Penguin Books, 1999.
Serres, Michel. *Angels: A Modern Myth*. Translated by Francis Cowper. Paris: Flammarion, 1995.
Shaberman, R. B. *George MacDonald: A Bibliographical Study*. Winchester: St. Paul's Bibliographies, 1990.
Sheley, Erin. "From Eden to Eternity: The Timescales of Genesis in George MacDonald's 'The Golden Key' and *Lilith*." *Children's Literature Association Quarterly* 29, no. 4 (2004): 329–44.
Sidney, Edwin. *The Life of the Reverend Rowland Hill*. London: Seeley, Burnside, & Seeley, 1844.
Sontag, Susan. "Notes on 'Camp.'" In *Against Interpretation*, edited by Susan Sontag, 275–92. London: Eyre & Spottiswoode, 1967.
Soto, Fernando. "Mirrors in MacDonald's *Phantastes*: A Reflective Structure." *North Wind* 23 (2004): 27–47.
———. "Unearthing Ancient Sources in MacDonald's 'The Golden Key.'" *North Wind* 26 (2007): 99–120.

Stott, Andrews. *Comedy*. London: Routledge, 2005.
Thackeray, William. *The Newcomes*. Leipzig: Bernhard Tauchnitz, 1854.
Tolkien, J. R. R. *A Tolkien Miscellany*. New York: SFBC, 2002.
Trimmer, Sarah. *Fabulous Histories*. London: J. G. & F. Rivington, 1838.
Trueblood, Elton. *The Humor of Christ*. New York: Harper & Row, 1964.
Wallace, James Buchanan. *Snatched into Paradise (2 Cor 12:1-10): Paul's Heavenly Journey in the Context of Early Christian Experience*. Berlin: de Gruyter, 2011.
Welborn, L. L. *Paul, the Fool of Christ: A Study of 1 Corinthians 1-4 in the Comic-Philosophic Tradition*. London: T&T Clark, 2005.
Welsford, Enid. *The Fool: His Social and Literary History*. London: Faber & Faber, 1968.
Whybray, R. N. "Qoheleth, Preacher of Joy." In *Wisdom: The Collected Articles of Norman Whybray*, edited by Katharine J. Dell and Margaret Baker, 141–52. Aldershot: Ashgate, 2005.
Wilczek, Frank. *The Lightness of Being*. London: Penguin, 2010.
Wilde, Oscar. *Complete Shorter Fiction*. Oxford: Oxford University Press, 1979.
———. *De Profundis and Other Writings*. London: Penguin, 1986.
———. *The Happy Prince and Other Stories*. London: Penguin, 1994.
———. *The Picture of Dorian Gray*. Leipzig: Bernhard Tauchnitz, 1908.
Williams, Rowan. *The Wound of Knowledge: Christian Spirituality from the New Testament to St. John of the Cross*. 2nd rev. ed. London: Darton, Longman & Todd, 1990.
Wilson, R. Rawdon. *In Palamedes' Shadow: Explorations in Play, Game, and Narrative Theory*. Boston: Northeastern University Press, 1990.
Wolff, Robert Lee. *The Golden Key: A Study of the Fiction of George MacDonald*. New Haven: Yale University Press, 1961.
Wordsworth, William. "Essay Supplementary to the Preface." In *The Poetical Works*. New Haven: Peck & Newton, 1836.
Worringer, Wilhelm. *Abstraction and Empathy: A Contribution to the Psychology of Style*. Translated by Michael Bullock. New York: International Universities Press, 1980.
Wright, A. "The Riddle of the Sphinx: The Structure of the Book of Qoheleth." *CBQ* 30 (1968): 313–34.
———. "The Riddle of the Sphinx Revisited: Numerical Patterns in the Book of Qoheleth." *CBQ* 42 (1980): 35–51.

Wright, T. R. *The Religion of Humanity: The Impact of Comtean Positivism on Victorian Britain*. Cambridge: Cambridge University Press, 1986.
Zipes, Jack. *Fairy Tales and the Art of Subversion*. New York: Wildman, 1983.
Žižek, Slavoj. *The Puppet and the Dwarf: The Perverse Core of Christianity*. Cambridge, Mass.: MIT Press, 2003.

INDEX

Adam, 14, 26, 130, 137, 176, 233n132
Adela Cathcart, 108–16, 121, 125, 147, 170, 175, 178, 182, 184, 226n8, 227n21, 240n24
Agamben, Giorgio, 42, 65
Aging (within fairyland), 128–31
ambiguity, 86–89, 96–97, 206, 222n73
anarchy, 3, 21, 53, 123–24, 160, 162, 164, 165, 237n70
Anderson, Hans Christian, 115
angels, 9–21, 23–24, 30, 84, 117, 118–19, 123, 133, 134, 169, 176, 194, 203, 239n94, 240n12
Annals of a Quiet Neighbourhood, 136
Aquinas, Thomas, 31, 33, 152
Aristotle, 12
Arnold, Matthew, 80–82, 221n42
as if, 41–43, 149, 183, 216n25
ascent and ascension (images of upward movement), 11–12, 13, 21, 24, 27–28, 31–32, 34–35, 59, 60, 100, 102, 141, 149, 155–61, 165, 192, 242n56
At the Back of the North Wind, 2, 99, 112–13, 138, 222n78, 228n47, 232n112, 239n94
Auden, W. H., 44–45, 63, 90–91
Augustine, St., 26–27, 32–33, 37, 176, 213n19, 214n39

Bakhtin, Mikhail, 40, 53, 55, 57, 58, 60–61, 62, 63, 65, 124, 125, 127, 217n9, 219n5

Balthasar, Hans Urs von, 24, 31, 34
baptism, 135, 198, 206
Barbauld, Anna, 86
Barth, Karl, 44, 48, 49, 56, 60, 62, 65, 134, 195, 213n19, 229nn53, 55
beauty, 16, 27–28, 63, 93, 98, 116, 129–30, 138, 150–51, 188–89
Bede, the venerable, 116
Beerbohm, Max ("The Happy Hypocrite"), 46–48
Bentham, Jeremy, 76
Berger, Peter, 30
Bernini, Giovanni Lorenzo (*The Ecstasy of St. Teresa*), 22, 23–24, 159–60
Bible, The, 39, 80–81, 138, 237n71
Blake, William, 21, 180
borders (of fairyland and of miracles), 146–47, 163–65, 182, 199, 235n19
Bradley, Ian, 79
Browning, Robert, 93–96; "Browning's 'Christmas Eve,'" 93–96, 114, 144–45, 227n10
Butler, Alban (*Lives of the Saints*), 25
butterflies, 13, 18–19, 21, 30, 44, 96, 193–95, 199, 201
Byron, Lady, 108
Byron, Lord, 43–46, 52, 81

Caillois, Roger, 55

Index

camp, 15, 192, 211n15
"Carasoyn, The," 131–33, 135, 137–38, 144, 145, 146, 161, 165–66, 229n47, 232n112, 240n23
carelessness (divine), 21, 31, 33, 47–48, 111–12, 114, 128, 153, 198; of fairytales, 98; of Jesus, 103–4, 112, 197
Carlyle, Thomas, 77–78, 81, 220n28
carnival, 18, 51–67, 122–27, 129, 141, 147, 217n9, 218n15, 231n93, 236n39
Carroll, Lewis, 1, 16, 85, 89, 91, 101–2, 225n110, 230nn64, 66; *Alice in Wonderland*, 86–88, 107, 109, 115, 119–20; *Through the Looking Glass*, 101
Castle Warlock, 185, 231n93
Chaucer, 15, 81
Chesterton, G. K., 2–4, 10, 14, 18–19, 58–59, 63, 67, 73, 75, 81, 91, 98, 130, 143, 197, 203–5, 207, 209n9, 210n11, 222n73, 231n79, 243n5
childlike, 3, 32, 47, 99–105, 109, 110–12, 114, 125, 130, 145, 146, 160, 165, 174, 203, 239n91
Christianity, 4, 24–32, 51–53, 55–56, 64–66, 71–72, 92, 138, 140–41, 212n13, 213n19; Roman Catholic, 52, 71–73, 199; in Victorian Britain, 72–73, 78–82
Christmas, 93, 108–16, 120, 122, 124–25, 134, 135, 141, 163, 178, 226n8, 227nn11, 21, 228nn38, 45, 228–29n47, 233nn141, 145; MacDonald family Christmas, 115–16
Chrysostom, John, 27
cleverness (trait of witches), 135
Coleridge, Samuel Taylor, 188, 236n56
Comte, Auguste, 83, 221n50
confession, 62, 181, 206
Congreve, Richard, 82
Cowper, William, 79
Cox, Harvey, 59
"Cross Purposes," 118–20, 137, 145, 149–50, 161, 164, 183, 226n8, 230n64, 235n19
Cruikshank, George, 73, 86

Dante, 1, 10–18, 21, 78, 81, 84–85, 138–39, 140, 155, 176, 192, 194, 210n13, 242n56
David Elginbrod, 102, 109
Davis, Philip, 77, 220n21

death, 2, 30, 39, 40–41, 42, 59–60, 65–66, 91, 107, 114, 116, 117, 123, 126–33, 134, 141, 153, 154, 159, 162–63, 165, 168, 184, 190, 232n117, 233n132
Derrida, Jacques, 39, 97, 215n12
Dickens, Charles, 73, 75–78, 83, 86, 147
Donne, John, 62, 181, 206
Dostoevsky, Fyodor, 34, 214n40
dreams, 54, 119–22, 131–32, 156–57, 162, 184–85

Easter, 62, 65, 108, 134
Ecclesiastes, 38–41, 43, 51, 111, 149, 175, 180, 200, 215nn6, 7, 11, 216nn15, 18
ecstasy, 17, 23–35, 37–38, 46, 110, 119, 128, 130, 150–61, 172, 176, 212nn12, 13
Eden, 48, 130, 134, 136, 232–33n132; childhood as, 101–2, 146
Edgeworth, Maria, 85–86
Eliot, George, 82–85, 92, 220n40, 221n50
Engels, Friedrich, 72
Enlightenment, the, 10, 71–73, 76, 92, 99, 165, 219n6
Erasmus, Desiderius, 25
eschatology, 31, 48, 49, 65, 117, 138, 168, 201; inaugurated, 134–35, 233n149
evangelicalism, 72, 78–82, 86, 99
evil, 26, 89–91, 116, 127, 135–37, 140, 141, 147–48, 169, 176, 180, 228n36

fairytales: *see under specific titles*
"Fantastic Imagination, The," 96–99, 112, 193–94, 234n2
fantasy, 1, 16, 48, 91, 96, 108, 121, 140, 173, 184–85, 196, 237–38n72
fear and fearless, 42, 61, 103, 123–24, 133, 136, 138, 157, 163, 164, 165–67, 188
festival, festivity: *see* carnival
folly (fools, foolishness), 18, 23–35, 46, 64–65, 97–98, 99, 111, 138, 147–48, 149, 153–54, 200, 213nn22, 31; holy fools, 24–25, 27–30, 137–38, 153–54
frame (narration), 40, 108, 113, 114, 116, 147, 150, 170, 178, 182
François de Sales, St., 26

Gadamer, Hans-George, 44, 47–48, 111, 226n7, 227n24

Genesis (book of), 38–39, 60, 117, 130, 216n18, 232nn116, 117
Giantland, 147, 149, 235nn18, 19
"Giant's Heart, The," 112, 127, 145, 146–48, 226n8
gnostic and Gnosticism, 26, 43, 154, 161, 171, 172
Goethe, Johann Wolfgang von, 81, 94, 125
"Golden Key, The," 90, 117–18, 126–27, 129–31, 138–40, 145, 149, 168, 175, 183, 198, 200, 229n47, 232nn112, 116, 117, 234n153
Good Things for the Young of All Ages, 99, 224n105, 229n47, 233n141
Gosse, Philip, 80
gravity (metaphorical or literal), 1–4, 10, 12, 14, 20, 26–27, 31, 39, 42–43, 52, 72–73, 74–75, 85, 89, 113, 115, 126, 139, 152, 154, 170, 176, 181, 203, 207
Gray, Donald, 73, 74, 75
grotesque, the, 3, 55, 63–73, 82–85, 89–91, 95, 114, 122–26, 146–47, 166, 177, 199, 230–31n79, 231n90

harmony (in general, between body and spirit, within and without), 31, 56, 103, 116–17, 119, 145, 163–72, 199
Hart, David Bentley, 24, 28
Hein, Rolland, 105, 185, 233n132
Hill, Rowland, 79
"History of Photogen and Nycteris: A Day and Night Mährchen, The," 136–37, 138, 140, 145, 146, 148, 150, 157–61, 183, 190, 207, 233n141, 240n5
Holy Spirit, 157, 160, 191, 192, 239n102
home (quest for, emblem of peace), 103–4, 144–48, 152, 155, 156–57, 171, 180
Hood, Thomas, 73, 74–75
hope, 65, 100, 102–3, 105, 136, 137–41, 163, 185, 189, 225n111, 234n153
Hope of the Gospel, The, 103, 169
humor, 17, 30, 73–75, 94–95, 126, 213n30

imagination, 76, 80–81, 83, 89–90, 96, 104, 156–57, 158, 192, 193, 204, 206
indeterminacy, 89, 97–98, 207
Industrial Revolution, the, 77–78

inward turn (bent inwards), 26, 176–77, 181, 198, 200
isolation, 148–53, 155, 172, 236n45

Jesus Christ, 11, 24, 27–35, 42, 48, 55–56, 59–60, 65, 97, 103–4, 110–11, 112, 115, 125, 134, 135, 137, 149, 151, 153–54, 165, 167, 171, 188, 192, 195, 196–98, 199, 236n45, 239n91; miracles of, 31, 66–67, 162–64, 195–98; transfiguration of, 30–32, 162–64
John of the Cross, St., 34
Joseph of Cupertino, 25
journey, 31–32, 100, 102, 110, 124, 130, 131, 139, 144–48, 156, 173
joy, 2–3, 16, 35, 40–41, 53, 60, 67, 92–93, 110–11, 126, 128, 131, 154, 160, 163, 170, 199, 205–6

kenosis, 28, 33–34, 65, 214n40
Kirk, Robert, 118
Knoepflmacher, U. C., 101, 223n79, 227n14, 228n34, 230n64
knowledge, 32–34, 151, 160, 171; arrogance of, 135–36; comes through the senses, 63, 64, 82
Kott, Jan, 57, 64
Kundera, Milan, 39

laughter, 14, 16, 17–18, 60–62, 65, 67, 73–75, 127, 152, 166, 200, 217n9
law (in fairyland), 161–62; and miracles, 164–65, 166, 168
Leech, John, 73
letting go (of the self, seriousness), 47, 48, 62, 189, 195, 205–7
levity, *passim*; 1, 4–5, 9–21, 26, 30–32, 42, 62, 71–75, 91, 93–99, 105, 120, 121–22, 126, 157, 160, 181, 183, 195, 197–99, 200–201, 203–7; levitation, 10–12, 14, 17, 19, 24–25, 28
Lewes, George, 82
Lewis, C. S., 1–2, 15, 48, 140, 149, 174, 203, 205–7, 234n161, 244n9
"Light Princess, The," 112–13, 125–26, 127, 133, 135, 138, 145, 148, 152–55, 168, 169–71, 190, 225n111, 227n14, 228n34
lightness, 13, 17, 18–19, 31, 38–41, 47, 62,

95, 96–99, 103, 126, 141, 198–99, 206; *see also* levity
Lilith, 2, 91, 127, 165, 185, 209n8, 222n78, 234n162
"Little Daylight," 112–13, 135, 138, 140, 145–46, 148, 150–51, 152, 154, 168, 190, 198, 228nn 36, 38, 232n112
love (in general and divine), 18, 26, 28–30, 32, 33–35, 59, 64, 80, 103, 111, 128–29, 151, 153–55, 161, 164, 169–73, 197, 199–200; romantic/erotic, 25, 46–47, 54, 61–62, 120, 150–55, 189, 190, 212n10
Lüthi, Max, 145, 148, 173–74, 197, 198, 228n33

Mabille, Pierre, 173, 174
MacDonald, George: life, 91–93
MacDonald, Greville (son), 91–92, 228n41
MacDonald, Lily (daughter), 87–88
madness, 24, 25, 102, 124, 200
Marion, Jean-Luc, 41–42, 151, 175–76, 215n5, 216n25
masks, 25, 34, 39–40, 46–48, 53, 61–62, 63–64, 65
Massey, Gerald, 74–75
McIntosh, Mark, 32
Milbank, Alison, 84, 226n126, 235n3
Milbank, John, 126
Mill, John Stuart, 76
Milton, John, 20–21, 74
miracles, 25, 55, 66–67, 162–65, 167–68, 171, 195–200, 237nn71, 72, 243n83
Miracles of Our Lord, The, 162–65, 167–68, 195–200
mirrors, 46–47, 53, 130, 176–77, 180, 182–84, 187–88, 190–93, 240nn12, 14
Moltmann, Jürgen, 42–43, 48, 56, 65, 71, 138, 200, 233n149
morality, 9, 80, 86, 89, 91 98, 100, 156–57, 201; and seriousness, 1, 2, 73–75, 79, 81
morals (of fairytales), 85–91, 94, 147–48, 174, 194–201; moralistic, 3, 147
Morris, William, 91
"My Uncle Peter," 113–14, 228n38
mysticism, 2, 3, 10, 26, 32–35, 37, 38, 43, 110, 146, 150–51, 164, 171, 214n40, 237n69, 242n58

nature, 92–93, 103, 160, 161–72, 188
Neaves, Charles, 51–52, 66, 72
Neoplatonism, 31–32, 33, 213n16
Nesbit, Anthony, 80
Newman, John Henry, 72–73, 85, 93, 99
Newton, Isaac, 10, 210n4
Niebuhr, Reinhold, 62
Nietzsche, Friedrich, 95
nonchalance, 136, 153–54, 198
nonsense (literature), 3, 16, 67, 85, 88, 101
Novalis, 144, 161, 162

parables, 28–30, 35, 97, 151, 183, 188
Paul, St., 28, 32–35, 42, 48, 65, 159, 171, 192, 198, 212n13, 214n38
Peter, St., 31, 125, 157
Phantastes, 1, 2, 91, 108, 115, 119, 125, 156, 162, 165, 181, 185–89, 190–93, 205
Pickstock, Catherine, 116–17
Plato, 25–26, 27, 30–31, 44, 156, 157, 188, 212nn10, 13
play, *passim*; 1–4, 17, 37–49, 51–52, 57–59, 88–91, 97–98, 101–5, 123–24, 131–33, 175, 185, 199–201, 205–7, 215n12, 226n6
Plotinus, 212n13, 213nn16, 23
Portent and Other Stories, The, 169, 184
positivism, 81, 82–83, 84
preposterous, 58–60, 65, 136
Prickett, Stephen, 84, 186, 206, 221n42, 244n9
pride, 12–14, 21, 26, 161, 177
Pridmore, John, 100, 237–38n72
Princess and Curdie, The, 140, 225n113, 232n112, 233n141
Princess and the Goblin, The, 99, 135–36, 204, 232n112
prophecy, 27, 150, 157, 168–72
Pseudo-Dionysius, 17–18, 19–20, 26, 28, 31
Pullman, Philip, 161

Qoheleth: *see* Ecclesiastes
quest, 118, 127, 132, 144–46, 148, 155, 172, 180, 206

Rad, Gerhard von, 117
Raeper, William, 96
Raphael (*Transfiguration*), 31

rapture, 26, 33, 37, 119, 150, 152, 236n; *see also* ecstasy
revelation, 16, 44, 60, 63–65, 94, 126, 132, 151, 154, 155, 161, 169–70, 180–84
Robert Falconer, 107, 226n2
Romanticism, 92, 99–101, 188; German, 125
room (sense of space), 100, 105, 110, 150, 155–61, 172; for the reader, 89, 97, 205
Rowling, J. K., 161
Ruskin, John, 82, 83–85, 89–90, 92, 95, 123–24, 199, 228n34, 231n84

Sabbath, 52–53, 55–56, 59, 60, 62, 65–66, 116–17, 120–22, 125, 130, 132, 135, 137, 168, 184–87, 229nn53, 57
sacramental, 169
sacrifice, 125, 141, 154, 170, 190–91
Satan, 13–14, 20, 176, 180
Schiller, Friedrich, 37–38, 46
seriousness, 1–4, 10, 14–16, 21, 34, 38, 39, 41–43, 46, 47–49, 53, 60–61, 62, 71–105, 113–14, 122–23, 126, 136, 185, 195, 197, 200, 209n8, 211nn13, 15
Serres, Michel, 20
"Shadows, The," 113–15, 121, 122–25, 145, 155–56, 161, 175–82, 187, 228nn41, 45, 240nn12, 23, 24
Shakespeare, William, 9, 27, 81; *A Midsummer Night's Dream*, 54, 57–59, 63–64, 118
Shelley, Percy Bysshe, 189, 241n45
sin, 11–14, 26, 27, 79, 93, 101, 134, 163, 176–77, 206, 213n19, 215n7
Sir Gibbie, 111, 138,
solemnity: *see* seriousness
solipsism, 120, 154, 159, 160, 164, 184
style, 197–99
symbols/symbolism, 19, 20, 66, 97, 158, 170–71, 192–93

Tennyson, Alfred Lord, 80
Teresa of Avila, St., 23–24, 35, 152, 159–60
Thackeray, William, 73, 79
Thousand and One Nights, The, 116
time (narrative importance, theological significance), 51–66, 107–41 *passim*, 162, 185, 186
Tolkien, J. R. R., 2, 107, 108, 126, 143, 161, 166, 170, 173, 186, 226n3, 235n3, 239n97, 239–40n4
transfiguration, 128; of Jesus, 30–32, 162–64
transformation, 13, 20–21, 24, 31, 45–49, 122, 126–29, 151, 154, 165–66, 168, 174 ; of readers, 173–201 *passim*, 203–7
Trimmer, Sarah, 86, 222n62
Trinity, the, 16, 28, 138–39, 239n102
twilight, 109, 116–23, 125, 133–34, 137, 140, 184–85, 187–89

Unspoken Sermons, 104, 126, 129, 192, 242n58
Utilitarianism, 75–78, 82, 86, 220n21

vanity, 37–49, 51, 149, 151, 169, 175–84, 186, 189, 215n5
Vaughan, Henry, 100
Victorians, 72–105 *passim*, 113, 115, 120, 147, 196
Virgil, 1, 13–14
vulnerability, 33, 97, 98, 111, 112

Weil, Simone, 90–91, 214n40
Wender, Wim, 18
What's Mine's Mine, 155–56
Wilde, Oscar, 1, 15, 85, 88–89, 133, 188, 192, 222n73
"Wise Woman, The," 127–29, 145, 146, 166–68, 183–84, 229n47, 232n112, 240nn5, 23
Within and Without, 108, 125, 231n93
wonder, 76, 104, 122, 124, 140, 156, 159, 186, 187, 188, 195
Wordsworth, William, 81, 99–100, 101, 102, 104, 188, 191, 194, 224n106, 242n62
worries (as burdens), 42, 111, 115, 116, 131, 133, 136, 157, 182
Worringer, Wilhelm, 197

Žižek, Slavoj, 64

www.ingramcontent.com/pod-product-compliance
Lightning Source LLC
Chambersburg PA
CBHW030615230426
43661CB00053B/1995